the POLITICAL SEDUCTION of the Church

How Millions of American Christians Have
Confused Politics with the Gospel

MICHAEL L. BROWN

VIDE

VIDE

Unless otherwise noted, all Scripture quotations from The Holy Bible, English Standard Version. ESV® Text Edition: 2016. Copyright © 2001 by Crossway Bibles, a publishing ministry of Good News Publishers. Scripture marked NIV is taken from the Holy Bible, New International Version®, NIV® Copyright ©1973, 1978, 1984, 2011 by Biblica, Inc.® Used by permission. All rights reserved worldwide. Scripture marked NKJV is taken from the New King James Version®. Copyright © 1982 by Thomas Nelson. Used by permission. All rights reserved. Scripture marked NLT is taken from the *Holy Bible*, New Living Translation, copyright © 1996, 2004, 2015 by Tyndale House Foundation. Used by permission of Tyndale House Publishers, Inc., Carol Stream, Illinois 60188. All rights reserved. Scripture marked NASB is taken from the New American Standard Bible®, Copyright © 1960, 1971, 1977, 1995 by The Lockman Foundation. All rights reserved.

Vide Press
6200 Second Street
Washington D.C. 20011
www.VidePress.com

PB ISBN: 978-1-954618-49-7
e-Book ISBN: 978-1-954618-50-3

Printed in the United States of America

Contents

Preface

As I write these words on May 29, 2022, the lead headline on the widely read Drudge Report website stands bold and clear: "Christian Nationalism on the Rise." The headline links to an Associated Press article by Peter Smith and Deepa Bharath, "Christian nationalism on the rise in some GOP campaigns," which begins with these words:

> The victory party took on the feel of an evangelical worship service after Doug Mastriano won Pennsylvania's Republican gubernatorial primary this month. As a Christian singer led the crowd in song, some raised their arms toward the heavens in praise.
>
> Mastriano opened his remarks by evoking Scripture: "God uses the foolish to confound the wise." He claimed Pennsylvanians' freedom would be "snatched away" if his Democratic opponent wins in November, and cast the election in starkly religious terms with another biblical reference: "Let's choose this day to serve the Lord."

According to Smith and Bharath, "Mastriano, a state senator and retired Army colonel, has not only made faith central to his personal story but has woven conservative Christian beliefs and symbols into the campaign — becoming the most prominent example this election cycle of what some observers call a surge of Christian nationalism among Republican candidates."[1]

Last month, on April 6, 2022, the *New York Times* ran an article written by Elizabeth Dias and Ruth Graham titled "The Growing Religious Fervor in the American Right: 'This Is a Jesus Movement'." The subtitle claimed that, "Rituals of Christian worship have become embedded in conservative rallies, as praise music and prayer blend with political anger over vaccines and the 2020 election."[2] The very next day, John Fea, a Christian university professor (and persistent critic of Donald Trump), posted this question on the Current website, linked to the Dias and Graham article, asking, "Is there a difference between an evangelical worship service and a right-wing political rally?" His answer? "Sometimes it's really hard to tell."[3] This is a cause for concern.

Do I believe that Christians should be involved in politics? Absolutely. Do I prefer the policies of one main political party over those of the other main party? Definitely. Do I believe that the spiritual and political realms often overlap? Certainly. But to the extent we confuse the gospel with the politics or identify one party as "God's party" or seek to advance the goals of the gospel largely through politics, to that extent we will fail.

That's why I have written this book, urging us to learn the lessons from the Donald Trump presidency, in particular from the 2020 elections and the events that followed. I voted for Trump in both 2016 and 2020, and while I was always concerned about the destructive aspects of his personality, when it came to opposing abortion, fighting for religious freedoms, standing up to tyrannical China, facing down world terrorism, and standing with Israel (among other things), it was an easy choice for me to make. I chose Trump rather than Hillary Clinton or Joe Biden.

At the same time, I became increasingly concerned that many Christians were putting too much trust in Trump as the man uniquely raised up by God to save America, that they were becoming more fervent about partisan politics than about the gospel, that they were becoming as mean-spirited and divisive as their president, that they were in danger of selling their souls for a seat at the table of power, and that the growing chorus of prophetic voices guaranteeing four more years of Trump would lead to massive disappointment and tremendous spiritual reproach.

Sad to say, all those concerns have been realized, and to this day, there are prominent Trump prophets who continue to call Biden a "fake president" and who proclaim that, in God's sight, Trump is the sitting president, enthroned in heaven by God. The deception and confusion run very deep.

In fact, on May 15, 2022, a pastor with a large internet following issued this strong warning to those on the left: "You keep on pushing our buttons, you low down, sorry compromisers. You God-hating communists, you'll find out what an insurrection is because we ain't playing your garbage. We ain't playing your mess. My Bible says that the church of the living God is an institution that the gates of hell shall not prevail against it. And the Bible says they will take it by force."[4] And when I called him out publicly for his words,[5] many of his followers blasted me, saying that our Founding Fathers would be proud of him and ashamed of me.[6] The fact that this pastor subsequently appeared on my radio show to clarify that he was *not* calling for a violent uprising did little to dampen the enthusiasm of some of his followers.[7] They were quite ready to take up arms.

It is the purpose of this book to get to the root of this deception and confusion, to understand the true role of the church in the society, to expose the false prophetic spirit, to paint a picture of the healthy intersection of the gospel and politics, and to show us a biblically based way forward—and I write this as someone deeply committed to a gospel-based moral and cultural revolution in the society. I also write as someone who has deep concerns about the radical leftist agenda and who has very little trust in much of the secular media. But I do not write as a Republican (and certainly not as a Democrat), nor do I write simply as a social conservative (although I am anything but a liberal). I write as an unashamed, Bible-believing, follower of Jesus and as one who believes that, through the gospel, the church should be changing the world rather than the world changing the church. The simple question is how. How are we called to bring about this change?

Having written more than two thousand op-ed pieces over the last decade, with most of them appearing in the *Christian Post*, I am pleased to publish this book in the *Post*'s publishing arm, Vide Press. My appreciation to Tom Freiling for pursuing this project, for CEO Chris Chou's enthusiastic support, and for the masterful editorial work of Geoff Stone. My appreciation also to the entire AskDrBrown Ministries team, to my faithful intercessors and supporters worldwide, and to my wonderful bride since 1976, Nancy, who has shed buckets of tears over the issues I address in this book. May Jesus be glorified in His people!

—Michael L. Brown

CHAPTER ONE

When Evangelical Christians Were Blamed for the Storming of the Capitol

The scene will be etched in our collective American consciousness for decades to come. Thousands of Trump supporters stormed the Capitol building with both houses of Congress in full session. The vice president speedily evacuated, followed by congressional leaders, all of them fearing for their lives. It was a picture of chaos and confusion as the police were quickly overwhelmed by the surging crowd. And it all played out on live TV, on internet feeds, and on cell phones to the utter shock and horror of the nation.

Soon enough, the protesters, stoked and inspired by the words of their leader, took over the building in an effort to "take back" the stolen election. After all, it was just minutes before that President Trump had said to tens of thousands of loyalists:

All of us here today do not want to see our election victory stolen by emboldened radical-left Democrats, which is what they're doing. And stolen by the fake news media. That's what they've done and what they're doing. We will never give up; we will never concede. It doesn't happen. You don't concede when there's theft involved.

To concede would be to capitulate to evil. We can never let that happen! Trump continued:

> Our country has had enough. We will not take it anymore and that's what this is all about. And to use a favorite term that all of you people really came up with: We will stop the steal. . . . .
> And we fight. We fight like hell. And if you don't fight like hell, you're not going to have a country anymore. . . . .

Yes, this was a matter of freedom or bondage. This was about the future of our nation. And so, the president concluded,

> we're going to, we're going to walk down Pennsylvania Avenue. I love Pennsylvania Avenue. And we're going to the Capitol, and we're going to try and give.
> The Democrats are hopeless—they never vote for anything. Not even one vote. But we're going to try and give our Republicans, the weak ones because the strong ones don't need any of our help. We're going to try and give them the kind of pride and boldness that they need to take back our country.
> So let's walk down Pennsylvania Avenue.
> I want to thank you all. God bless you and God Bless America.[8]

But the peaceful march the president envisioned soon turned unruly, and within minutes, there were casualties: scores would be injured, some would even die. A policeman screamed in agony as his arm was crushed in a door; a female military veteran was shot by an officer as she attempted to climb through a window. She collapsed to the ground where she breathed her last breath. Yes, this was the scene in

Washington, DC, on January 6, 2021, a scene we thought we would never see in our lifetimes. Our Capitol was under siege by patriotic supporters of the president. How could this be?

In testimony before Congress July 2021, two policemen recounted what happened to them on that fateful day as they sought to defend the Capitol:

> "The mob of terrorists were coordinating their efforts… shouting 'heave, ho,' as they synchronized pushing their weight forward crushing me further against the metal doorframe," [Dennis] Hodges said. "A man in front of me grabbed my baton… he bashed me in the head and face with it, rupturing my lip and adding additional injury to my skull."
>
> MPD Officer Michael Fanone, meanwhile, detailed how he was "electrocuted again and again and again with a taser. I am sure I was screaming, but I don't think I could hear my own voice."[9]

How on earth did this happen, right here in our country, as impassioned Americans in the name of patriotism viciously attacked these DC policemen? What in the world went wrong?

Yet it gets even worse since, in the eyes of the watching world, this was a *Christian* event, more specifically, an *evangelical Christian* event. And it was called an insurrection — *an evangelical Christian insurrection on behalf of Donald Trump.* At least that's how the secular media presented it.

Writing for *Rolling Stone* on January 31, 2021, Sarah Posner began her article with these words:

The January 6th Save America March, where then-President Donald Trump incited a crowd to attack the U.S. Capitol, opened with a prayer. Trump's longtime spiritual adviser and White House adviser, the Florida televangelist Paula White, called on God to "give us

3

a holy boldness in this hour." Standing at the same podium where, an hour later, Trump would exhort the crowd to "fight like hell," White called the election results into question, asking God to let the people "have the assurance of a fair and a just election." Flanked by a row of American flags, White implored God to "let every adversary against democracy, against freedom, against life, against liberty, against justice, against peace, against righteousness be overturned right now in the name of Jesus."

And this was just the opening paragraph. She continued:

Within hours, insurrectionists had surrounded the Capitol, beaten police, battered down barricades and doors, smashed windows and rampaged through the halls of the Capitol, breaching the Senate chamber. In video captured by *The New Yorker*, men ransacked the room, rifling through senators' binders and papers, searching for evidence of what they claimed was treason. Then, standing on the rostrum where the president of the Senate presides, the group paused to pray "in Christ's holy name." Men raised their arms in the air as millions of evangelical and charismatic parishioners do every Sunday and thanked God for allowing them "to send a message to all the tyrants, the communists and the globalists, that this is our nation, not theirs." They thanked God "for allowing the United States of America to be reborn."[10]

In similar fashion, on January 8, 2021, Emma Green's article in the *Atlantic* was titled "A Christian Insurrection." She wrote:

The name of God was everywhere during Wednesday's insurrection against the American government. The mob carried signs and flag declaring Jesus saves! and God, guns & guts made America, let's keep all three. Some were participants in the Jericho March, a gathering of Christians to "pray, march, fast, and rally for election integrity." After calling on God to "save the republic" during rallies at state capitols and in D.C. over the past two months, the marchers returned to Washington with flourish. On the National Mall, one man waved the flag of Israel above a sign begging passersby to say yes to Jesus. "Shout if you love Jesus!" someone yelled, and the crowd cheered. "Shout if you love Trump!" The crowd cheered louder. The group's name is drawn from the biblical story of Jericho, "a city of false gods and corruption," the march's website says. Just as God instructed Joshua to march around Jericho seven times with priests blowing trumpets, Christians gathered in D.C., blowing shofars, the ram's horn typically used in Jewish worship, to banish the "darkness of election fraud" and ensure that "the walls of corruption crumble."

And what did all this indicate? What did this say about the relationship between Trump and American Christians? Green opined,

The Jericho March is evidence that Donald Trump has bent elements of American Christianity to his will, and that many Christians have obligingly remade their faith in his image. Defiant masses literally broke down the walls of government, some believing they were marching under Jesus's banner to implement God's will to keep Trump in the White House. . . . . . . White evangelicals, in particular, overwhelmingly supported Trump in 2016 and 2020. Some of these supporters participated in the attack on the Capitol on Wednesday. But many in the country hold all Trump voters responsible—especially those who lent him the moral authority of their faith.[11]

Not to be outdone, Matthew Avery Sutton's article in the *New Republic* on January 14, 2021, was titled "The Capitol Riot Revealed the Darkest Nightmares of White Evangelical America. How 150 years of apocalyptic agitation culminated in an insurrection." He wrote,

> White evangelicals believe they see truths that you and I cannot.
> While Americans around the country watched an inflamed mob overrun the Capitol on January 6, the evangelical participants in that mob saw something else: a holy war. Insurgents carried signs that read "Jesus Saves," "In God We Trust," "Jesus 2020," and "Jesus Is My Savior, Trump Is My President." One man marched through the halls of Congress carrying a Christian flag, another a Bible. They chanted, "The blood of Jesus covering this place."

According to Sutton,

> These Christians apparently believe that they had no choice but to try to overthrow the Congress. For months, various evangelicals have claimed in sermons, on social media, and during protests that malicious forces stole the election, conspired to quash Christian liberties, and aimed to clamp down on their freedom to worship and spread the Christian gospel. They felt sure that the final days of history were at hand and that the Capitol was the site of an epochal battle. As one evangelical from Texas told *The New York Times*, "We are fighting good versus evil, dark versus light."[12]

As for the *New York Times* article just cited, it was written by Elizabeth Dias and Ruth Graham and published on January 11, 2021. It, too, carried a provocative headline: "How White Evangelical Christians Fused With Trump Extremism." And it, too, made very strong claims. Dias and Graham wrote,

> A potent mix of grievance and religious fervor has turbocharged the support among Trump loyalists, many of whom describe themselves as participants in a kind of holy war.
>
> Before self-proclaimed members of the far-right group the Proud Boys marched toward the U.S. Capitol on Wednesday, they stopped to kneel in the street and prayed in the name of Jesus.
>
> The group, whose participants have espoused misogynistic and anti-immigrant views, prayed for God to bring "reformation and revival." They gave thanks for "the wonderful nation we've all been blessed to be in." They asked God for the restoration of their "value systems," and for the "courage and strength to both represent you and represent our culture well." And they invoked the divine protection for what was to come.
>
> Then they rose. Their leader declared into a bullhorn that the media must "get the hell out of my way." And then they moved toward the Capitol.
>
> The presence of Christian rituals, symbols and language was unmistakable on Wednesday in Washington. There was a mock campaign banner, "Jesus 2020," in blue and red; an "Armor of God" patch on a man's fatigues; a white cross declaring "Trump won" in all capitals. All of this was interspersed with allusions to QAnon conspiracy theories, Confederate flags and anti-Semitic T-shirts.[13]

This was how the "insurrection" looked in the eyes of journalists writing for these prominent, secular publications.

But it was not just the secular media bringing these charges. David French, himself an evangelical Christian and political commentator (as well as an outspoken Never Trumper), claimed that a "violent *Christian* insurrection invaded and occupied the Capitol" (his emphasis). He wrote, "Why do I say this was a Christian insurrection? Because so very many of the protesters told us they were Christian, as loudly and clearly as they could." He also noted that there "was a giant wooden cross outside the Capitol" and added that "'Jesus saves' signs and other Christian signs were sprinkled through the crowd. I watched a man carry a Christian flag into an evacuated legislative chamber."

One of his colleagues pointed out "that Christian music was blaring from the loudspeakers late in the afternoon of the takeover. And don't forget," he wrote, "this attack occurred days after the so-called Jericho March, an event explicitly filled with Christian-nationalist rhetoric so unhinged that I warned on December 13 that it embodied 'a form of fanaticism that can lead to deadly violence.'" French also pointed to some of the rhetoric that helped fuel the fires of the storming of the Capitol, including: "America will end if Trump loses"; and, "The fate of the church is at stake if Joe Biden wins."[14]

Similarly, Ed Setzer, another respected evangelical thinker, called for an evangelical reckoning on Trump. Appearing on NPR, he was asked by Rachel Martin, "You write that 'many evangelicals are seeing Donald Trump for who he is.' Do you really think that's true? There have been so many other things that Trump has said and done over the past four to five years that betray Christian values, and their support didn't waver. You think this time it's different?"

Setzer responded,

I think it's a fair question, and I've been one for years who was saying we need to see more clearly who Donald Trump is and has often not been listened to. But I would say that for many people, the storming of the Capitol, the desecration of our halls of democracy, has shocked and stunned a lot of people and how President Trump has engaged in riling up crowds to accomplish these things. Yeah, I do think so. I think there are some significant and important conversations that we need to have inside of evangelicalism asking the question: What happened? Why were so many people drawn to somebody who was obviously so not connected to what evangelicals believe by his life or his practices or more.

His biggest question was simply How did we get here? As he said in the interview, " 'Part of this reckoning is: How did we get here? How were we so easily fooled by conspiracy theories?' We need to make clear who we are. And our allegiance is to King Jesus, not to what boasting political leader might come next."[15] How, indeed.[16]

After all, many in the large crowd that day were Christians, specifically evangelical Christians. They had come to DC to pray for the reversal of the elections, believing that Trump was divinely appointed to serve a second term. Some had arrived days earlier, calling out to God for His anointed servant, Donald Trump, while others had been singing hymns and worshiping with raised hands, while others carried banners with words of Scripture or images of the cross. Even among those who made their way into the halls of Congress there was a small group of radicals who stood triumphantly in the very place from which our elected officials had fled, offering up prayers of thanksgiving *in Jesus' name*. Yes, they prayed in the name of Jesus.

No wonder the secular media reported that this "insurrection" was an evangelical Christian event. No wonder this confirmed their greatest fears about evangelical supporters of Trump and supported their ugliest accusations. After all, the handwriting was already on the wall.

Barely one month earlier, Rod Dreher, another respected conservative Christian commentator described what he saw as he watched the six-hour, Jericho March in DC live online. As he explained, "I watched because I wanted to see how far the Christian Right—for the record, I am an Orthodox Christian and a conservative—would go to conflate Trump politics and religion. Pretty far, as it turns out. Right over the cliff. You had to see it to believe it."

At one point Dreher recounted,

> Fr. Greg Bramlage, a Colorado priest who says he is an exorcist. He shamanically prayed down heaven to deliver America from demons. These were real deliverance prayers. He is saying, in effect, that to oppose Trump and his re-election is to be an agent of Satan. This was the first time I got really angry. As regular readers know, I believe in the power of exorcism. I believe the demonic is real. But there was this Trumpy priest deploying holy prayers of deliverance from the demonic on behalf of a politician, and did it in a way that logically locates doubters within the shadow of Mordor. It felt sacrilegious.

Then, at the height of retired Gen. Michael Flynn's speech,

> Trump appeared overhead in Marine One. Like an apparition! After Trump choppered off to the Army-Navy game, Flynn resumed his address. *Every time they attack Trump,* he said, *they're attacking you!* Total identification of the collective with the individual

man, Trump. I despise facile comparisons, but this is a core fascist trope. At the 1934 Nuremberg Party rally, Nazi functionary Rudolf Hess told the faithful, "The Party is Hitler! But Hitler is Germany, as Germany is Hitler!"

To be perfectly clear, Dreher wrote, "No, I don't think Donald Trump = Adolf Hitler. My point is simply that political rhetoric that turns a political movement into a personality cult, and unites the masses in this psychological way with the leader, are never headed to a good place. You see what Flynn also did here: trained people in the crowd to reject any criticism of Trump as a personal attack on them."

Another speaker that day was Alex Jones of Infowars fame:

"Humanity is awakening! Jesus Christ is King!" he screamed. And: "This is the beginning of the Great Revival before the Antichrist comes! ... Revelation is fulfilled!"

Jones . . . denounced Mark Zuckerberg and a litany of elites as "miserable slaves of Satan."

"World government is here! The system is publicly stealing this election from the biggest landslide and the biggest political re-alignment since 1776!" he ranted.

"GOD IS ON OUR SIDE!" he bellowed. Then: "We will never bow down to the Satanic pedophile New World Order!"

The Christians in the crowd cheered him. Alex Jones, you may recall, is being sued for defamation by families of children killed in the Sandy Hook massacre, which Jones for years denied on his radio show. Alex Jones is a profoundly evil man. But today, he was a hero to these Christians.

Later came "a pastor with an outfit called the Black Robe Regiment."

> He compared Trump supporters to the Israelites about to cross the Red Sea. Pharaoh's army is coming, he said, but just you wait. "God is about to do something in this country that is going to take the threats we're dealing with and put it [sic] down."
>
> Real pastors, he said, lead their flock into battle. He wasn't speaking metaphorically. The pastor denounced separation of church and state ("What is this separation of church and state?" he sneered). This was truly extraordinary: the conflation of shedding blood, seizing the government, and serving God. This was a great gift to the Left, this speech. The entire day was. A very conservative Christian friend e-mailed me during all this to say, "My God, this is the kind of stuff that drove me away from Christianity for 25 years!"
>
> Another speaker, a man wearing a black cowboy hat, called on Trump to "invoke the Insurrection Act" to "drop the hammer" on "traitors." He said that Trump should know that the "militia" is with him.
>
> "Let's get it on now, while [Trump] is still the commander in chief," said the speaker.[17]

And this is just a sampling from Dreher's lengthy and detailed article. How on earth did this happen? Another pastor, with an American flag draped over his shoulders, also made specific reference to the Black Robe Regiment and the militaristic uprising of our Founding Fathers, shouting loudly to the crowd, "It is time for war! Let us stop the steal!"[18]

What makes this even more troubling is that I know some of the leaders who participated in the Jericho March event, and they are God-fearing, Jesus-loving, men of integrity. Some had no idea the event would turn so political, and they should not be held responsible for what happened that day. Their own comments were gospel-oriented and sound. But others seemed to go right along with the flow without criticism or hesitation. To ask again: How on earth did this happen? Or, in Setzer's words, "How did we get here?"

Personally, I do *not* believe the storming of the Capitol was a Christian event, let alone an evangelical Christian insurrection. That's why I wrote an article in response to David French (with whom I often agree), titled "No, It Was Not Jesus-Loving Evangelicals Who Vandalized the Capitol."[19] That's also why, in February 2021, "More than 1,400 evangelical pastors and other faith leaders have signed an open letter decrying 'radicalized Christian nationalism,' arguing that the religious expressions by insurrectionists during the Jan. 6 attack on the U.S. Capitol are 'heretical' and a 'perversion of the Christian faith.'"[20]

As I explained in my article, every Christian I spoke to who attended the January 6 rally was absolutely shocked by the events that transpired as the Capitol was stormed and attacked.[21] They were mortified and appalled beyond words. It did not reflect who they were, and they had no clue such things would take place. That's why I made an important distinction between the serious Jesus followers who were in D.C. to pray for a righteous outcome to the election and those who came ready to do battle. (When I polled my Twitter followers, 79 percent did not know a single Christian who approved of the attack on the Capitol.)[22]

Take a few minutes to research where the violent, pre-rally chatter came from online. Was it from solid evangelical sites where the Word of God is honored, and Jesus is preached? Or was it from right-wing extremist websites? The latter may profess to be Christian, but they have little to connect them to the Christian faith. As the *Washington Post* observed, "The planning for Wednesday's assault on the U.S. Capitol happened largely in plain view, with chatters in far-right forums explicitly discussing how to storm the building, hand-cuff lawmakers with zip ties and disrupt the certification of Joe Biden's election—in what they portrayed as responding to orders from President Trump."[23]

Even the description of a terrorist insurrection was exaggerated, as argued by Tucker Carlson on September 23, 2021, after reviewing some of the video footage of the January 6 event: "So it turns out, the vast majority of people inside the Capitol on January 6 were peaceful. They were not insurrectionists. They shouldn't have been there, they weren't trying to overthrow the government, that's a total crock."[24]

At the same time, there is no question that we—meaning evangelical Christians—got way too close to these dangerous, potentially violent flames and that, in the previous months and days, we became way too identified with Donald Trump and way too caught up in a partisan political spirit. Worse still, the incendiary rhetoric at events like the December 2020 Jericho March in DC *did*, in fact, reflect the sentiments of a significant portion of evangelicals. This cannot be denied.

That's why, despite the fact that the vast majority of evangelicals are not part of the alt-right, the optics on January 6 were very bad, leading to a January 8 tweet that stated, "One aspect that hasn't been picked up on by the media about the #CapitolRiots: the obvious and increasing overlap between the Christian Right and the alt-right. There were Proud Boys & Oath Keepers right alongside Trumpists waving 'Jesus 2020' flags as they stormed the Capitol."[25] (The tweet featured a picture of the Jesus 2020 banner in front of the Capitol.) So, was it "Jesus 2020" or "Jesus through His Man Donald Trump in 2020"?

As the trials unfolded for some of those who stormed the Capitol, this disturbing report was published in the *Washington Post* on July 6, 2021, featuring this provocative headline: "A horn-wearing 'shaman.' A cowboy evangelist.

For some, the Capitol attack was a kind of Christian revolt." The article stated,

> Late last month, one of the accused Jan. 6 Capitol insurrectionists told a D.C. judge that she didn't recognize his authority and was making a "divine special appearance." Another one of the accused streams a solo religious service each week that he calls "Good Morning Sunday Morning." A third runs a 65,000-subscriber YouTube channel where she shares Bible verses and calls herself a "healer of deep inner wounds."

Specifically,

> Pauline Bauer, Stephen Baker and Jenna Ryan were among the thousands who descended on the Capitol in protest of what they falsely called a stolen election, including some who saw themselves engaged in a spiritual war. For many, their religious beliefs were not tied to any specific church or denomination – leaders of major denominations and megachurches, and even President Donald Trump's faith advisers, were absent that day. For such people, their faith is individualistic, largely free of structures, rules or the approval of clergy.[26]

And there was this headline from July 9, 2021: "Additional Church Leaders Arrested in Relation to January 6 Attack on U.S. Capitol."[27] The article provides details of evangelical pastors who were either arrested or were under investigation or who had resigned from their pastoral role after entering the Capitol in January. They were *not* accused of engaging in violent behavior, but they *were* among the thousands who entered the building and walked through the halls, some of them taking pictures and videos. What on earth were they doing there?

That's why, in December 2020, I posted an article responding to a Gen. Flynn editorial which I titled "Sorry, but the American Flag Is Not Directly Related to the Banner of Christ." Flynn had written, "We the people are proud to proclaim that the United States of America is 'One Nation under God'—in this public profession of faith in God, we recognize his Lordship over our country, and we proudly stand beneath the banner of Christ and our flag in which millions have sacrificed their very lives for. In scripture through the strength and commitment of Matthew, he said, 'Whoever is not with Me is against Me'."[28]

But was Jesus, as quoted in Matthew, actually saying that the Left was against Him and the Right was for Him? Isn't that a massive oversimplification, to say the least? And does the fact that we recognize the lordship of Jesus over all of life mean that we can require others to do the same? And how, pray tell, is the banner of Christ directly connected to the American flag? And did the countless Americans who fought in our wars all fight under the banner of Christ?

Decades ago, Christian philosopher Francis Schaeffer issued this important warning: "We must not confuse the kingdom of God with our country. To say it another way: 'We should not wrap Christianity in our national flag.' "[29] But that is exactly what so many of us did, with Donald Trump becoming the man we put our trust in to help us change the nation. I ask again: how did we fall so far?

On November 30, 2020, Trump attorney Joey diGenova said of Chris Krebs, Trump's former cyber-security director, "That guy is a Class A moron. He should be drawn and quartered, taken out at dawn and shot."[30] This was because Krebs had claimed that the presidential election was "the most secure in American history."[31] (Not surprisingly, he was fired by President Trump.)[32]

In response to diGenova's irresponsible rhetoric, I asked my social media followers to denounce his words, since this was not the time for reckless speech. Not when tens of millions of Americans believed the election was stolen and not when the president himself was egging them on.

Some responded by saying to me, "Come on! Everyone knows this was just hyperbole. The guy's a New York lawyer. This is just street talk. Don't be such a snowflake." But that was not really my concern since diGenova obviously did not intend his words to be taken literally. My focus instead was on the response of the larger, pro-Trump, Christian public, and my concern was that, with emotions running so high and anger reaching a boiling point, it would not take much to push people over the edge. We were in danger of losing our bearings completely.

That's why it was heartbreaking to see comment after comment saying, "Krebs has committed treason! He deserves to die!" And many of these comments came from evangelical Christians. To be sure, these people were not calling for gang violence. But they *were* calling on the government to execute this allegedly evil man who betrayed our commander in chief. And they *were* quite serious.

My specific request on Facebook[33] and Twitter[34] simply stated: "If you're the world's most ardent Trump supporter, please tell me you denounce this comment from Trump lawyer Joey diGenova that Chris Krebs, Trump's fired cyber-security head, 'should be drawn and quartered. Taken out at dawn & shot.' Can you denounce this without qualification?"

Instead of denouncing the statement, many poured out anger and hatred, even stating that execution was too small a price to pay for a man like Krebs. This was despite the fact that not one charge had ever been brought against Krebs. Not one. He was simply tried and convicted in the eyes of the people for the crime of saying the election was conducted fairly. "Off with his head!" said the mob in response.

For all we know, Krebs might be one of the most honest men who served in Trump's administration. Or he might be an outright liar. Either way, at the time of this writing, we have zero evidence that he was a terrible traitor worthy of death. Yet the howls of the angry mob kept rising. "Away with him!" they shouted. And again, these were the howls of people who had Bible verses on their social media accounts and offered praises to Jesus for Donald Trump. That's why I poured out my heart on a Facebook video that night, asking if we had completely lost our minds and our souls.[35] How could so many Christians get worked up into such a frenzy?

Barely five weeks later, "Hang Pence" was trending on social media. Yes, the vice president apparently was also guilty of treason, and he deserved to die too. "Coward! Traitor! String him up!" And as "Hang Pence" was trending online, radical Trump supporters were storming the Capitol, traumatizing the nation, and potentially threatening the lives of our elected officials, including Vice President Mike Pence.

So I ask yet again: how did so many of us fall so far? Looking back at this almost two years later, it is not just fair to ask this question, it is necessary to ask it. Coming up with the right answers and then learning from our errors is a matter of life or death.

CHAPTER TWO

The Church of Jesus Is Transcendent

The Church of Jesus—meaning the community of believers worldwide through all generations —is utterly transcendent. It has been purchased at the highest imaginable price —the blood of the Son of God —and it consists of hundreds of millions of redeemed men and women from every background and ethnicity and color. Those who are part of this blood-bought community live in every nation on the earth, yet their ultimate citizenship is in heaven. In the words of Prof. Gerald Sittser, rather than being resident aliens, they are alien residents.[36] They are in this world but not of it.

Those of us who are part of this community are united, but not by any earthly creed or national anthem. We are united based on our shared citizenship in God's heavenly kingdom and our joint status as sons and daughters in His heavenly family. And our real hometown is not the city of our natural birth or current earthly dwelling. Rather, it is a city that is, quite literally, out of this world. As the author of the letter to the Hebrews states,

> you have come to Mount Zion and to the city of the living God, the heavenly Jerusalem, and to innumerable angels in festal gathering, and to the assembly of the firstborn who are enrolled in heaven, and to God, the judge of all, and to the spirits of the righteous made perfect, and to Jesus, the mediator of a new covenant,

and to the sprinkled blood that speaks a better word than the blood of Abel (Hebrew 12:22–24).

We are even called the bride of Christ in Scripture, meaning that corporately we are joined with Him in spirit as a husband and wife are joined together by mutual love. As Paul explained, Jesus the Messiah "loved the church and gave himself up for her, that he might sanctify her, having cleansed her by the washing of water with the word, so that he might present the church to himself in splendor, without spot or wrinkle or any such thing, that she might be holy and without blemish" (Ephesians 5:25–27). What a bright future awaits this sacred community of believers, a future in which we will be completely holy and without fault or blemish of any kind.

We are also likened to a body—specifically, the body of Christ—meaning that we become one with Him, extensions of His very person, functioning in this world as His hands and feet and eyes and ears and mouth, so to speak. To quote Paul again, "Now you are the body of Christ and individually members of it" (1 Corinthians 12:27). That's why it is a grave sin to join ourselves to that which is unclean and defiling. As Paul wrote to these very same Corinthians,

Do you not know that your bodies are members of Christ? Shall I then take the members of Christ and make them members of a prostitute? Never! Or do you not know that he who is joined to a prostitute becomes one body with her? For, as it is written, "The two will become one flesh." But he who is joined to the Lord becomes one spirit with him. Flee from sexual immorality. Every other sin a person commits is outside the body, but the sexually immoral person sins against his own body. Or do you not know that your body is a temple of the Holy Spirit within you, whom you have from God? You are not your own, for you were bought with a price. So glorify God in your body. (1 Corinthians 6:15–20)

But do we grasp the seriousness of these words? Do we really believe what Paul is saying? Do we recognize that our physical bodies belong to God and are part of the body of Christ? Do we understand that if we have sex with a prostitute —or with anyone we are not married to—we defile both ourselves and our Lord? I hear Paul shouting to us again to be sure he has our attention, "Shall I then take the members of Christ and make them members of a prostitute? Never!"

Writing to this same audience in another letter, Paul put it like this (it's a lengthy passage, but please chew on every word):

Do not be unequally yoked with unbelievers. For what partnership has righteousness with lawlessness? Or what fellowship has light with darkness? What accord has Christ with Belial [meaning, Satan]? Or what portion does a believer share with an unbeliever? What agreement has the temple of God with idols? For we are the temple of the living God; as God said,

"I will make my dwelling among them and walk among them, and I will be their God, and they shall be my people. Therefore go out from their midst, and be separate from them, says the Lord, and touch no unclean thing; then I will welcome you, and I will be a father to you, and you shall be sons and daughters to me, says the Lord Almighty."

Since we have these promises, beloved, let us cleanse ourselves from every defilement of body and spirit, bringing holiness to completion in the fear of God. (2 Corinthians 6:14–7:1)

Coming from a different angle, with an emphasis on our calling to be priests and living stones in God's temple, Peter writes: "As you come to [Jesus], a living stone rejected by men but in the sight of God chosen and precious, you yourselves like living stones are being built up as a spiritual house, to be a holy priesthood, to offer spiritual sacrifices acceptable to God through Jesus Christ" (1 Peter 2:4–5). He continues, "But you are a chosen race, a royal priesthood, a holy nation, a people for his own possession, that you may proclaim the excellencies of him who called you out of darkness into his marvelous light" (1 Peter 2:9).

What a lofty calling and sacred vocation. What a weighty responsibility and awe-inspiring privilege. Not only are we the Messiah's family; the Messiah's bride; children of God; citizens of an eternal, heavenly kingdom; and members of the Messiah's body; but we are also a chosen race, a royal priesthood, a holy nation, a people for his own possession.

That's why Peter writes to us as sojourners and exiles, meaning that we are just passing through this world. And that's why he urges us not to mingle with the sins of the world. Instead, he calls us to live differently in order to bring glory to God, writing: "Beloved, I urge you as sojourners and exiles to abstain from the passions of the flesh, which wage war against your soul. Keep your conduct among the Gentiles honorable, so that when they speak against you as evildoers, they may see your good deeds and glorify God on the day of visitation." (1 Peter 2:11–12).

Once again, we live in this world, but we are not of this world. Our spirit is different. Our mentality is different. Our greatest goals are different. Our methods are different. Even our ultimate allegiance is different since for us there is something higher than the national flag or the team motto or the company slogan. Jesus and Jesus alone is our Lord, and we do not bow the knee of ultimate submission to anyone but Him.

Paul even states that right now, while we live our lives here on earth, eating and drinking and working and having families, our "citizenship is in heaven" (Philippians 3:20). And—get this—Paul says that we are "seated in heavenly places" together with Jesus, as if, spiritually speaking, we were now ruling and reigning with Him at the right hand of God (see Ephesians 1:20–23, 2:6). Talk about being transcendent. Talk about a sacred calling. Talk about what it means to be sons and daughters of Almighty God.

Yet is this very thing that makes our passionate political alliances so grievous. We join the heavenly with the earthly, the sacred with the profane, the pure with the polluted, thereby lowering ourselves and even prostituting ourselves, which means that, in a sense, we lower and prostitute our Lord. To paraphrase Paul's words quoted earlier, "Shall I then take the members of Christ and make them members of the political system? Never!" As expressed by Aleksandr Solzhenitsyn at his commencement address to Harvard University June 8, 1978, "We have placed too much hope in political and social reforms, only to find out that we were being deprived of our most precious possession: our spiritual life. In the East, it is destroyed by the dealings and machinations of the ruling party. In the West, commercial interests suffocate it."[37]

To be clear, we *should* have political involvement since politics intersects with culture and culture intersects with morality and the kingdom of God intersects with politics and culture and morality. But we interact as citizens of a heavenly kingdom not owned by a party or a politician, standing for causes and issues more than for people or parties. We are above politics, even while we vote and lobby and work within politics. We breathe a different spirit and carry a different identity, one that is beyond party affiliation. As for our witness to our communities, we are to be far better known as followers of Jesus than as supporters of a candidate. Yet all too often the opposite is true. Everyone knows who we are voting for, but far fewer know whom we worship. The signs in the front of our yard say it all, as do the hats and shirts we wear and the bumper stickers on our cars. We shout our support for Trump (or Obama or Biden) for the world to hear while we virtually whisper our solidarity with Jesus. (We must use wisdom we say.) And worst of all, we become just like the political system at its worst — crude and cruel, boisterous and bigoted, divisive and demeaning, merciless and mocking.

What has happened to our heavenly calling? What has become of our union with the Lord? Instead of a beautiful aroma there is a stench. Instead of the Holy Spirit there is carnality. Instead of peace and joy there is turmoil and strife. We resemble bickering children more than priests in God's temple, carrying ourselves like angry sports fans rather than like His sacred bride. We sound more like nasty political pundits than the people of God or the members of Messiah's body. How did this happen to us?

God's Word calls us to live like this: "Therefore be imitators of God, as beloved children. And walk in love, as Christ loved us and gave himself up for us, a fragrant offering and sacrifice to God" (Ephesians 5:1–2). How different this is than the spirit of politics. But, to repeat, this does not mean that we disengage from politics, especially when we live in a Democratic Republic like America. (We'll return to this subject often in the pages that follow.) It's the *way* we engage that matters. We never sell our souls. We never compromise our values. We never trade expediency for ethics. In short, we do not lower ourselves into the muddy waters of the political system—and they are muddy; shall we call them a swamp?

Instead, we get involved as members of a third, higher party, casting our votes and calling for action in keeping with our moral and ethical values. We transcend politics just as a disciplined, elite athlete transcends the jeering of the crowd. He or she doesn't run into the stands and scream at a heckler. To do so is both demeaning and dangerous. In fact, if a professional athlete acted that way, they would be fined and disciplined. They are expected to be above such squabbles, bigger than the fans and their petty insults.

Ask yourself for a moment how you would feel if the Queen of England jumped into a crowd of protestors, screaming out profanities and swinging her fists. The Queen? It is the same with us as God's people, except infinitely more so. Our royal status is much higher than that of any earthly monarch. How dare we stoop so low.

So, we pray for our national leaders, but we are not politically partisan (meaning we don't identify primarily with a party rather than an issue), which is why Rev. Billy Graham was invited to counsel both Democratic and Republican presidents. He may have voted Republican all his life (I'm not saying he did; I'm simply saying he might have). He certainly opposed some Democratic policies later in life, quite openly (see chapter 11 for more details) because he was a Christian leader rather than a political leader. But when you thought of him, you didn't think of politics, you thought of the gospel. That's the way it should be with us, both as leaders and as followers of Jesus. As for those of us who are called to be on the front lines of politics, and some of us certainly are, our conduct should be in keeping with the gospel, and we should be identified as disciples more than as appendages of a political party.

Unfortunately, we often lose our way here, joining ourselves to the spirit of the age, becoming as partisan as the political system and as nasty (and childish) as the worst attack ads. We gleefully repost all kinds of mocking memes and loudly castigate those who differ with us—even our fellow Christians—insulting them in the basest of ways. And we do this, we claim, because God has emboldened us, because we are full of the Spirit, because we will not back down. What a deception. What a severe degrading of our holy calling. What a pathetic compromise. In reality, when we, God's people, fight primarily with political or worldly weapons, we forfeit our supernatural strength. We dilute our spiritual authority, and like Samson with his hair shorn, we become like other, mere human beings. And what lasting fruit do we have to show for it?

Look again at the verses about us being citizens of the heavenly Jerusalem (Philippians 3:20), about us being members of the body of Christ (1 Corinthians 12), about us being His bride (Ephesians 5:25–32), about us being priests in His holy temple (1 Peter 2:4–5), and then look at what we have become through our political unions. When you see it and grasp it and feel it, it is a truly heartbreaking picture.

The truth is that the church should be leading the way in moral and cultural reformation. We should be on the front lines of confronting evil and calling out injustice. And politicians should be appealing to us for our vote and our support, recognizing that they need us more than we need them. As for Christians who are called to political office, the moment they compromise their values for the sake of political gain is the moment they have sold their souls for the sake of power. They, along with each of us, are called to something much higher.

Probably the most grievous thing that has taken place in recent years in our conservative evangelical circles is that some Christian politicians have sold out. We became more identified with Trump (or another candidate) than with Jesus. Or perhaps worse still, we equated Trump with Jesus, meaning that if you were for Jesus, then you were for Trump. It even felt as if we were equally passionate about both, if not even more passionate politically than spiritually. And in the eyes of a watching world (a world with millions of young people who were paying careful attention), we resembled disciples of Trump more than disciples of Jesus. What a costly failure for the people of God. And what a tragedy for those we were called to reach.

Of course, it is not too late to turn to God in repentance (many of us have already), and it is not too late to repair the breaches. But we can only do that when we recognize the full extent of our fall, and we can only see the extent of that fall when we realize the lofty nature of our call. Do we?

CHAPTER THREE

God, Guns, and Our Great White Country? Not So Fast

It is very easy to paint a caricatured picture of Trump's conservative Christian supporters as if they were all gun-toting, immigrant-hating, xenophobic, homophobic, white supremacists. But to do so would be grossly inaccurate, not to mention missing the whole point of political *seduction*. In other words, if the relationship between Trump and American evangelicals was as natural as peanut butter and jelly, then there would be no need to write a book like this. If that were the case then Trump and his Christian followers would be made for each other, fitting together like a hand and glove. No mystery, no surprise, and certainly no seduction. Politically motivated evangelicals were waiting for a man just like Donald Trump. When he finally rose up on the scene, they joyfully embraced him. But is that accurate?

In her 2020 book *Jesus and John Wayne: How White Evangelicals Corrupted a Faith and Fractured a Nation*, Kristin Kobes Du Mez argued that

> evangelical support for Trump was no aberration, nor was it merely a pragmatic choice. It was, rather, the culmination of evangelicals' embrace of militant masculinity, an ideology that enshrines patriarchal authority and condones the callous display of power, at home and abroad. By the time Trump arrived proclaiming himself their savior, conservative white

evangelicals had already traded a faith that privileges humility and elevates "the least of these" for one that derides gentleness as the province of wusses. Rather than turning the other cheek, they'd resolved to defend their faith and their nation, secure in the knowledge that the ends justify the means. Having replaced the Jesus of the Gospels with a vengeful warrior Christ, it's no wonder many came to think of Trump in the same way. In 2016, many observers were stunned at evangelicals' apparent betrayal of their own values. In reality, evangelicals did not cast their vote despite their beliefs, but because of them.[38]

In short, Du Mez claims, "Donald Trump did not trigger this militant turn; his rise was symptomatic of a long-standing condition,"[39] a statement she supports with extensive polling data along with interesting contrasts with conservative black Christians in America, an important sector of believers who largely do *not* identify as evangelicals precisely because of their differences with white evangelicals on a number of key points.[40]

Similarly, in her 2019 book *Red State Christians*, Angela Denker explained why, in her view, so many evangelicals quickly warmed up to Trump:

Cheering his dark and dire depiction of America were millions of Red State Christians, many of them weaned on church traditions that taught Christian Nationalism, the importance of America as a Christian country, and the fear that America was being destroyed for its apostasy. Somehow, despite being raised a millionaire's kid in New York City, Trump spoke their language. He understood their colloquialisms and appealed directly to Red State Christians across America, whether by eating a taco bowl on Cinco de

Mayo, shouting "Merry Christmas," bragging about his Big Mac consumption, or saying things that sounded racist, sexist, and rude. While Trump was connecting through the power of shared language, Democrats sounded like foreigners to Red State Christians across the South and rural America. Leading liberals didn't understand the language, much less speak it.[41]

Again, however, these statements represent an oversimplification, if not actually mischaracterizations, of these issues, although both Du Mez and Denker have accurately described *some* of Trump's support. (We'll return to both of these books in the pages that follow.) The fact is that there were deeper issues involved, issues of genuine Christian concern, issues with biblical foundations, and issues which could not be dismissed simply based on a shallow, carnal form of macho Christian nationalism. (For our discussion of Christian nationalism, see chapters 12 and 13.)

Is It Really So Simple?

It is true that major evangelical leaders like Mike Huckabee, a former presidential candidate as well as the former governor of Arkansas, have written books with titles like *God, Guns, Grits, and Gravy* (2014) and *The Three Cs That Made America Great: Christianity, Capitalism, and the Constitution* (2020).[42] But again, there is much more going on in these books than the titles suggest (note that the second title does not equate Christianity with Capitalism or the Constitution, as if the three were the same), and it is all too easy to caricature. After all, isn't that what the Right does to the Left and the Left does to the Right? Isn't that why we often pass each other like ships in the night, not talking to one another but rather talking through one another?

The reality is that—in the eyes of many fine, Christian Americans—the nation has been going in a very dangerous direction for quite some time. Racial diversity is not the issue, as many of these Americans live in racially diverse neighborhoods, have racially diverse circles of friends, or attend racially diverse churches. These Christians don't fall asleep at night draped in the American flag, nor do they recite the pledge of allegiance as a family after breakfast. And while many might be gun owners, unless they are avid hunters or they fear the government is trying to strip them of their right to bear arms, guns are hardly ever a major topic of conversation.

Instead, they are grieved over the ongoing slaughter of the unborn. To them, it is a monstrous evil and a cause for real grief and concern. And, they wonder, can we overturn *Roe v. Wade* and develop a culture of life, or will divine judgment overtake us first?

To them, the sexualizing of our children—from overt sex-ed curricula beginning in elementary schools to drag queens reading to toddlers in libraries, and from the endless stream of sensual music videos to the ubiquitous presence of online porn—is beyond obscene. Have we completely forgotten how to blush?

To them, as much as they welcome all people into their churches to hear the gospel, LGBTQ activism has emerged as a real threat to their freedoms of speech, religion, and conscience and is also contributing to the downgrading of the sanctity of marriage. Opposing this activism has nothing to do with homophobia and everything to do with believing that God's ways are best. Should they not care?

To them, having secure borders is simply a matter of common sense, in harmony with policies previously advocated by Democratic presidents such as Bill Clinton and Barack Obama. What nation can survive without secure borders? Legal immigrants will always be welcome, but everyone must abide by the same rules.

To them, America plays an important role in the world, and without strong leadership from the White House down, China will only increase as a dangerous, oppressive world power; Iran will flex its muscles against Israel and the Middle East; and murderous terrorism will spread unchecked. A healthy America means a safer world. What is so wrong or unchristian about values like this?

Yet every day these same Christian conservatives watch with real concern as people with radically different agendas and worldviews gain more and more control of our nation. Some of them are openly anti-Christian, yet they are now professors at our top universities and leaders in the fields of commerce, finance, media, and technology. Do these Christians just sit back and do nothing?

Indeed, people who seem even to hate America, people who despise our past and disdain our present, people who seem ashamed to be Americans, people who glorify socialism, people who want the government to micromanage every area of our lives—these people seem to be taking over the nation. Were evangelicals so wrong in feeling concerned? And were they so wrong in cheering on a surprising champion despite his many flaws?

These Christians also see the degree to which Big Tech is cooperating with the Left, censoring their posts, blocking them on social media, banning their books, even telling them which apps they can and cannot use. Who put Big Tech in charge of the world?[43]

Try to Put Yourself in the Shoes of Christians Who Voted for Trump

Then there is the constant mantra of the liberal media not only painting Trump in the worst possible light but doing the same thing to his followers. Not only is Trump a racist but so are all his supporters. Not only is he a womanizing pig but so are all his followers. Not only is he a xenophobic bigot but so are all his voters. "You're all a bunch of vile, white supremacists," says the steady stream of attacks. "You should be ashamed of yourselves."

Truth (at least, the "truth" as we heard it day and night during the Trump presidency) be told, the man can be compared to Hitler. What does this say about all those who voted for him? And what about when Hillary Clinton made her infamous comment about Trump supporters, likening them to a "basket of deplorables"? That became a term of honor: "Yes, I'm one of those deplorables too!"

From the perspective of Trump voters, we were being labeled as racists and bigots and haters—even the people of color among us—when, in fact, we were simply Christians who loved and appreciated our country. And because we were demonized as human beings simply for voting for Trump, things became personal. When others attacked him, it felt like they were attacking us, and this only got worse after January 6, 2021, when all Trump supporters were being blamed for "the insurrection." Yes, despite the fact that we were beyond mortified by the storming of the Capitol, if we voted for Trump, we were there in DC that day, we were part of the crowd that broke through the police lines, and we were all guilty of treasonous crimes.

And this was not an accusation made in the heat of the moment in the immediate aftermath of January 6. To the contrary, this became an oft-repeated narrative, to be echoed and embellished in the months to come, as on August 1, 2021, when commentators on CNN likened Trump supporters to the Jonestown cult that resulted in the coerced suicide of more than nine hundred devotees of Jim Jones.

Speaking with Rep. Jackie Speier, who herself survived a shooting at the airport near Jonestown, CNN's Brian Stelter said, "These citizens in other countries sometimes email me, and say you know why doesn't the American media just call out Trump for what he is? Call Trump fandom for what it is? Sometimes they use the word 'cult.' I know that's a sensitive word, doesn't come up a lot in American news coverage, so I wanted to put it to an expert, an unfortunate expert."

Stelter said that he "wanted to hear her thoughts about the comparison, the notion of the cult of Trump, especially in the light of January 6 and the mass delusion that led to a riot of lies on Capitol Hill."

Representative Speier responded, "There's no question that you could compare Jim Jones as a charismatic leader who would bring his congregation together. And the only difference between Jim Jones and Donald Trump is the fact that we now have social media, so all these people can find themselves in ways that they couldn't find themselves before."[44]

Note those words carefully: "the only difference between Jim Jones and Donald Trump is the fact that we now have social media." Then ask yourself how this makes you feel if, after much careful consideration and even prayerful reflection, you felt that Trump was a better choice for president than either Hillary Clinton or Joe Biden. You would not be feeling too kindly right now towards CNN. Fake news indeed!

When former President George W. Bush spoke on the twentieth anniversary of 9/11, comparing the Islamic terrorists who murdered thousands of our people to the people who stormed the Capitol on January 6, 2021, many Trump supporters felt as if they were being personally attacked. President Bush had said, "There is little cultural overlap between violent extremists abroad and violent extremists at home. But in its disdainful pluralism, in their disregard for human life, in their determination to defile national symbols, they are children of the same foul spirit, and it is our continuing duty to confront them."[45] Yet Trump supporters took this personally, not simply pointing out the ill-advised nature of the comparison, but saying, "You're talking about us, aren't you?"

Joe Kent, a Republican congressional candidate tweeted sharply:

> The only place Bush should be on 9/11 is answering to the American people for all his lies.
>
> Instead he's just showing us that the regime is not just one party, it's the ruling class that despises us & is not done exploiting us.[46]

And Jack Posobiec, senior editor of the major conservative publication *Human Events*, tweeted:

> Bush is publicly comparing 9/11 to Jan 6
>
> They want Trump supporters treated like jihadists.
>
> Are you paying attention yet?[47]

So, even though former president Bush was specifically pointing to those who stormed the Capitol, it felt as if he was attacking all of us who supported Trump, and this, nine months into the Biden presidency. The divide between them against us—between the elite ruling class and those who truly cared about our nation—was growing wider and deeper.

Evangelical Christians and the Origins of America

As for the Christian origins of America, we were fully aware that we had a very checkered past, and we made no excuses for it. At the same time, we were proud to be Americans and we knew there was a reason that people all over the world were trying to become citizens of our great country. We understood why the American flag represented freedom and hope to many oppressed peoples worldwide, and we knew that, to whatever extent we were a blessed nation, it was because of the Christian principles that helped inspire our founding. There was nothing xenophobic here, let alone racist.

We took exception to those who hated our flag and wanted to undo the very things that made us great. Sure Donald Trump was crude, vulgar, prideful, self-centered, and narcissistic, but he stood up as our unexpected champion and was willing to fight for many of the things that were important to us. He even seemed more interested in protecting our religious freedoms than some of our own Christian leaders. In our two-party system, what was so wrong in supporting him? And wasn't a vote for him a vote against Hillary Clinton or Joe Biden?

Obviously, I can't speak for all evangelical Trump supporters, and I'm not trying to paint a comprehensive picture here. But the reality is that the reasons that tens of millions evangelicals became such ardent Trump supporters are much more complex than meet the eye, and if we oversimplify the issues from the past, we will never learn the right lessons going forward.

The fact is I have lived in the evangelical world for decades. I'm friends with a number of the evangelical leaders who were close to Trump. I've spoken at countless evangelical churches and spent many hours in private meetings discussing the pressing needs of our nation. And the vast majority of the men and women with whom I have worked do not fit the description given by the mainstream media at all. In reality, the relationship that developed between my colleagues and Donald Trump was a surprising one, to the point that I often heard, "Out of the seventeen Republican candidates, Trump was my seventeenth choice." The fact they eventually voted for him and did their best to support him was hardly a fait accompli.

As for the storming of the Capitol, I knew quite a few believers who were in DC on that day, praying for a fair outcome to the election, having deep concerns that it had truly been stolen. But to a person, they were horrified by the events that unfolded. This was not who they were, and it did not express their views. Not in the least.

Blacks and Hispanics Who Supported Trump

What do we say about the many black and Hispanic Trump voters, people who, quite obviously, do not fit the mold of xenophobic white supremacists? Writing for the *New York Post*, Gianno Caldwell, himself black, asked, "Why the supposedly racist Trump grew his numbers with black and Latino voters"? He observed:

> They called Donald Trump "the grand wizard of 1600 Pennsylvania Avenue." They said Donald Trump is a "racial arsonist." They even warned that if you support Donald Trump, you're a racist, too.
>
> Democrats have been demonizing the president as a bigot since he descended his golden escalator in 2015. Indeed, many say that no black or Latino American should ever support Trump and that if they do, they are self-hating sell-outs.
>
> Rep. Maxine Waters (D-Calif.), for example, said recently that young black men who "think somehow they can align themselves with Trump" are betraying their race.

Yet, Caldwell continued:

> Despite statements such as Waters', President Trump has invested heavily in the black and Hispanic communities. Policies like the First Step Act, opportunity zones and funding for historically black colleges and universities have paid off. As of this writing, exit polls conducted by Edison Research show President

Trump won at least 18 percent of black men this year, up from 13 percent in 2016, and 8 percent of black women, doubling his percentage from four years ago.

The president also increased his support among Latino Americans. According to Edison Research, he captured 36 percent of Latino men and 32 percent of Latino women. These votes helped Trump secure victories in Texas and Florida.

Trump received historic levels of black support not seen since 1960, and record-breaking Latino support suggests people value policy over rhetoric.[48]

Well, what do you know! Shall we factor all this into the larger picture as well? Could it be that things are not as simple as some people make them out to be? Could it be that we have lost our sense of nuance, thereby losing our grasp of the truth? Not everything is a matter of good versus evil or integrity versus corruption. Often there is a mixture, one in which many factors are weighed and considered. To caricature is to do a disservice.

Does it matter that Trump took historic strides in prison reform, something that affected minorities in particular? Does it matter that, as Caldwell noted, Trump showed real solidarity with our black colleges and universities? And shouldn't this matter to followers of Jesus? Even Trump's emphasis on a healthy economy was not simply a matter of greed or a crass appeal to American carnality. To the contrary, a healthy economy creates more potential opportunities for all Americans and makes a way to provide more help to our struggling inner cities. What's so evil about this?

By no means was all evangelical support of Trump misguided. To the contrary, much of it made sense, excellent sense. The problem is that many of us lost our perspective and went way too far in our support—let alone our adoration—of Trump. The problem is that many of us compromised our ethics in the process, failing to recognize the real damage that Trump was doing (while also doing much good). The problem is that many of us confused patriotism with spirituality. The problem, in short, is that many of us got seduced.

But how exactly does seduction take place? We'll take that up in the next chapter.

CHAPTER FOUR

The Subtlety of Seduction

It started so innocently, with no evil intent. After all, Alan had been in pastoral ministry for more than twenty years, counseling hundreds of couples with marital troubles, and he had established strict safety guidelines. He never counseled the opposite sex alone. He never played emotional games. He never took advantage of a vulnerable, hurting person. After all, he was in the ministry, and this was sacred work. He would never bring reproach to the name of the Lord.

As Alan had done countless times before, he sat down to counsel yet another couple, hearing them out, sharing his wisdom, giving them some practical homework to do, and agreeing to see them again in two weeks. But this time, things were different. The woman, whom we'll call Sarah, was about ten years younger than Alan and very attractive, and she was close friends with his personal secretary, who gave both Sarah and her husband his personal email address. Yet it was Sarah, not her husband, who liked to communicate via email, and before he knew it, Alan was answering multiple emails a day from this pretty gal. Of course, all the communication was spiritually based and completely above board. Still, just to be safe, Alan blind-copied his wife too. Better safe than sorry! Sarah so appreciated Alan's sermon on Sunday. It gave her a lot to think about. His counseling session also made her realize where she was falling short. She absolutely wanted to make this marriage work. Every day, she thanked God for Alan!

Soon enough he decided there was no reason to bother copying his wife on the emails. Why give her something else to read? Plus, if he was being honest with himself, he was feeling a slight emotional attachment to Sarah, waiting eagerly for the next email to come in so he could respond at once. Best to keep that to himself. Still, that was as far as it went. He was a pastor and a married man. Under no circumstances would he ever commit adultery. Not a chance!

Unfortunately, his home life was not that great. His wife, Elaine, was super busy juggling the responsibilities of being a mother of four while serving as the wife of a pastor who was in high demand. She was also leading the women's ministry in the church and helping in the community. With the ministry hours he kept as the senior leader of his church, Alan and Elaine weren't connecting that much. They were quietly drifting further apart and experiencing less and less intimacy.

As for the counseling sessions with Sarah and her husband, Alan could not believe that her husband was so insensitive and seemed uninterested in making her happy. Alan would never treat her like that. And she was so sexually frustrated. She said it openly when the three of them met.

Soon enough, Alan and Sarah were texting each other throughout the day. Then they were having lengthy, secret phone calls and sharing their feelings and desires openly. Then they were in bed together. Alan, the pastor of a church, a husband, and a father was having sex with another woman. And it all started so innocently, with no evil intent. But that is how seduction works. That is how we get dragged into something we never intended to get dragged into. We start off with the best intentions. We end up somewhere we never intended to go. That's exactly what happened with many of us and Donald Trump.

Seduction Has Been Here Since the Beginning

Pointing back to the garden of Eden, Paul warned the Corinthian believers about the subtlety of seduction, writing, "But I am afraid that just as Eve was deceived by the serpent's cunning, your thoughts will be led astray from your sincere and pure devotion to Christ" (2 Corinthians 11:3). And how exactly did Satan deceive Eve? Was it with an outright call for her to rebel against God's command? Did he simply say, "Don't listen to the Lord. Just do whatever you want to do"? Not at all. Instead, it was through subtlety, by planting a seed of doubt and suspicion in her mind and by giving her an excuse to focus on the appealing nature of the forbidden fruit. Only then did she consider disobeying her creator, whose command she had likely received from Adam.

That is how seduction normally occurs: in covert ways through the back door. The beginning of the seduction is nuanced and, in some ways, can even appear justifiable. It is only over time that we lose our way, often dramatically. That's when the seduction can become overt. We have lost our will to resist, or, perhaps worse still, we don't even realize that we need to resist. Consider some everyday examples, things many of us can relate to.

Because of your love for God and His Word, you get more and more interested in theological studies, ultimately going to seminary. There, you revel in the riches of the Scriptures and the beauty of the Christian tradition. It is only gradually that you substitute intellectual stimulation for spiritual fervor. Eventually, you find your joy in tearing down those who differ with your beliefs, glorying in your orthodoxy. "How zealous I am for the Lord!" you think to yourself. The tragedy is that you might go on like this for many years—or, even, until the end of your life—without realizing that you have gone backward rather than forward, having left your first love. This is hardly an uncommon occurrence.

Or perhaps you have a real burden for the mission field, wanting to give your life to reach the lost overseas. But you don't want to rely on anyone else's support, so you decide to be a "tentmaker," meaning you will start your own business and become self-supporting. Then, once your business is doing well, you will turn the company's operation over to a colleague and relocate to the foreign field to fulfill your life's calling. Only you never make it overseas. In fact, you don't even reach out to the people in your own neighborhood. That's because you became so prosperous that making money became your mission. This, too, is hardly an uncommon occurrence.

Or maybe you want to use sports as a platform for preaching the gospel, since you are both athletically gifted and a bold witness. You work hard in your sport, sacrificing some of the enjoyments of life to stay ahead and at the same time never compromising your witness. As you get to higher and higher competitive levels, you need to find something new to keep you ahead of the increasingly tough competition. Before you know it, you are taking performance enhancing drugs and have compromised your testimony and integrity, something you would never have dreamed of years earlier when you were so fervent and pure in faith. The pull was just too strong.

Or maybe you were frustrated with the direction of your local school district and with the "good old boys" political scene. As a political outsider strongly opposed to the compromised system, you ran for office and, based on your integrity and your independent thinking, you won. Before long, you were headed to bigger and better things, recognizing the impact you could make on the political scene. You were a breath of fresh air! But as you started to swim in deeper waters, you realized that, without a little compromise here and there, you were destined to remain a big fish in a small pond. Soon enough, you were as corrupt as the very system you rejected, one of the "good old boys" yourself, seduced by the very power you once pledged to fight.

That is how seduction works: it starts off subtly and often progresses gradually. In all these examples, from the pastor and Sarah to the corrupting influence of power, and from the obsession with theological studies to making money or wining in sports, something else took first place in their hearts, getting them out of balance. That is called idolatry, and that is exactly what happened to many of us with Donald Trump—and I write this as someone who voted for him in both 2016 and 2020 and often supported him when he was reviled and attacked.

To put it another way, I understand why many of us supported Trump, and I do not criticize anyone who chose to vote for him. That's why I wrote an article on November 3, 2020, the day before the elections titled "The Case Against Trump and Why He Still Gets My Vote."[49] And that's why, just one mother earlier, on October 5, 2020, I wrote another article titled "Once Again, Why So Many Evangelical Christians Strongly Support Trump."[50]

At that time, the president was battling COVID, and there was a massive groundswell of prayer on his behalf, reflecting the loyalty of his large Christian base. Yet his performance at the first presidential debate one week earlier had been miserable and immature, raising the question again: Why are so many evangelical Christians still so loyal to this man who often behaves in such unchristian ways, trashing people close to him, maligning his opponents in the crudest ways, and, just a few days earlier acting like a little baby in one of the most important debates of his life? Why did we remain so doggedly loyal, more loyal than we had been to any of our presidents in recent decades?

Why We Got Behind Such an Unlikely Candidate

Back in 1998, when evangelical Christians were fed up with the antics of President Clinton, the Southern Baptist

Convention issued a strongly worded resolution on the moral character of public officials, ending with this: "Be it finally RESOLVED, That we urge all Americans to embrace and act on the conviction that character does count in public office, and to elect those officials and candidates who, although imperfect, demonstrate consistent honesty, moral purity and the highest character."[51] And now we were embracing President Trump with tremendous enthusiasm, even claiming that God had raised him up? How did this happen?

Christian historian Randall Balmer, himself an Episcopal priest wrote:

> The number was staggering to anyone who took seriously the Religious Right's claim to be the guardians of probity and "family values." In the 2016 presidential election, 81 percent of white evangelicals supported Donald Trump, a thrice-married former casino operator, and self-confessed sexual predator. How could this possibly be true? Leaders of this movement, after all, had excoriated Bill Clinton for his tawdry encounters with Monica Lewinsky. How could they turn a blind eye to Trump's multiple extramarital affairs and hush payments to a porn star and a Playboy model?[52]

During the Clinton presidency, Dr. James Dobson, one of the most respected and influential evangelical leaders in America, wrote:

> At any given time, 40 percent of the nation's children list the President of the United States as the person they most admire. What are they learning from Mr. Clinton? What have we taught our boys about respecting women? What have our little girls learned about men? How can we estimate the impact of this scandal on future generations? How in the world can

7 out of 10 Americans continue to say that nothing matters except a robust economy? . . .

In his farewell address to the Congress in 1796, George Washington said:

"Of all the disposition and habits which lead to political prosperity, Religion and morality are indispensable supports . . . And let us with caution indulge the supposition, that morality can be maintained without religion . . . reason and experience both forbid us to expect that national morality can prevail in exclusion of religious principle."[53]

Yet two decades later, Dobson, like many other, major evangelical leaders, was also an enthusiastic supporter of President Trump. Wasn't this a deep contradiction? Weren't these Christian conservatives demonstrating their hypocrisy by condemning Clinton while praising Trump? In my October 2020 article, I used the following illustration to help answer these very important and totally justified questions.

Let's say that you and your spouse were committed Christians, raising your four children to honor the Lord and live by biblical principles. Included in those principles are the words of Jesus, who taught that the meek would inherit the earth and the peacemakers would be called children of God. That's one reason that you eschew violent entertainment, from graphic video games to blood-and-gore movies to extremely violent sports.

You just moved into the suburbs, and your next-door neighbor had become famous years ago as the toughest bar fighter in the region, cracking open many a skull in the process. He then transitioned to cage fighting where he has made an excellent living in mixed martial arts, ultimately getting the nice home he now enjoys. And while he is a decent neighbor in some ways, he is not a good role model for your kids. He uses all kinds of profanity. He drinks. He has multiple girlfriends. And he makes his living by inflicting physical damage on others, competing in mixed martial arts.

One day, two of your kids come home from school quite shaken. They were cursed out by some older teens who mocked their Christian faith. They were spat on. And they were threatened. They were also told, "Just see what our dad is going to do your parents! He hates Christians even more than we do. There's a good reason they call him Crazy Ted!"

Later that night, to your shock, Crazy Ted shows up at your door with three of his friends, all of them looking ominous and angry. They begin to scream threats against you, and you can see they have tire irons and knives in their hands. But before you can respond, your neighbor comes running over, ripping into Crazy Ted and his cronies. Although he gets stabbed and struck in the process, he beats them up with his bare hands, elbows, knees, and feet until they are subdued, disarmed, and helpless.

As the police arrive to clean things up, your neighbor leaves the attackers with a threat: "If you ever come near this family again—and that includes your kids coming near their kids—I will tear you apart with my own hands. I mean it!" And with that, he walks back into his house.

How would you feel about your neighbor now? Would you see him in a different light, violence and all? Would you recognize that God just used this profane character, who makes his living beating people up, to save your lives? You still might not approve of his professional career, but you would have a deep sense of gratitude and even loyalty toward him. Your whole perspective would change. And the next time someone criticized him, you would actually stand up on his behalf. After all, he risked his life to save yours. You feel a sense of allegiance. Who else would do what he did? (Now that you think of it, the really sweet neighbors who lived across the street, the ones with a Scripture verse hanging over their door, saw what was happening and didn't even come outside. They were too terrified to move. Yet this foul-mouthed pagan saved your lives.)

Trump Fought for Us So We Fought for Him

Of course, this is meant as an illustration rather than a precise analogy, but the application to Trump, with all his failings and warts and shortcomings, is clear. It was not just that Trump had the guts to fight. It was that *Trump fought for us*. He was, as one of my colleagues said so well, "the people's champion."

That's exactly how a large number of Americans, including many non-evangelicals, felt about Donald Trump, beginning in 2015 and then all the more once he was elected president. Trump was speaking for them and fighting for them. Trump was willing to put himself in harm's way for their sake. He was willing to challenge the lying media. He was willing to take on the political establishment. He was willing to confront the radical leftists who wanted to disfigure our nation. He was willing to call out Big Tech. So what if he lied. So what if he was nasty in the process. So what if he created deeper divisions along the way. No one said this was fun and games, and besides, the future of our nation was at stake. There will always be collateral damage during times of battle and conflict. But when it came to assessing Trump's presidency, his supporters determined that the good far outweighed the bad. This was not the time to play nice. It was time for war, and Trump was our warrior in chief.

When it came to Christian conservatives, the feelings ran just as deep. There were hostile leaders who wanted to wipe us off the map. They despised our beliefs. They wanted to silence us in the public square. They wanted to indoctrinate our children in the schools. They wanted to steal our most fundamental liberties. They also stood for the most egregious sin in our nation, namely the slaughter of the unborn. At last, in Donald Trump we had someone fighting back for us—and for the unborn. At last, we had someone tenacious enough to keep his word no matter what.

And do you really think a baby girl who had been spared from abortion would be upset to know that the man who helped save her life was a profane narcissist? Or that a protester in Hong Kong who risked his life standing up to Communist China would be distressed to learn that the courageous man standing up for him in DC was undisciplined in his tweets?

Yes, Trump was the last person most of us would have chosen for the job, just like the cage-fighting neighbor was the last person we would have chosen for a neighbor and thought would have come to our aid. But, when it came to our nation and Trump, these were existential issues he was fighting for, from the life of the unborn to our religious liberties, and from standing up to Communist China to facing down Islamic terrorism. We appreciated him fighting on our behalf, and the more he was attacked in the process, the more we defended him, even if his words or actions were indefensible. "Don't dare speak against our man!"

In the process, we became apologists for Trump, reacting more to criticism of our president than to criticism of our Lord. In the process, we lost our focus, putting more emphasis on politics than on prayer and becoming more passionate about the elections than about being God's elect. (If you think I'm exaggerating, go back and reread the social media feeds of Trump-supporting Christians in the months before and after November 2020 and tell me what subject was front and center. Or perhaps you can simply review your own social media feeds.)

In the process, we became idolatrous, looking to Trump as God's uniquely anointed man raised up to save America, without whom we were doomed. In the process, we even became drunk with our close connection to power, reveling in the fact that evangelical Christians had a seat at the table right next to Trump, closer to him, it seemed, than any other group in the country. (For the record, I'm not saying the president's evangelical advisers became drunk with power. I'm saying that this was an almost unconscious feeling that permeated our national evangelical psyche. "We" were on the inside, influencing the most powerful man on the planet. That, indeed, is intoxicating.)

This ethos was summed up well by Never Trump evangelical David French,

> The top levels of the bureaucracy filled with Evangelicals, and the administration granted an almost unprecedented amount of access to Evangelical activists. During the 2020 campaign, it was routine to read ministry leaders sharing their "personal" insights into Trump based on time spent in the Oval Office.
>
> Images of Trump surrounded by large numbers of praying Christians sent a clear message to the Evangelical public: *Look how many of us are in the room where it happens.* The word got out—no president in modern times had been more welcoming to Christian ministries. No president has granted Christians greater access.[54]

But with the unprecedented access came many hazards and temptations, which is why I wrote in my October 2020 article that we cross a dangerous line "when we become apologists for Trump. When we defend his indefensible and even destructive behavior. When we look to him rather than to the Lord. When we are better known as Trump supporters than as Jesus followers."

Unfortunately, for many of us, that is exactly what happened: our loyalty went too far. But that is the subtlety of seduction, and that is how so many of us were led astray, to the point of believing crazy, pro-Trump conspiracy theories (discussed in Chapter 9), to the point of insisting the Trump prophets were right and that he would be restored to the presidency in 2021 even after Biden was inaugurated (discussed in Chapters 7 and 8), to the point of being divisive and carnal ourselves (discussed in Chapter 11).

The more the left attacked Trump, the more we defended him. The more they lied about him, the more he became a saint and a martyr in our eyes. The more he kept his promises, the more he merited our unwavering trust. The more he appeared to be the only bulwark that would stop the onslaught of a radical, leftist, even Marxist agenda, the more he became our bigger than life hero. "Yes," we shouted without any sense of shame or self-contradiction, "we love Jesus, and we love Trump! Only Trump can save America! Only Trump can preserve our freedoms!"

In the end, we even began to mirror Trump in our own attitudes and words, acting in ways that we would have deplored just years or even months before, ways that were in violation of our faith and morals. We, too, engaged in mockery and name-calling. We, too, savaged those who rejected Trump's leadership. We even questioned the spirituality of those who could not vote for Trump, as if they were being disloyal to God. And ultimately we took on some of Trump's most unchristian characteristics, just as Psalm 115 declares that those who worship idols become like the idols they worship. Some of us seemed to lose our very selves in the process.

A few weeks after the elections, when emotions were still at a fever pitch and Trump supporters were feeling robbed and raw, I was up late one night reading some online posts written by friends of mine. These were people whom my wife, Nancy, and I had known for years, people of good character, people who were gospel-first in their orientation. But not that night. As I read their pro-Trump posts containing the most ridiculous claims, attacking other believers with angry words, reflecting extreme political biases, I broke down weeping. "What has become of us?" I asked my wife. "These are our friends."

Those posts reflected just the tiniest tip of a massive iceberg. On a national level we had drifted seriously off course, deeply damaging our Christian witness in the process and becoming something we never intended to become. As the pastor of a thriving, mainly millennial church told me early in 2021, he never lost as many people in as short a period of time as he did in the months following the elections. Hundreds of young people walked out the doors of his building disgusted over the evangelical adoration of Trump, which was summed up in a biting (although exaggerated) meme that said (looking ahead to the 2024 elections): "You want to know what's pathetic? There are more Christians looking for the second coming of Trump than the second coming of Jesus Christ."

Yet the whole thing happened so subtly, which is exactly how seduction works. In the rest of this book, we will explore the subtle process of political seduction, not for the purpose of condemning but for the purpose of recovering our way. This is not a mistake we can afford to make again.

The Sword of Political Seduction Cuts Both Ways

Before we analyze how so many of us on the right lost our way, it's important to point out that the sword of political seduction cuts both ways. Plenty of Left-leaning Christians and Never Trumpers lost their way as well. Plenty of professing believers on the Left justified their own hateful words and attitudes—after all, it was Trump and his followers they were reviling—just as professing believers on the right justified their hateful attitudes and words—after all, it was

Trump they were defending. And how many Christians today have embraced the latest woke talking points with passion and zeal and determination somehow confusing the PC agenda with an awakened biblical faith. How many have turned the BLM movement, with all its Marxist tenets, into an arm of the gospel? How many have uncritically imbibed CRT as if it were the new spiritual orthodoxy and adhering to it was the proof of true allegiance to Jesus?

Hypocrisy is not hard to find, be it on the left or right or middle, and self-righteousness is not a rare commodity. So, in the words of Jesus, before you take out the splinter in your brother's or sister's eye, be sure to take out the plank in your own eye first (Matthew 7:1–5). All of us do well to get low at a time like this, searching to see where our own hearts may have been seduced rather than pointing a gloating finger at others. God shows no favoritism and tips the scales for no one.

To cite a case in point, Obery Hendricks, a highly regarded religious scholar and Christian activist, begins his 2021 book, *Christians Against Christianity: How Right-Wing Evangelicals Are Destroying Our Nation and Our Faith*, with these scathing words:

> A travesty. That's how I would characterize Christianity in America today. A travesty, a brutal sham, a tragic charade, a cynical deceit. Why? Because the loudest voices in American Christianity today—those of right-wing evangelicals—shamelessly spew a putrid stew of religious ignorance and political venom that is poisoning our society, making a mockery of the Gospel of Jesus Christ. Their rhetoric in the name of their Lord and Savior is mean-spirited, divisive, appallingly devoid of love for their neighbors and outright demonizes those who do not accept their narrow views—even fellow Christians. Perhaps most shocking is their enthusiastic, almost cultish support

for the cruel, hateful policies and pronouncements of President Donald Trump, whose words and deeds more often than not have been the very antithesis of Christian faith.

He continues:

I do not make these claims lightly. And I can't be dismissed as a contentious outsider; I offer these observations as an ardent insider of the faith. I am a proudly ordained elder in the African Methodist Episcopal Church, a former president of its flagship theological seminary, and a dedicated biblical scholar trained at the highest levels of academia. But most significantly, I speak from a lineage of faithful Christians who know the Gospel of Jesus Christ that right-wing evangelicals seem to have left behind: the Gospel that tells us to love our neighbors, to respond to the cries of the poor and the vulnerable, to accept the immigrant stranger, to seek fairness and justice for all. Some might call me a "progressive" Christian, although I reject that and all other labels. I simply believe in the life-affirming, justice-insistent message that Jesus proclaimed and died for. I have little interest in the doctrinal bells and theological whistles that drive so much of Christendom today.[55]

These are strong, confrontational words, and I affirm some of what Dr. Hendricks writes. In fact, I could add my hearty amen to many passages in his book. Yet Dr. Hendricks also devotes a whole chapter to the subject of abortion, challenging the evangelical pro-life position and writing, "Those who take seriously the call of Jesus to love our neighbors must ask the Christians whose unyielding abortion obsession imbues our society with such division and rancor: How can you care so deeply about the unborn, yet show so little compassion and concern for the children of God who are already here?"[56] Seriously? "Unyielding abortion obsession"? Tell that to the slaughtered little ones and to their moms with lifelong scars.

As for allegedly showing "so little compassion and concern for the children of God who are already here," the fact is, "Religious Americans adopt children at two and a half times the overall national rate, and they play a particularly large role in fostering and adopting troubled and hard-to-place kids."[57] When you do more research into the subject of foster care too, you'll see that evangelical Christians, the very ones decried in *Christians Against Christianity*, are among those leading the way here as well.[58]

It is true that Dr. Hendricks writes with erudition and sensitivity, explaining "that the purpose of this chapter is not to pass moral judgment on the painfully divisive issue of abortion. Both pro-choice and antiabortion advocates offer arguments that deserve much greater consideration than I can offer here. Nor is my purpose to question or challenge the sincerity of the everyday people who hold dear those positions."[59] Yet in the process he demonizes millions of pro-life evangelicals, especially those who give themselves tirelessly to fight for the life of the unborn, painting a caricatured picture that does not apply to virtually any of the pro-life leaders I know and fails to recognize their compassionate outreach to the mothers (and born children) too. In doing so, he fails to acknowledge that these same evangelicals often lead the way in ministries of compassion to the hurting and poor worldwide, also giving more to charitable causes than do "progressive" Christians.[60] Once again, the sword of truth cuts both ways.

Similarly, Dr. Hendricks referenced the Moral Majority's "support for school prayer and opposition to abortion, gay rights, feminism, the Equal Rights Amendment, and anything they believed militated against 'family values,' including social welfare programs, which they decried nearly as heartily as they decried pornography and illicit drugs. But," he added, "however sincere their concern for these issues, looming over them was the goal of imposing on all of American society a Christian nationalist agenda, with its ever-present undercurrent of white supremacy. True to the values of its founders, racism remained a driving subtext of the Moral Majority movement."[61]

Once again, while I would second his concern about "a Christian nationalist agenda" (see Chapters 12 and 13), and while I would agree with many of his caveats concerning the Moral Majority (while appreciating the good as well), I strongly differ with his claim that racism, or, more specifically, white supremacy, "remained a driving subtext" of the movement.[62] Or is it only "progressive" Christians or African-American Christians or non-Christians who get to point out the faults of "right-wing evangelicals," especially white right-wing evangelicals? Are there no blind spots in the other groups and camps?

Dr. Hendricks even defends same-sex "marriage," devoting a whole chapter to that subject and concluding that "the biblical passages used to support the claim that homosexuality is a sin are simply too ambiguous, and the supporting evidence too slim and much too open to dispute to be used as the determining factor of even one person's happiness and life chances, much less the lives of untold millions." And he writes, "I've never understood why it is a scandal that two people who plan to spend the rest of their lives in loving communion would seek to consecrate their love in the name of God."[63] He also claimed that, "Nowhere in the Gospel does it say anything about whom we should and should not love, only that we *should* love."[64]

Once again, despite his great learning and his effort to speak with sensitivity, he misses the mark badly in his treatment of the biblical texts. He ignores the very meaning of marriage as the distinct union of a man and woman established by God at creation and reaffirmed by Jesus, and he fails to see the implications of the larger LGBTQ+ agenda, which is causing anguish and pain to millions of families and individuals. And once again, he demonizes "right-wing evangelicals" both anecdotally and philosophically, as if there were not millions of Christian conservatives who oppose homosexual practice *because* of their love for Jesus and their love for their neighbors and who hold to their positions with grace, sensitivity, and compassion.

It is ironic that in a book filled with prophetic insights about the failings of Trump-supporting Christian conservatives, two whole chapters are devoted to making a biblical case *for* abortion (when it is allegedly justified) and *for* same-sex marriage, while many of the author's best statements are marred by exaggerated and even inflammatory claims. To say it once more: the sword of truth (and political seduction) cuts both ways.

In that light, all of us on all sides of the conversation should get low. Very low. Only God is God, and it is His affirmation we seek. May He help us to remove the plank from our own eyes before we point out the speck in our neighbor's eye.

CHAPTER FIVE

How Donald Trump Went from President to Superhero to Political Savior

Pastor Andrew Brunson and his wife, Norine, served as missionaries in Turkey for twenty-three years, doing what missionaries do: preaching the gospel, teaching new converts, serving their community, ministering to the hurting and the poor. Then suddenly and without notice, in October 2016, they were arrested by the Turkish police and put in prison with the understanding that they were about to be deported. Then just as suddenly, Norine was released while Andrew was kept behind bars.

Ultimately, he was charged by the government of Prime Minister Erdogan with terrorist activity and plotting a coup. In fact, he was accused of being the head of a major organization that controlled the FBI, the CIA, and more, not to mention head of the Mormon Church. Of course, the charges were completely bogus—they were beyond ridiculous—but they were used to keep Brunson in Turkish prisons for two long years, with the real threat of life-long imprisonment hanging over his head and filling him with fear.

He was a political hostage—more specifically, a *Christian* political hostage—locked up because of his faith. Thankfully, his case came to international attention, leading to a world-wide prayer movement for his release. It also came to the attention of American leaders, with some of our senators, including Thom Tillis and Lindsey Graham, coming to visit him in prison, and two secretaries of state, Rex Tillerson and Mike Pompeo, fighting for his release in person in Turkey.

But it was President Trump who took it on himself to get Brunson out of jail and back to America, doing what very few national leaders would do, to the point of asking Erdogan to release Brunson and return him to the States not once but three times in their first twenty-three-minute, face-to-face, meeting in DC. Rather than agreeing to Trump's request, Erdogan figured this missionary must be important, and he now had leverage to use against America.

Brunson learned from his wife that when Erdogan had repeated the charges against him to Trump, claiming that Brunson was a terrorist and spy, "Trump's response was vehement and forceful: 'Cut the BS. We know it's not true.'"[65] And when Brunson was subjected to a show trial in Turkey, gaining the attention of the nation, Trump tweeted, "They call him a spy, but I am more a spy than he is."[66] Trump also tweeted that Brunson was a hostage and was being held for no reason at all.[67]

When Erdogan wouldn't budge, Trump turned up the heat, instituting economic sanctions that devastated the Turkish economy. This president was not going to let a foreign strongman mess with one of his own citizens, especially when that citizen was a Christian pastor. When Tony Perkins from the Family Research Council came to visit Brunson, he bought him a personal letter from Trump:

> *Dear Pastor Andrew,*
> *We are praying for you, and we are working to bring you home.*
> *Keep the faith. We will win!*
> *God bless you.*
> *Sincerely,*
> *Donald Trump*[68]

In a matter of weeks, Erdogan caved, Brunson was released, and this beleaguered pastor was on his way back home. He actually met with Trump in the White House the day after he arrived in the States. Trump, along with his team, including Vice President Pence, Secretary of State Pompeo, had come through. Trump stood up to the bully and won—and he did it for a Christian pastor.

How many other presidents would do such a thing? How many would take such personal interest in an imprisoned, American missionary, a man previously unknown to the world? How many would refuse to give an inch to Erdogan's hardnosed tactics, taking him on publicly? But that was Donald Trump doing what he did best, standing up as a champion for beleaguered Christians.

Trump may not have been politically correct, but he got the job done, and millions of Christians were grateful beyond words. In Brunson's own words, "President Donald Trump intervened for me again and again, taking unprecedented steps to secure my release."[69]

By October 2018, Trump had already become somewhat of a legend in the eyes of his conservative Christian supporters. This guy backed his words with action. This guy was a champion for religious liberties. This guy was our friend. Rather than use us to get elected and then drop us once in office—something that had happened to us before—Trump did the exact opposite, opening his door even more once he was in the White House and surrounding himself with solid Christian leaders.

Setting the Stage in June 2015

In June 2015, about one thousand evangelical leaders met with Trump in New York City where he presented his views and answered some of their questions. Although I was unable to attend, quite a few of my friends and colleagues were there. Many of us were quite skeptical, thinking that Trump was doing what any savvy conservative politician would do, namely appealing to this large Christian base. But why should we trust him? Did he suddenly have some kind of epiphany? Were his values now changing? How convenient!

At that meeting, Trump asked how many evangelicals there were in America. He was surprised to hear the number, asking, "Why don't you speak out more?" If there were so many of us, why were we often so silent? Why did we act as if we were a small minority? Why had we lost our voice? Why didn't we work together as one?[70]

Trump promised to help us get our voice back. He would take on the infamous Johnson Amendment that hinders pastors from speaking out more on political issues. He would face down those who sought to steal our religious freedoms. Trump would be our defender and friend—at least that's what he promised. But would he follow through? The answer, to our surprise, was absolutely, categorically yes.[71]

Just look at these news stories from 2016 through 2018. Trump was making promises, and Trump was keeping promises:

- August 8, 2016: "When Donald Trump addresses the Values Voters Summit on September 9th, he will tell the assembled Christians that it is time to get the IRS out of the pulpit. And he will encourage the assorted evangelical and Catholic activists, who have gathered in Washington, D.C. for this event, to surge out of their churches and reoccupy the public square."[72]
- February 2, 2017: "President Donald Trump praised America's faith-based values, vowing to defend them from an increasingly dangerous world, in a speech at the National Prayer Breakfast Thursday. 'America will thrive as long as we continue to have faith in each other and faith in God,' Trump said. 'That faith in God has

inspired men and women to sacrifice for the needy, to deploy to wars overseas, and lock arms at home to ensure equal rights for every man, woman, and child in our land.'"[73]

- May 10, 2017: "On May 4, 2017, *President Trump* signed an executive order that directs the executive branch to limit its enforcement of the '*Johnson Amendment*.' As previously reported, the Johnson Amendment prohibits organizations that are exempt under section 501(c)(3) of the *Internal Revenue Code* from engaging in political campaign activities."[74]

- October 14, 2017: "Tony Perkins, the president of the Family Research Council, said on Friday that President Donald Trump is keeping the most important promise he made on the campaign trail. 'I believe that the defense of our religious freedom is the most important,' Perkins told Breitbart News at FRC Action's Values Voter Summit in Washington, DC."[75]

But Trump was just getting started. As reported by NBC News February 24, 2019,

A NBC News and Columbia Journalism Investigations review of dozens of court cases found that in its first two years the Trump administration's Justice Department submitted more friend-of-the-court briefs in religious liberties cases than the Obama administration and the Bush administration during their first two years. It has also filed briefs at lower, trial court levels faster than both of the two previous administrations.

The filings are in keeping with the Trump administration's forthright position on religious liberty. "A dangerous movement, undetected by many, is now challenging and eroding our great tradition of religious freedom," then-Attorney General Jeff Sessions said at the Department of Justice's Religious Liberty Summit last July. "This president and this Department of Justice are determined to protect and even advance this magnificent heritage."[76]

Whether he was posturing or not, whether he was just being a smart politician, either way he was getting the job done, and in unprecedented fashion at that. We never had a president like Donald Trump before. At least that's what a lot of evangelicals were saying after years of feeling used and then neglected or abandoned by previous leaders.

Marc A. Thiessen, a columnist with the *Washington Post* and a senior fellow with the American Enterprise Institute expressed things well in a March 29, 2018, article titled "Trump might be the most pro-religion president ever." He wrote:

> Conservative Christians are being accused of hypocrisy. How can so-called "values voters" continue to stand with President Trump despite revelations that he allegedly had affairs with a porn star and a Playboy model, and paid them for their silence?
>
> No doubt some Christian leaders have gone too far in rationalizing Trump's past personal behavior and excusing his offensive comments while in office. He is a deeply flawed man. But Trump does have one moral quality that deserves admiration: He keeps his promises.
>
> During the 2016 campaign, Trump pledged to defend religious liberty, stand up for unborn life and appoint conservative jurists to the Supreme Court and federal appeals courts. And he has done exactly what he promised. The abortion-rights lobby NARAL complains that Trump has been "relentless" on these

fronts, declaring his administration "the worst ... that we've ever seen." That is more important to most Christian conservatives than what the president may have done with a porn actress more than 10 years ago.[77]

Thiessen hit the nail on the head. He asked the right questions. He did not downplay Trump's flaws. (But why would he? Thiessen is not a political conservative.) He acknowledged that some Christian leaders had gone overboard in their defense of Trump. And he put into perspective just why we were standing with him.

He also underscored how radical and extreme the left had become and how so many Christians were feeling that their most fundamental liberties were under assault, explaining:

> Trump's election came as religious liberty was under unprecedented attack. The Obama administration was trying to force the Little Sisters of the Poor to violate their religious conscience and facilitate payment for abortifacient drugs and other contraceptives. During oral arguments in the Obergefell v. Hodges case, President Barack Obama's solicitor general told the Supreme Court that churches and universities could lose their tax-exempt status if they opposed same-sex marriage.
>
> Hillary Clinton promised to escalate those attacks. In 2015, she declared at the Women in the World Summit that "religious beliefs ... have to be changed"—perhaps the most radical threat to religious liberty ever delivered by a major presidential candidate. Had Clinton won, she would have replaced the late conservative Justice Antonin Scalia with a liberal jurist, giving the Supreme Court a liberal judicial-activist majority.[78]

Significantly, Thiessen also noted that, "The president is moving at record pace to fill the federal appeals courts with young conservative judges who will protect life and religious freedom for decades."[79] Yes, for decades.

The implications of all this were huge. We could either support this unruly, often profane, even reckless president who would help preserve the liberties of our children and grandchildren and who would fight tirelessly for the lives of the unborn, or we could get self-righteous and petty, refusing to back the most pro-Christian president in our lifetimes. For most of us, the choice was obvious.

Writing for the *New York Times* on September 12, 2019, Jeffery C. Mays explained, "Nearly two years ago, the New York City Council celebrated when it passed a far-reaching ban on conversion therapy, a discredited practice to change a person's sexual orientation or gender identity." Of course, his opening words expressed his own liberal biases, using the standard talking points, including the term "conversion therapy" (a term used by critics of sexual orientation change efforts) and parroting the lie that people cannot see changes in their orientation or gender confusion with the help of professional counseling.

He continued:

> On Thursday, Corey Johnson, the Council speaker, who is gay, said the Council would act swiftly to repeal the ban.
>
> The move is a gambit designed to neutralize a federal lawsuit filed against the city by a conservative Christian legal organization; if the case were to be heard by the Supreme Court, advocates for the L.G.B.T. community fear that the panel could issue a ruling that could severely damage attempts to ban or curtail conversion therapy.[80]

This unrighteous and unethical ban on counseling freedom had been challenged by a New York-based Orthodox Jewish counselor, with the help of the Alliance Defending Freedom. As Mays reported,

> "This law was a textbook violation of free speech and the right of individuals to pursue the lives and identities they want to exercise," said Roger Brooks, a senior lawyer for the group, which says its mission is to defend religious freedom.
>
> "We went in with confidence that the courts would agree with us," he said. "This move by the city suggests that on mature consideration, they think that would be the outcome as well."[81]

The reality, of course, is that New York City only made this abrupt about-face because of Trump-appointed justices, who were willing to hear the case because they knew the ban was unconstitutional. If they overturned the ban, they knew an appeal would likely lose in the federal courts (and/or the Supreme Court), hopefully striking a blow against similar bans throughout the country.

Trump was still in his first term, and the trickle-down effect of his leadership was already being felt. What would happen over the next ten or twenty or thirty years? And what about Trump's promises to Israel, beginning with moving our embassy to Jerusalem, something that Presidents Bill Clinton and George W. Bush and Barack Obama all failed to do, even though our government officially recognized Jerusalem as the capital of Israel back in 1995? Others talked about doing it. Trump did it. Speaking in August 2018, he explained that he moved the capital of Israel to Jerusalem "for the evangelicals."[82]

As American-Israeli anti-terrorist activist David Rubin pointed out, "The out-of-the-box move by the Trump administration was groundbreaking. As opposed to the expected uptick in terrorism and war, it led to a surprising peace process between Israel and its Muslim neighbors." Yes, rather than the move leading to the collapse of the Middle East, it led to the Abraham Accords. What's more, Rubin notes, Trump was also responsible for:

- The closing of the PLO shadow embassy in Washington, DC.
- The withdrawal from the dangerous Iran nuclear deal.
- The (ignored) demand that the Palestinian Authority stop paying salaries to terrorists.
- The official recognition of Israeli sovereignty over the strategic Golan Heights.
- The official recognition that there is nothing illegal about Israeli communities in Judea and in Samaria.[83]

No president in our history had done what Trump had done. He was becoming bigger than life. And he did all this while fighting off the daily attacks of the mainstream media and the ongoing attempts of Democratic leaders to remove him from office. Where did he get such resolve?

He also voided our disastrous nuclear treaty with Iran, faced down tyrannical China, stood with the Hong Kong protesters, took out major Islamic terrorists, and when threatened by the rogue leader of North Korea, who pointed to the nuclear button on his table, Trump responded by calling him Rocket Man and telling Kim Jong-un that his own button was "much bigger" and "more powerful."[84] You don't mess with Donald Trump and the USA.

And so this philandering, thrice-married, New York City businessman, this narcissistic wheeler-dealer who made money off casinos with strip clubs, this man accused by numerous women of sexual harassment or assault, this profane character whose verbal attacks were beyond crass and demeaning, this divider and disruptor, *this same Donald Trump* had done in a few short years what other presidents and sessions of Congress had not done in decades.

And his door was always open to us for input, for prayer, for counsel. This meant that we could continue to help him grow and mature, since he did, after all, profess faith in Jesus. We could urge him to step higher and treat others more kindly. But when it came to life-and-death policies, when it came to our essential freedoms, when it came to making the world a better place for our children and grandchildren, Donald Trump was our man, and we had his back. Four more years of Trump!

As for other, potential Republican candidates who might run for president in 2020, none of them had a chance. Trump was getting the job done. The others were politicians. Only Trump could be trusted.

The Left Swings Farther Left

At the same time, the leftist agenda was becoming more extreme. There was talk of packing the Supreme Court, which would effectively undo all the good that Trump and his conservative predecessors had done, virtually guaranteeing decades (or generations) of anti-Christian decisions. Candidate Joe Biden had said that, should *Roe v. Wade* be overturned, he would turn it into federal law. He also tweeted that transgender rights had become *the* civil rights issue of our day, something that can sound quite innocent but in reality has harsh implications for children in schools, for women's sports, and for religious liberties.

There was also the very real concern that our borders would be opened wide to a flood of illegal immigrants, who would quickly become US citizens and be recruited to vote as Democrats, effectively tipping the balance of power to the point of no return. Republicans might never win a national election again. And what of the outright socialist agenda of

candidates like Bernie Saunders, seconded by populist representatives like Alexandria Ocasio Cortez? Should we not take
this seriously? Wasn't the very direction of our nation at stake?

While all this was being discussed on a theoretical level,
our cities were literally on fire, set ablaze by anarchist mobs.
They just might march into your city (or neighborhood)
next! Plus, if the Democrats have their way, you won't have a
weapon with which to defend yourself. As Rich Kiper wrote
in an op-ed piece published July 16, 2020,

> Remember that moment in September 2019 when
> Democratic presidential candidate Beto O'Rourke
> threw his hand in the air? He yelled, "Hell, yes, we're
> going to take your AR-15, your AK-47."
>
> That was a precursor to what the Democrats really
> want. Now they are coming after your handguns, too.
>
> Probably most of us have read about or watched
> the video of protestors destroying a gate to gain access
> to private property. When told to leave, they did not.[85]

What will happen when one of these mobs comes
storming into your community and threatens your family? If
the Democrats are in power, you might not be able to defend
yourself, which means that your only defense is to keep them
out of power. And the only way to do that was to vote for
Donald Trump. Only he could stop this onslaught of evil.
Only he could stand up to the forces on the left. Only Trump
could save America.

It was just that simple, and tens of millions believed that if
you wanted freedom and order, you voted for Trump. If you
wanted anarchy and chaos, you voted for Biden. If you cared
about the future of America and you cared about the kind
of world your children or grandchildren would live in, you
voted for Trump. If you wanted to throw away your country
as you knew it, you voted for Biden. If you wanted to stop the

slaughter of the unborn, you voted for Trump. If you wanted the blood of those babies on your hands, you voted for Biden.

If you wanted peace in the Middle East. If you wanted to continue to push back against Islamic terrorism. If you wanted to stop Communist China from taking over the world. If you wanted to give hope to persecuted believers around the globe. If you wanted economic hope for America's poor. If you cared about biblical values—you voted for Trump. Only he could get the job done. Only he could save us.

And that's how Donald Trump, with all his glaring failings and flaws, went from president to superhero to political savior. In the moment, it seemed so right. After all, what alternative did we have?

On the day that New York Governor Andrew Cuomo resigned (August 10, 2021), a very sober-minded Christian attorney sent this text to a group of ministry colleagues:

> Every election is described as the "most important" of a lifetime. But 2022 – a non-presidential year – may turn out to be just that.
>
> If they get those seats, and hold the House, the progressive wish list will come with a vengeance – federal control of elections, the Equality Act, a full-blown Green New Deal, surrender of national sovereignty to international interests, and a packed Supreme Court to approve all of it. Part of the goal will be rigging election "reform" to never lose another national election. I don't see how we recover from these as a nation for a very long time. It may well be judgment time.[86]

This is how many of us were feeling before the 2020 elections and then, as reflected in this text, how we were feeling in 2021. This is how many of us are feeling in 2022, as the stakes seem to be getting higher and higher each day. And what of

2024? For some, the answer was—and still is—simple: it's either Trump or judgment day, Trump or the end of America, Trump or else.

And fanning these dangerous flames was Donald Trump himself, a master marketer and a man who knew how to push the right buttons. He had this down to a science. Create mistrust in everyone and everything else. Create trust in him alone.

You can't believe the fake news. You can't listen to the other politicians, not even the Republicans.[87] Big Tech is against us. The world is against us. The truth be told, even the Supreme Court, with three Trump appointees, cannot be trusted. You can only trust Trump! Only Trump can save us!

To be sure, I have never met anyone who confuses Trump with Jesus or who looks to him for forgiveness of sins or personal redemption. Many Christian supporters of Trump have told me in no uncertain terms, "I don't worship Donald Trump. I worship God. And Jesus, not Trump, is my Savior. Who doesn't know that?"

They bristle at the idea that there was anything idolatrous in their wholehearted support of Trump. Yet idolatry, just like seduction, is often subtle as well (see chapter 4). Idolatry does not simply say, "Bow down to this piece of wood or stone. Make this inanimate object into your god. Worship something that your own hands have made."

Instead, idolatry can be as subtle as putting too much trust in a method or system or person as opposed to trusting fully in God. As the fourth-century Christian Saint Jerome wrote sixteen hundred years ago, "Idolatry is not confined to casting incense upon an altar with finger and thumb or to pouring libations of wine out of a cup into a bowl." In keeping with this thought, I've never met anyone who had a shrine to Trump in their house. Nor do I know of anyone who offers sacrifices and incense to an image of Trump or who worships him as God. Obviously not.

Yet the apostle Paul actually wrote that covetousness (or, greed) is idolatry (Colossians 3:5). Chew on that one for a minute. As one online Bible study explains, "Whatever we treasure more than God, whatever drives our thoughts and actions, becomes an idol, and these idols dull our spiritual hearing and harden our hearts to things of God."[88] This means that we can make an idol out of our job, our reputation, our bank account, or our social media following. It becomes the thing in which we put our trust, the thing that consumes our energy and attention, the object of our affections. That is what makes it into an idol. Only God is God. Only God is triumphant and ultimate. Everything else is created and dependent. Yet we often ascribe almost supernatural powers to that which is here today and gone tomorrow.

On some level, whatever takes a place in our hearts and lives that should only belong to the Lord is an idol. That's why we can also make idols out of people, making them bigger than life, looking to them to do what only God can do, glamorizing them and glorifying them and adoring them beyond all proportion, lauding their strengths while overlooking (or even ignoring) their weaknesses. That is the kind of idolatry that should concern us, the subtle idolatry of the heart rather than the overt idolatry of worshiping a statue.

We rarely admit to ourselves that we are committing idolatry, and when it comes to outright acts of worship, kneeling before statues or praying to statues, we will tell ourselves, "You are not worshiping a statue or praying to a statue. Of course not! The statue is simply a way of helping you to fix your attention on the invisible being you worship. It is not idolatrous. It is transcendent." To the contrary, God calls it idolatry. And throughout the Scriptures, God commanded His people to get rid of all idols, throwing them away or smashing them to bits. All idols must go.

Again, when I say that Trump is not our savior, the Christian response is always the same: "Only Jesus is my

Savior. Trump is just a man that we support and appreciate, the best man for the job. We all know that."

But if that were truly the case, why the despair and near panic over his defeat? Why the crushing emotional letdown? Why the persistent hope among many of his supporters that he would miraculously displace Biden within the next few months (or years)? Why the inability for so many Trump supporters to move on from him to any other potential candidate? And why the virtual denial of the amount of damage he did during his presidency, damage which largely offset the good?

In Numbers 21, the Bible records that when the children of Israel sinned against God, He sent venomous snakes as a judgment against them, with many people dying as a result. When they pleaded for mercy, the Lord instructed Moses to make a bronze snake similar in appearance to the snakes that were attacking the people, and then to put it on a pole. As a result, whoever looked to the snake would be healed (see Numbers 21:4–9). It was God's vehicle of deliverance, packaged in a highly unusual way. But centuries later, we read that the Israelites were offering sacrifices to this bronze snake, even calling it Nehushtan (see 2 Kings 18:4). How extraordinary.

So, rather than discarding (or, at the least, hiding it away somewhere) the bronze snake once it had served its unique purpose, they worshiped it. Rather than putting their total faith in the God who used the snake as an unexpected means of healing, they looked to the snake itself. Rather than leaning on the Deliverer alone, they leaned on the object He had used for deliverance.

But this was not a one-time event (although the godly king Hezekiah did cut Nehushtan into pieces). Instead, this is a recurring pattern among the Lord's people. God performs miracles through a man-made, lifeless, bronze snake, and we glorify the snake as if it were endued with healing powers. God works through a human vessel, and we look to that person almost as much as (or even more than) to the Lord. God raises up a very flawed leader, and we put our hope in the leader, as if without him our cause would be sunk. This is the essence of idolatry, and this is what many of us have done with Trump.

Unfortunately, as human beings, we tend toward idolatry, exalting other mortals into almost godlike status, looking for the next superhero (we do this with our Christian leaders too), finding substitutes for the one true God. In antiquity God gave Israel judges to help govern the nation, with the Lord Himself being their one true King. This worked for a while, but after a number of years, the people said, "We want a king"—meaning an earthly king rather than the heavenly King. Having leaders is not enough. We must have a king.

Again, I've never met anyone with a shrine to Trump in their house, nor do I know of anyone who offers sacrifices and incense to an image of Trump. Obviously not. But just as Israel looked to the impotent and powerless bronze snake as the deliverer rather than as the means of deliverance, much of the Church has looked to Trump in ways that belong only to the Lord.

Coming from a Jewish perspective, and written decades before Trump was a factor, Rabbi Louis Jacobs, citing a famous Hasidic leader, Shneur Zalman of Liady (1745-1813) explained idolatry like this: "Pride is truly equivalent to idolatry. For the main root principle of idolatry consists in man's acknowledgement of something existing in its own right apart and separate from God's holiness, and does not involve a complete denial of God" (*Tanya*, chapter 22).[89] Did you see that? Idolatry "does not involve a complete denial of God" but rather attributing to others what should only be attributed to Him.

This, I believe, was one of the great sins that many Christian Trump supporters committed, giving him the glory (even in small measure) that belongs to God alone, hailing him as he if were a political messiah, putting all our eggs in his basket as the only real hope of America. And this, coupled with Trump's own self-will and pride, made for a toxic mix. As Acts 12 records,

> Now Herod was angry with the people of Tyre and Sidon, and they came to him with one accord, and having persuaded Blastus, the king's chamberlain, they asked for peace, because their country depended on the king's country for food. On an appointed day Herod put on his royal robes, took his seat upon the throne, and delivered an oration to them. And the people were shouting, "The voice of a god, and not of a man!" Immediately an angel of the Lord struck him down, because he did not give God the glory, and he was eaten by worms and breathed his last. (Acts 12:20–23)

Again, I understand that among the tens of millions of Christians who zealously supported Donald Trump none of them thought that Trump died for their sins and rose from the dead on the third day. In that sense, none of them confused Trump with Jesus. At the same time, I heard Christian leaders quote verses in the Bible that applied to Jesus as the Messiah and apply those very verses to Trump, including Psalm 2, a psalm that ultimately applies to the coronation of Jesus as the messianic King, including these verses, spoken by the Messiah, who is quoting the words of God: "I will proclaim the LORD's decree: He [meaning, the Lord] said to me, 'You are my Son; today I have become your father. Ask me, and I will make the nations your inheritance, the ends of the earth your possession. You will break them with a rod of iron; you will dash them to pieces like pottery' " (Psalm 2:7–9 NIV).

Yes, this psalm, in which the Messiah is described as God's Son, the one who will rule the nations, was applied to Trump by a Bible teacher with a large online following—not that he was Jesus, but that the spirit of the psalm could be applied to him. This is not only a blatant misuse of the Bible. It is dangerous. Under no circumstances should we put such hope in a man.

The opening verses of Psalm 2 were also applied to God and Trump, in particular, to the attempt to steal the election from him: "Why do the nations conspire and the peoples plot in vain? The kings of the earth rise up and the rulers band together against the LORD and against his anointed, saying, 'Let us break their chains and throw off their shackles' " (Psalm 2:1–3 NIV). So, this psalm, which originally applied to David, who was installed by God as Israel's king, and ultimately applied to Jesus the Messiah, was applied to Donald Trump.

On November 29, 2020, less than one month after the elections, I wrote:

> Right now, tens of millions of Americans, including many Christian conservatives, are more likely to question Trump-appointed judges or Republican governors or the FBI or the DOJ or anyone in Trump's doghouse before they will question a word that Trump says. Why? What power does he exert that makes him the only one whose words we can trust? And does he have such a perfect record of always telling "the truth and nothing but the truth"?
>
> These things concern me, not as a Trump-basher, but as a Trump-supporter. They concern me as someone who has also warned about the dangers of the radical left and is concerned about the real attack on our freedoms, as someone who believes that Trump can be a bulwark against the left and its threats.[90]

It's almost as if we came under a spell, a cultlike spell in which we could only trust our beloved leader, as if he alone was out for our good and everyone else—right up to Mike Pence—was suspect. Only Trump could be trusted. Only Trump would fight the system. Only Trump could save. Only Trump! Is not this idolatrous? And what of the many memes depicting an almost supernatural Trump, virtually walking on the water and carrying the nation on his shoulders? What of the golden Trump statue, brought to a major, conservative political event?[91]

And what of the billboard that went up in Georgia in September 2021? It had the image of an American flag in the background with Trump to the right, and in big, bold letters these words: "UNTO US A SON IS GIVEN AND THE GOVERNMENT SHALL BE UPON HIS SHOULDERS"—the very words of famous messianic prophecy about Jesus in Isaiah 9:6–7, celebrated in Handel's *Messiah*.[92] Beneath that were the words "JOINT HEIRS" and the accompanying Scripture reference, Romans 8:17, which speaks of us being joint heirs with Jesus the Messiah. Talk about exalting a man into godlike status, yet for some (even if their numbers were small), this is how they saw Donald Trump.

I also wrote in a November 2020 article how legendary actor Jon Voight release a video

> raising grave concerns about a Biden presidency. He said, "We're heading down a street that has no name now. We must not allow our nation to crumble. Let me warn you all that we are in great danger if we fall under a Biden administration."
>
> Yes, "The left are burning and destroying our cities. We are willing to fight for freedom, not freedom to burn down our flag but to raise her up with the glory of this land of the free."

These are certainly grave concerns, which were only underscored by Voight's reference to the destructive California policies implemented by Gov. Newsom.[93]

But Voight didn't stop there. As I noted in the article, Voight also said this: "Let the truth show itself that President Trump is the only man that can save this nation." And that is where Voight crossed the line. That is where his allegiance became unhealthy. And to the extent that others shouted their "Amens" to Voight's words, that is where they exposed the idolatry of their own hearts as well.

I closed the article with this:

> With all respect to Voight's vision for a free America, I do not believe that Trump is the only man who can save the nation. Absolutely not.
>
> Had Voight said, "I believe Trump is the best man for the job," that would be one thing, and we could have a healthy discussion about it. Had he said, "Trump, not Biden, can stop our descent into socialism and government overreach," I would have concurred.
>
> But to say he's the only man who can save the nation (or as I've heard others say, save the free world), is to engage in dangerous hyperbole.
>
> The stakes are certainly at an all-time high in terms of which direction America could go, and in certain ways, Trump has been a wedge in the door, delaying some of the lurch to the left.
>
> But we do him a disservice, not to mention dishonor God, when we speak of him or pray for him in Messianic terms. Such devotion to a mere human never ends well. When will we learn?

The question remains the same: When will we learn?

From the World's Perspective

As far as the perspective of the secular media, there is no question about it: conservative Christians, especially white conservative Christians, worshiped Donald Trump. This headline, which is representative of many others, say it all: "False Idol — Why the Christian Right Worships Donald Trump" (Alex Morris, *Rolling Stone*, December 2, 2019). But once again, it was not only the secular media bringing such charges. Respected Christian commentators (and frequent Trump critics) raised similar concerns, as reflected in headlines like this: "The Dangerous Idolatry of Christian Trumpism" (David French, *The Dispatch*, December 13, 2020). As expressed by the well-known Christian ethicist Stanley Hauerwas, "Trump is quite pious and his religious convictions run dangerously deep. But his piety is not a reflection of a Christian faith. His piety is formed by his understanding of what makes America a country like no other."[94]

Back in 2016, the controversial conservative commentator Ann Coulter published the book *In Trump We Trust*, proclaiming with her typical overstated bombast that she worships him like the "people of North Korea worship their Dear Leader—blind loyalty." In an interview with *Daily Caller*'s Alex Pfeiffer she also said, this time with some seriousness, "I got to tell you when I wrote 'Adios America' I thought there was a 10 percent chance of saving the country. On the evening of November 8 [2016], I thought, 'Wow we have a 90 percent chance now, this is a chance that comes along once every thousand years, we can save America now.'"[95]

A few years later, she had turned on Trump, mocking him savagely as a "defective man" and worse[96]—actually, much worse.[97] This is what happens when we over-exalt a man. This is what happens when we look to a person to save us. This is what happens when we become idolatrous: sooner or later, there is a crash, a great big crash. To ask one more: when will we learn?

Yet there were other factors involved as well, factors which made the political seduction of the Church all the more possible, including false prophecies, a flood of conspiratorial theories, and an unhealthy Christian nationalism. But before we address those issues, let's examine how even our prayers became polluted because of our over-the-top devotion to President Trump.

CHAPTER SIX

When Even Prayer Became Partisan

The atmosphere was electric, as tens of thousands of Christians descended on Washington, DC, on September 26, 2020, for two large prayer gatherings, both scheduled for the same day but without any prior coordination between them. These were two separate events. One, called The Return was organized by bestselling, messianic Jewish author Jonathan Cahn. The other was organized by Rev. Franklin Graham. Both events were nonpolitical, devoted instead to prayer and non-partisan preaching.

To be sure, prominent Republicans, including Vice President Pence, joined together with Rev. Graham for his event. And you can safely assume that the vast majority of participants at both events were Trump supporters, but neither event was devoted to partisan politics or to praising Trump or bashing Biden. The main focus was crying out to God for mercy on America, praying for the Lord's outcome in the elections, and repenting of our own sins.

My brief message at The Return was focused on God's eternal purposes for Israel, and I heard Jonathan Cahn's keynote message firsthand. It was God-glorifying and repentance-based, calling out our corporate sins and directing us to the only one who could save us: the Lord Himself. So far, so good.

In the weeks that followed, many other prayer events were held, some in DC and some in other key cities. Christians in other nations were even praying for the elections. Surely, these were the most important elections in our lifetime. Surely, it was crucial that the right man was elected president. And God certainly knew who that man was!

But it gets more interesting still since these prayer rallies continued *after* the November 3 elections. It appeared that something was very wrong with the results since Trump was well on his way to victory when we went to sleep on election night. How on earth did Joe Biden pull ahead while we slept? Perhaps the steal was real? Perhaps this was what Trump was warning about for months, saying he could only lose by fraud? And what about all the prophetic words guaranteeing Trump's second term? This was not the time to stop praying. No, this was the time to pray even more: "God, intervene and bring justice!"

And so it was that prayer circuits were organized in the key cities where fraud was alleged. "Rise up, Lord, and give us a righteous outcome!" Christians were mobilized in unprecedented numbers, praying online together, praying on prayer calls, praying at organized prayer meetings. The fate of the nation hung in the balance. Our freedoms were on the line. Only God could turn the tide.

But let's not kid ourselves. We were desperate because Trump had lost—or at least that's where things stood at that moment. We were praying around the clock and in city after city because Trump *had* to win if America was to be saved. Even if we didn't say the words out loud, what we were really saying was this, "Lord, give us four more years of Donald Trump. And under no circumstances let Joe Biden be certified as president. In Jesus' name, amen!"

During one post-election prayer call, a Christian leader claimed to have received a stunning revelation. Our prayers were not being answered because we were not praying with enough aggression. Instead, we needed to begin praying imprecatory prayers—meaning, prayers that called down curses on others—in this case, against those who allegedly stole the elections. In other words, "Lord, we're asking you to curse and destroy all those who were complicit in stealing this election from Donald Trump. Hurt them! Destroy them! Crush them! Make them yield and tell the truth!" With my own eyes I watched a Christian leader pray prayers just like this online, with thousands of viewers adding their words of affirmation.

These were followers of Jesus praying these prayers, followers of the One who asked the Father to forgive those who crucified Him, the One who taught us to pray for our enemies (not against them), the One who instructed us to bless those who cursed us. And now, in His name, we were praying down curses and judgments on those who allegedly committed election fraud. If you dared to differ with their prayers, that's because you were weak and spineless. Was this really happening?

Even after Biden's inauguration, the same attitudes prevailed. That's why, on February 28, I posted this comment on Facebook and, in slightly shortened form, on Twitter:

My prayer for President Biden:

"Father, I ask you to reveal Yourself to him, to convict him of his sin, to save him and transform him, to give him a heart for righteousness, and to use him for the good of America."

Can I get an Amen? Is there anything in that prayer that we, as God's people, cannot come together and pray?[98]

What was the response? As of this writing, on our Facebook page alone, there are more than 7,000 likes, along with more than 2,700 comments, most of them being an amen to the prayer. Others, however, could not add their amen. For some, it was simply objecting to the words "President Biden." They still did not see him as legitimate.

Others could not agree fully with the prayer because they were convinced we should pray down curses on Biden. As Stephen wrote, "Sure! I'll add this prayer from Psalm 109":

> When he is tried, let him be found guilty, and may his prayers condemn him. May his days be few; may another take his place of leadership. May his children be fatherless and his wife a widow. May his children be wandering beggars; may they be driven from their ruined homes. May a creditor seize all he has; may strangers plunder the fruits of his labor. May no one extend kindness to him or take pity on his fatherless children. May his descendants be cut off, their names blotted out from the next generation. May the iniquity of his fathers be remembered before the LORD; may the sin of his mother never be blotted out. (Psalm 109:7–14 NIV)

And to these words, Stephen added his amen.

My friend, that is *not* how God wants us to pray for President Biden (or his successor). It is completely contrary to the directives of the New Testament, and it is a blatant violation of the spirit of Jesus. But the seduction of the church also meant the seduction of our prayers. Even in what should be the least partisan area of our lives, when we kneel down before Almighty God and cry out to Him to have His way and do His will and cause His kingdom to come, and as we confess our ignorance and our shortsightedness, the seduction prevailed. This is the one place where all partisanship should cease. Yet in the aftermath of the elections, even our prayers were hijacked by Trump fever.

When it comes to praying imprecatory prayers, such as those found in Psalm 109, let's flesh this out for a minute and ask ourselves: Should we pray for Biden's death, for his wife to be a widow? Should we pray for his children to be despised, homeless, beggars on whom no one has pity? Should we pray for his parents' sins to be remembered? Should we pray for future generations of his descendants, which would include his grandchildren, to be cut off and blotted out? God forbid we pray like that!

It is one thing to be grieved over a sinful agenda and to pray for God to stop that agenda. It is another thing to pray down curses on someone's children and grandchildren. What on earth happened to our Christian spirit?

Few human beings who lived were more evil than Hitler, but even at the height of his powers, if he had children or grandchildren, I would not be praying down curses on them. Instead, I would pray for his reign of evil to be stopped, for God to rescue the innocent, and for him to repent and face justice or be taken out of the way.

Yet sadly, in recent months the trend has emerged—the latest Christian fad, it appears—to pray down curses on our political enemies.[99] This is a fad we must resist. It does not come from the Spirit of God. It does not represent the heart of our Father. And it is not the Jesus way.

Of course, it is good to pursue justice, to pray for corruption to be exposed, and to take godly action. The last thing I'm advocating is passivity and faithless resignation. But what has happened to our own souls as followers of Jesus? We seem to be moved by malice more than by mercy, forgetting how much grace God showed us when we were living in ignorance and rebellion, as if political divisions give us the right to act in unchristian ways. Isn't that the truth?

There's a fascinating account preserved in Luke's Gospel that speaks to our situation today. Jesus and His disciples were on their way to Jerusalem shortly before He would be crucified, and they needed to pass through Samaria. But the Samaritans refused entry to Jesus and His group since the Jews looked down on the Samaritans and considered them half-breeds. Plus, Jesus was on His way to Jerusalem, the sacred city of the Jews but not the Samaritans.

Indignant that their Master should be dishonored, Jacob (James) and John asked Jesus, "Lord, do You want us to command fire to come down from heaven and consume them, just as Elijah did?" (Luke 9:54 NKJV). Basically, they were saying "They deserve it, don't they, Lord? And isn't this what Elijah the prophet did to his enemies in the Old Testament? Shall we zap them with fire, like he did, and kill them all?" (See 2 Kings 1).

But Jesus turned and rebuked them, saying, "'You do not know what manner of spirit you are of. For the Son of Man did not come to destroy men's lives but to save *them*.' And they went to another village." (Luke 9:55–56 NKJV; other ancient, Greek manuscripts do not have the actual words of Jesus preserved, but they are certainly true to the spirit of His teaching and example elsewhere.)

Jesus was saying to them, "No, we don't call down fire on those who insult us and mistreat us. That's not the purpose of My mission. I've come to save people, not destroy them."

It is true that one day He will return in blazing fire taking vengeance on His enemies. At that time, He will destroy those who have tried to destroy us, His faithful followers. But that time has not yet come. And even though God does judge wickedness in the present, if He judged every wicked person on the planet right now, most of the human race would be gone overnight, including a large percentage of the Church. Be careful what you wish for—and pray for.

In the Old Testament the Israelites were called to drive out the Canaanites. In the New Testament believers are called to drive out demons. There is quite a difference in terms of both our attitudes and our actions. The Israelites cursed their enemies. Jesus taught us to bless ours, saying, "You have heard that it was said, 'Love your neighbor and hate your enemy.'

But I tell you, love your enemies and pray for those who persecute you, that you may be children of your Father in heaven. He causes his sun to rise on the evil and the good, and sends rain on the righteous and the unrighteous." (Matthew 5:43–45 NIV).

I for one am glad that people didn't call down fire on me when I was a rebellious teenager stealing money from my own father and breaking into homes and a doctor's office for fun. Had that been the case, I would never have reached my seventeenth birthday.

I am glad that people didn't call down fire on my wife, Nancy, when she was a God-mocking atheist scorning religious people as stupid and weak, actively trying to pull them away from their faith. Had that been the case, we would have never met at the age of nineteen.

I am glad that people didn't call down fire on my dear Indian friend Yesupadam when he was a Marxist (Naxalite) terrorist. Instead, Jesus appeared to him, converting him with His love. Personally, I do not know a single person on the planet who has done more good to help more people than he. The world would be a much worse place without him.

I am glad that people didn't call down fire on Tass Saada, formerly a Jew-hating assassin for Yasser Arafat but now a devout Christian and great lover of Israel. And I am glad that people didn't call down fire on Saul of Tarsus when he was killing fellow Jews who believed in Jesus. Had that been the case, we would never have heard of the apostle Paul, and half of the New Testament would be missing.

Again, when it comes to the integrity of the elections, we should welcome thorough investigations into all credible charges of election fraud. For the sake of our freedoms and our integrity every vote must be counted fairly and accurately. But as we pray for justice and righteousness, we must pray with God's heart—a heart of love for our enemies, perceived or real. We must pray with a heart of compassion. A heart of longsuffering. A heart that longs to see everyone receive salvation and forgiveness through repentance and faith. Isn't this how God's heart was expressed to you and me when we were lost and in rebellion? Our attitude speaks even louder than our words. Unfortunately, our "righteous indignation" often stinks of the flesh and is filled with carnal anger, hateful attitudes, and double standards. Be careful before you curse, my friend.

The truth be told, to love your enemies while working against their perceived evil designs is a sign of strength not of weakness, a sign of courage not cowardice. This makes us bigger not smaller. But when we curse and revile them, we become just like them, if not even worse.

I have worked with suffering Christians in other parts of the world, sometimes during seasons of intense persecution. I can count at least five men I helped send out to preach overseas who were subsequently martyred. And on two occasions I had the extraordinary honor of spending hours with Richard Wurmbrand and his wife, Sabina, two of the saintliest human beings to ever grace our planet, both brutally tortured for their faith.

At no time did I ever hear any of these persecuted believers call down fire on their enemies. Instead, they prayed for the repentance and salvation of those very enemies. And during such times of intense testing, these Christians grew in their own faith and became more Christlike in their attitudes. This stands in stark contrast with many of us today. We have become as nasty and meanspirited as the very people we so self-righteously judge. How can this be?

Surely, during this critical time in American history, as God's people, we must rise higher and show the reality of our faith. As Paul wrote to the Philippians, "Do everything without grumbling or arguing, so that you may become blameless and pure, children of God without fault in a warped and crooked generation. Then you will shine among them like stars in the sky as you hold firmly to the word of life" (Philippians 2:14–16 NIV). It's time for us to shine and bring honor not reproach to the name of our Lord.

Look at these clear instructions from Paul as to how we are to pray for those in authority: "I urge, then, first of all, that petitions, prayers, intercession and thanksgiving be made for all people—for kings and all those in authority, that we may live peaceful and quiet lives in all godliness and holiness. This is good, and pleases God our Savior, who wants all people to be saved and to come to a knowledge of the truth" (1 Timothy 2:1–4 NIV).

Now, go back and read those words again, realizing that Nero—yes, Nero—was emperor of Rome when Paul wrote to Timothy. That's how he tells us to pray for a depraved maniac like Nero. Yet some Christians want to pray down curses on Joe Biden's children and grandchildren? How sick is that?

It is true that in Old Testament times under the Sinai Covenant, there may have been a situation when it was right to pray prayers like Psalm 109 against mortal enemies, who, with their descendants, were bent on doing evil. But that was then. This is now. And Jesus calls us to something much higher. The Lord—our Master—commands us to love our enemies not hate them. And Paul exhorts us to bless those who persecute us rather than cursing them back (see Romans 12:14).

Where we do see evil or unrighteousness or injustice, with God's help, we should oppose it with all our might. Let us do all we can to stand for what is right, both socially and politically. Let us be fearless, tireless, and courageous. Only let us not be consumed with hatred and carnal anger and vindictiveness in the process. The moment we do, we become part of the problem rather than the solution. Instead, let us have hearts filled with the hope of redemption. Let us pray for the leaders of our nation whether or not we voted for them and whether or not we respect them or agree with them. Who knows what God might do in answer to our prayers? At the very least, those prayers will change us, unless, that is, we turn the prayer into a partisan political exercise. May it not be!

Learning from the New Testament Leaders

The book of Acts recounts the persecution experienced by the first believers, including imprisonment, violent beatings, and death. But Acts also records their response to persecution, an attack which represented something far more hostile, direct, and life-threatening against these believers than alleged charges of election fraud. How then did these believers and leaders pray in the midst of persecution? Acts 4 records this account after the apostles were threatened by the religious leadership and ordered to stop preaching:

> On their release, Peter and John went back to their own people and reported all that the chief priests and the elders had said to them. When they heard this, they raised their voices together in prayer to God. "Sovereign Lord," they said, "you made the heavens and the earth and the sea, and everything in them. You spoke by the Holy Spirit through the mouth of your servant, our father David:
>
> "'Why do the nations rage and the peoples plot in vain? The kings of the earth rise up and the rulers band together against the Lord and against his anointed one.' [quoting Psalm 2:1–2]
>
> Indeed Herod and Pontius Pilate met together with the Gentiles and the people of Israel in this city to conspire against your holy servant Jesus, whom you anointed. They did what your power and will had decided beforehand should happen. Now, Lord, consider their threats and enable your servants to speak your word with great boldness. Stretch out your hand

to heal and perform signs and wonders through the name of your holy servant Jesus." (Acts 4:23–30 NIV)

Notice they did not curse their enemies (enemies who were guilty of far more severe sins than alleged election tampering). They did not call down fire on their adversaries. They did not invoke judgment on the children or grandchildren of those who opposed them. Instead, they asked God to take note of what was happening and give them boldness to preach Jesus in the power of the Spirit. That was it. And what was the result of their prayer? "After they prayed, the place where they were meeting was shaken. And they were all filled with the Holy Spirit and spoke the word of God boldly" (Acts 4:31 NIV).

Those are the kinds of prayers we need to be praying in America today—not prayers of cursing and malediction but prayers for boldness and courage to preach the gospel, empowered and backed by the Spirit. God will answer those kinds of prayers! And as a result of our Spirit-filled, fearless, Jesus-centered preaching, the nation will be shaken.

As for election reform and integrity in our government, we can pray for that as well, but, again, *not* by praying down judgment on the alleged election stealers. Rather, we can pray for the truth to emerge, for the courts to act fairly, for repentance when and if people have sinned, and for righteous and fair elections for all Americans in the days ahead. That's the kind of prayer God will answer as well.

Let's remember the example of Stephen, called to serve the needy in Acts 6 but also a man full of the Spirit, performing miracles in Jesus' name. As a result of his powerful ministry, he was called before the national leadership after being falsely accused. He then preached a strong message of rebuke, after which the listeners became enraged, gnashing their teeth against him before stoning him to death. And how did he pray as he was dying? Acts gives this account:

When the members of the Sanhedrin heard this [meanings Stephen's words of rebuke], they were furious and gnashed their teeth at him. But Stephen, full of the Holy Spirit, looked up to heaven and saw the glory of God, and Jesus standing at the right hand of God. "Look," he said, "I see heaven open and the Son of Man standing at the right hand of God."

At this they covered their ears and, yelling at the top of their voices, they all rushed at him, dragged him out of the city and began to stone him. Meanwhile, the witnesses laid their coats at the feet of a young man named Saul.

While they were stoning him, Stephen prayed, "Lord Jesus, receive my spirit." Then he fell on his knees and cried out, "Lord, do not hold this sin against them." When he had said this, he fell asleep. (Acts 7:54–60 NIV)

Do you see that? Even when being stoned to death for his faith in Jesus and his words of prophetic rebuke, Stephen did not curse his enemies or pray for their destruction. Instead, he prayed that the Lord would not hold their sin of murder against them.

That's the spiritual way of praying rather than the fleshly way of praying. It's the exact opposite of the partisan, mean-spirited, judgmental prayers that poured from some of our lips in the days and weeks after the 2020 elections. And it is that spiritual mindset we must embrace—the Spirit that moved Jesus and the apostles and Stephen to pray redemptive prayers rather than vindictive prayers—that could shake our nation from coast to coast. According to Paul, this was the spirit of the apostles: "When we are cursed, we bless; when we are persecuted, we endure it; when we are slandered, we answer kindly" (1 Corinthians 4:12–13 NIV). May that be our spirit as well. The fate of the nation is depending on it.

CHAPTER SEVEN

When the Prophets Prophesied Falsely

On April 30, 2021, Johnny Enlow, one of the most outspoken Trump prophets, posted an article on his Facebook page titled "The Prophets Were Right: Vision of a Golden Scepter."[100] To those outside of the pro-Trump prophetic circles, the post will sound shocking and even cult-like. But to those who fervently believed, several months into the Biden presidency, that Trump was about to be reinstated to office, the words of Enlow's post rang true, resulting in six thousand likes, almost three thousand comments, and more than fifteen hundred shares. Yes, Enlow declared, Trump did win the election, which certainly was stolen, but Trump will soon be reinstated. Thus, the prophets were right, and even now, in God's sight, Trump is the sitting president.

To be sure, there were many level-headed, sober-minded, spiritually solid Americans who believed that the election was stolen. They were convinced there was genuine evidence of serious fraud, and they believed that had more of the courts been willing to review the evidence the fraud would have been revealed.[101] Yet these same people understand that Joe Biden, not Donald Trump, is the sitting president, and they have no illusions about Trump's imminent return to the White House (short of running again in 2024). They don't like the outcome, but it is what it is. They have moved on (although they still advocate for election reform).

In stark contrast, the Trump prophets and their supporters believed that even in April 2021 (and later) Trump *was* the President of the United States and that, very soon, he was going to be restored to office. In their eyes, those who denied this were rank unbelievers and mockers of God's prophets, and when the prophets were proven right, those deniers would all be ashamed.

Of course, some of the prophets were quite sure that something big was going to happen well before April 30, 2021. Some spoke of major changes to come before the end of November 2020. Or December 2020. Or January 2021 (some time before the inauguration, for sure). When nothing happened within the prophesied dates, we were told that March of 2021 was going to be the next big month. No, make that April. Actually, it's August.[102] No, September.[103] That's when Trump would be restored. The goal posts kept moving, but the followers were committed: the prophets will be proven true!

Shortly before April 30, 2021, the date when the afore-mentioned Facebook page went up, a major statement calling for prophetic accountability was posted online. It was affirmed by hundreds of charismatic and Pentecostal leaders (meaning, people who believe that God still raises up prophetic voices today).[104] How did Johnny Enlow respond? What was his position now that it looked like the prophecies would never come to pass?

> Enough months have gone by since the election of 11/3/2020 that it is worth revisiting some important truth. There is actually no 'waiting to see' if the prophets were right who prophesied DJT winning the election. It happened. It happened BIGLY. By late night on the 3rd of November, it was all but announced that DJT had comfortably won the election. Prophesy fulfilled.[105]

In other words, since Trump really did win the election, all the prophets who predicted his victory were correct. Case closed, and nothing to wonder about or debate. Trump won fair and square just as the prophets predicted, but the election was stolen, plain and simple.

This, of course, begs the question, why weren't any of the prophets who prophesied Trump's victory informed by God that the election would be stolen from him? That's not a minor detail to overlook since what really matters is who is sitting in the White House and leading the nation not who was the theoretical winner of an election. In fact, I would dare say there was hardly a person on the planet who heard these prophets unanimously guarantee Trump's victory who then said to themselves, "Yes, these prophets are speaking truthfully and accurately, but the election will be stolen. And Biden will end up being the president." Not a chance. To the contrary, all of us who heard those prophecies (especially those of us who wanted them to be true, which included me) understood them to mean that Trump, not Biden, would be inaugurated on January 24, 2021. The question, "Who will win the elections?" was synonymous in our minds with, "Who will serve as our next president?" But of course.

For the Trump prophets and their ilk, however, the meaning was now something very different. There were saying Trump won the elections, and so he really is president no matter what the courts or Congress or anyone else says. It is so because we say it is so, and if the current reality alleges anything to the contrary, we reject that reality as unreal. You can readily see how scary this type of thinking is and where it can lead.

Enlow continued:

The ensuing, unparalleled in history, steal, that saw multiple states claim thousands more votes than registered voters (pause and let that register) is not going to stand. That becomes I suppose a second prophetic word— which also will be fulfilled. The fact Arizona is in a recount should tell you there is no expiration date on when a steal gets voided. The fact that the Dems have sent—at last estimate—100 attorneys, to try to stop it should tell you right there they understand that if the steal gets exposed in Arizona it will also happen in the other states. Who would be for stopping a recount done with 100% transparency in every step and every process? Only a thief and his den of thieves.

In retrospect, it looks like his post has not aged well. But he was just getting started:

In a related development, Mr. Pillow man has 100% percent proof of the national election steal— though the results will have to be searched for because the thieves have cohorts in big tech platforms trying to suppress the truth. It is yet another proof the prophets who prophesied DJT would win— were not wrong. Meanwhile, there is a leadership group in the Body of Christ upping the ante at going after the prophets that don't back down on what God said— and is still saying. They consider that if a thief has managed to hold the loot from a robbery for 5 or 6 months that it now has be considered fair and square his loot. They see it as a valuable service to the Body of Christ to "rein in" these prophets who keep agreeing with God. They have unwisely partnered with the thief while true prophetic voices have no choice but to agree with God. If God changes His mind we will too. If He doesn't we won't either. I'm guessing He won't change His mind.[106]

Here, this pro-Trump prophet launched a veiled attack against charismatic leaders who had called for prophetic accountability, claiming that we "unwisely partnered with the thief." In reality, of course, we were doing exactly what the New Testament told us to do, namely testing all prophetic words.[107] And in point of fact, many of us in the charismatic movement had been calling for accountability for years.

I devoted a whole chapter to the subject of Unaccountable Prophecies in my 2018 book *Playing with Holy Fire: A Wakeup Call to the Pentecostal-Charismatic Church*.[108] This, in turn, built on earlier chapters I had written in other, related books.[109] And on March 30, 2020, in the midst of prophecies claiming that COVID-19 would begin to dissipate by April 15 (meaning April 2020 not April 2021), I wrote that this would be a great time to test our prophetic words, calling for greater scrutiny.[110]

Then, on December 15, 2020, I posted an article titled "To My Prophetic Friends: You Were Either Right or You Were Wrong," in which I wrote:

> This is not the time for flights of spiritual fantasy. Either the charismatic prophets who declared unanimously that Donald Trump would be reelected to a second consecutive term were right or they were wrong. Either there is going to be some last minute, seemingly miraculous intervention that overturns the vote of the electoral college, or Trump will not serve a second consecutive term.
>
> There is no middle ground. There is no third option. There is no reality in which Trump actually did win but in fact didn't win. Or in which he's the president in God's sight but not in man's sight.
>
> Not a chance. To entertain possibilities like this is to mock the integrity of prophecy and to make us charismatics look like total fools. (To our critics, we already do look like fools, but that's another matter.

Sometimes truth itself can seem foolish to those who
reject it.)

I ended the article with this funny (but sad) story and a
clear appeal:

In the church where I came to faith in late 1971,
the pastor told us an amusing story.

A guest speaker was ministering to the congregation, and after the sermon, he had some personal
prophetic words for the people.

He told one woman standing in the front of the
building that God was calling her as a missionary to
India. He told another man standing in the back of
the building that God was calling him as a missionary
to China. What the guest speaker didn't know was
that they were married.

When they got in the car, they were both very
excited.

The wife said, "The man of God told me we're
called to be missionaries and we're going to India!"

He replied, "No, the man of God told me we're
called to be missionaries and we're going to China!"

Confused, they went back into the building to ask
for clarification, explaining to the speaker that he gave
them two conflicting prophecies.

He smiled and said, "No, there's no contradiction.
God is calling you to Indochina."

I appeal to my prophetic friends and colleagues
(and those I don't know personally), please don't play
spiritual games like this. Please don't bring further
reproach to the name of the Lord whom we love and
serve.

Either your words will come to pass with astonishing accuracy and the nation will witness the

miraculous reelection of Donald Trump, or your words will prove false.

Will you sign on the dotted line and make that "no excuses" and "no rationalizations" commitment today? The world is watching.[111]

I knew all too well that the longer things went and the clearer it became that Trump would not be inaugurated on January 20, 2021, some of these prophets would start to make excuses or put some hyper-spiritual interpretation on their words. That's why I told the Indochina story. It was easy to see this coming in advance.

I followed this up with a strongly worded article that was posted on January 21, 2021. I reproduce it here in full:

> January 20th is past, and Joe Biden, not Donald Trump, is the President of the United States. To all those who prophesied that Trump would serve a second consecutive term and assured us that he would be inaugurated on the 20th, I appeal to you in the strongest possible terms: admit your error, take full responsibility, and do not, under any circumstances, continue to put a false hope into the hearts of God's people.
>
> What you prophesied did not come to pass.
>
> There is not an alternative, spiritual reality in which Trump is still functioning as president.
>
> Nothing is going to change in a month or a year.
>
> It's over.
>
> Even if there was massive electoral fraud, the results of this election will not be overturned.
>
> Donald Trump will not serve a second, consecutive term.

Face the facts, be accountable before God and man, take the hits that will be coming, and humble yourself before the Lord and His people.

This is not the time for excuses. This is not the time to concoct spiritual myths. And this is absolutely not the time to blame others.

If you prophesied falsely, you and you alone are to blame.

Maybe you did not intend to mislead.

Maybe you were acting in sincerity and integrity, truly believing the Lord had spoken and doing your best to stand firm in faith no matter what. After all, you thought to yourself, isn't that what faith does?

Maybe you were so grieved over where the radical left was going that you prophesied what you desired, namely the reelection of Trump.

Maybe you sensed God's intent, namely that if Trump would repent of his pride and the church would repent of looking to him in an idolatrous way, God would give him four more years.

Maybe you got caught up in the power of the group, finding affirmation in others saying the same things.

Maybe you prophesied what your people wanted to hear, subconsciously tickling their itching ears.

Maybe you got caught up in a partisan political spirit.

Maybe you looked to Trump as a political messiah and God answered you out of the idolatry of your own heart.

Or maybe you fell prey to demonic deception.

Whatever the cause, you prophesied falsely, and now you need to own it. The last thing you should do is feel sorry for yourself and claim that you are being persecuted. Quite the contrary. The reality is that you have misled many.

As a result of your false prophecies, many believers are experiencing a crisis of faith right now. Who will be there to pick up the pieces?

After all, they wonder, how could all the prophets be wrong? (To the extent that you urged your hearers to hold on to the very end, to that extent you are responsible for bringing them to this point of crisis.)

Worse still, some of you issued prophetic threats to those who questioned your words, telling them they had to "believe the prophets" or else. And you did this while claiming to speak directly for God.

The Lord does not take it lightly when His people are abused like this. He will hold you responsible for misrepresenting Him.

So many of God's people are hurting, and the world is mocking us, thinking that our faith in Jesus is just as false as these failed Trump prophecies.

One young man posted online that he had been telling his family, none of whom were believers, that Trump would be reelected, based on the words of the prophets. He thought it would glorify the Lord when Trump was miraculously inaugurated. Now, he said, he doesn't think he can ever talk to them about the Lord again.

Do we realize the damage that has been done?

One woman who falsely claims to be a prophet said that God has been making a list, noting who is listening to the prophets and who is not. Those who are not, she warns — claiming to speak for the Lord — will lose their voice and their ministries.

This is deep deception and serious spiritual manipulation.

If God is making a list it is a list of those who misled His sheep. A list of those who threatened His children if they failed to "believe the prophets." A list of those who brought dishonor to the name of His Son.

Now is the time to repent, openly, publicly and forthrightly.

Now is the time to find accountability from other leaders in the Body who did not fall into this same error.

Now is the time for some serious soul-searching.

It's what the Bible calls bringing forth fruits worthy of repentance. This is no small thing.

If you continue to prophesy falsehoods and assure your followers that Biden will soon be replaced by Trump (and I don't mean in 2024), I warn you that you are moving into complete spiritual fantasy and leading others with you. Careful!

The reality is that I'm writing all this as a charismatic leader rather than as a charismatic basher, as a proponent of prophetic ministry rather than as an opponent. I'm writing as a friend, not an enemy.

In fact, it is a holy jealousy that drives me — jealousy for the honor of Jesus' name, jealousy for the health of His flock, and jealousy for the purity of prophetic ministry.

I also write out of a holy jealousy for your own ministry and calling.

All of us can make mistakes, even serious ones like this. Our God is a God of forgiveness, and redemption is the central message of our faith. You can come out of this closer to Jesus, deeper in the Word, godlier in character, and more in tune with the Spirit. And to the depth of your humility, to that degree the Lord will restore and rebuild.

But please, I appeal to you again.

Don't blame others. Don't make excuses. And don't perpetuate any further spiritual fantasy. It's over. Now, what are you going to do?[112]

And how did the followers of these Trump prophets respond? Here's a tiny sampling (and this really has nothing to do with me personally; it has to do with how these followers responded to the call for prophetic accountability):

- Dr. Brown attacking God's remnant.
- I believe Dr. Michael Brown is a false prophet.
- You really should stop doing this stuff Michael. You are going to have to eat a whole lot of humble pie when they come to pass. What you are doing is most decidedly NOT the work of the Lord. You would be better served doing something else.
- You will wish you had stood in faith. Trump is still president and soon he will be back.
- He [referring to me] rejected the prophets and accused the brethren standing for truth of being idolators. He believed the lying media on the election. They are his prophets. This is a man not worthy of a platform.
- You persist Dr Brown. For what purpose? There is AMPLE evidence against you and multiple brave prophets willing to look like fools in order to proclaim God's revelation. When will we witness YOUR repentance and apology? At this point NOTHING ELSE COULD RESTORE MY TRUST IN YOU!!!!![113]

Indeed, if I dared to say anything critical of Trump or the Trump prophets after the elections, responses like this were typical: "SHUT UP NEVER TRUMP COWARD." (I guess I must be one of the few Never Trumpers who voted for him twice and wrote scores of articles in support of him.) And when I announced on my radio show on January 6, 2021, (the day of the storming of the Capitol) that Trump would *not* be inaugurated in two weeks, the response was almost hysterical:

- You become our enemy by defending the lies and by riding the fence ... but now YOU know the future, right? I thought you were a debater. You're [*sic*] lack of being able to apply simple logic is quite astounding! Please go back to being an apologist, you're losing credibility moment by moment.
- Do us a favor and live stream yourself wearing sackcloth (burlap will work too) and throwing ash on yourself once this is all over and you're confronted with the realization of exactly what spirit you are of right now Dr. Brown.
- PRESIDENT TRUMP STILL MY PRESIDENT... BIDEN WILL NEVER BE A PRESIDENT...HE IS ONLY A PUPPET FOR SATAN.
- Dr. Brown you're a fraud and spawn of Baal.
- Shut the hell up. You're in a cult.

Isn't this remarkable? Fellow followers of Jesus were telling me that I was an enemy, a fraud, the spawn of Baal (a false god in the Old Testament), and a cult member. And some of them had been following my ministry for years. Now I was of the devil? Seriously? And all this for telling these Christians on January 6 that Trump would not be inaugurated on January 20? Really?

Again, I took none of this personally, since this wasn't about me at all, and I don't share it for sympathy. Of course not. I had simply hit a nerve, and the comments were illustrative of just how deeply deceived these followers of the Trump prophets were, often urged on by the prophets themselves. Yes, if you didn't agree with the prophecies guaranteeing that Trump would serve eight consecutive years in the White

House, even *after* the courts had refused to hear key cases alleging fraud, even *after* the Senate had certified the elections, even *after* the so-called insurrection, then you were the enemy, a virtual child of Satan. You were the one deceived. Talk about turning reality upside down.

Some of the Trump prophets even issued dire warnings, threatening those who would dare question their words. One of them claimed that God was "making a list" of those who failed to believe their words. (The woman making this claim had previously guaranteed that Trump would serve *eight consecutive years* in the White House, followed by eight years of Mike Pence. She issued this threat several months after Biden's inauguration.) Another claimed that there would be serious consequences for those who dared to "touch God's anointed"—meaning, the Trump prophets.[114] Talk about spiritual malpractice of the highest order. Talk about abusive manipulation.

And then there was the public response to some of the prophets who apologized for wrongly prophesying Trump's victory. They were attacked for apologizing! They were told that, under no circumstances should they ever back down from their words. A younger colleague of mine, Jeremiah Johnson, one of the first to issue a public apology, even received death threats for apologizing. He actually told me that people were unsubscribing from his email list in such large numbers that it crashed the server!

More than twenty-five hundred years ago, the Lord spoke through the prophet Jeremiah saying, "The prophets prophesy lies, the priests rule by their own authority, and my people love it this way. But what will you do in the end?" (Jeremiah 5:31 NIV). Johnson pointed out that, ironically, he was witnessing the same thing today. The people love it when the prophets prophesy lies but hate it when they tell the truth!

As for Johnny Enlow, the Trump prophet mentioned at the beginning of this chapter, on July 5, 2021, he received even more likes than to his April post, when he posted this on Facebook:

> Nope the Republic is not dead. God has just spoken "Come Forth" and the grave clothes are being pulled off. Soon the proof all are looking for will be evident. Meanwhile, let every dead hope in each of us rise into newness of life. A whole new era is straight ahead of us. The resetters are getting reset by the King of kings. Go ahead and arise with that reset now. The God of peace will crush Satan under our feet. Face/Chase the enemy in every way you can and start marching/stomping.[115]

Yes, the proof is coming "soon."

Thankfully, after President Biden's inauguration, many other charismatic leaders joined together in calling for accountability and repentance, grieved that some of our friends and colleagues (and others whom we did not know) were making a mockery of the gospel and bringing reproach to the things of the Spirit by continuing to hold to these failed prophetic words. Yet some prophets who gave very specifics dates about changes to come—such as blue states being switched to red states after the fraud had been revealed—or who guaranteed that Biden would not serve a single day in the White House simply entrenched themselves more deeply when their prophecies failed to come to pass. (Remember the Indochina story? I wrote about it back in December 2020 for a reason.)

Some of the Trump prophets simply ignored their past words and set new dates. Others rationalized their failure by arguing that Trump really was the president in God's sight, even after Biden's inauguration. Some claimed that there were now *two* presidents, the true president, Trump, as prophesied, and the false president, Biden, who was about to be removed by the military so that Trump could be restored.[116] That's why I told Ruth Graham of the *New York Times* that, in my forty-nine years as a believer, this was the most widescale deception I had ever seen.[117] And that's why my friend Dr. Joseph Mattera called this crisis "The Day of Reckoning."[118]

Yet the deception got even worse, tying in directly with the idolatrous exaltation of Trump. I can think of no better illustration than the very the same Facebook post from April 30, 2021, by Johnny Enlow where he recounted a vision of God's heavenly inauguration of Trump. And lest you dismiss what you are about to read as the misguided "revelation" of one individual, remember that *many* believers resonated with his words, posting a steady stream of affirmation, including comments like these, all of which were written on or after April 30, 2021, meaning that they were all written almost six months after the elections and more than three months after Biden's inauguration:

- I've never doubted for a minute who our President is ... I will never call the other person my President. Thank you Johnny for standing strong.
- Not only will DJT return, we will see a HUGE turn-over of the Supreme Court, and the trickle-down effect of the federal and state courts overturning, as well. The corruption will be exposed and rooted out! [This single comment received 647 likes.]
- I'm continuing to receive dreams and visions from people in other nations confirming Gods word. They are consistently saying the same thing from hundreds of angles. No matter how you slice it, it's never changed:-). [This one received 523 likes.]
- Come on!! WE THE PEOPLE will not be silent, we will not back down, nor sit down, nor shut up, nor relinquish what God has said. HIS will be done, on earth as it IS in heaven! [This one received 475 likes.]

And on and on it went, with some of the affirming comments even coming from people I knew, people who otherwise were solid in their faith. (For the record, there were plenty of other posts by Enlow on his page that were both edifying and non-political, which makes the deception all the more tragic.) The truth be told, some of these reader comments would not sound that extreme in other contexts, where Christians still believed God and His Word, such as, "Even though the doctors give mom only a 10 percent chance of survival, we're believing for a miracle!" But in the case of Trump, it was not faith. It was denial. And it was chilling to behold.

In that same April post, Enlow shared his vision of a golden scepter. Here it is, in full, without comment or edit of any kind (and note that the leadership group of which he speaks is the group I helped organize which produced the aforementioned document on prophetic standards). Read these words slowly and carefully, and feel free to let out a gasp along the way.

As I was praying today I saw a vision of DJT seated on a throne holding a golden scepter. He also had a golden crown on his head. This, I was shown, is his PRESENT status from heaven's perspective. That becomes all I need to know, as to should I back off saying "the steal will not hold". Heaven does not recognize JB having any scepter nor wearing any crown. From heaven's perspective, there is only the legitimacy of DJT. God has assigned a massive contingency of angels to that scepter and to that crown. They have not ceased assignment and anointed seers can see this. To repeat, the prophetic word has been true all the way from Nov 3. On that date, DJT won the election "as spoken by His servants the prophets". IT WAS FULFILLED. The only thing presently yet to be made visible is will an outrageous steal hold for a whole term. It will not! The answer from God to the question of when is—SOON. Do I have a date on that SOON? No, I don't.

DJT was called and anointed by God to lead our nation and the world into a new era. Most of the above-mentioned "leadership group" at one time believed some version of that reality. Now apparently, if a theft is outrageous and thorough enough, you must bow to that reality and actually congratulate and then even pray for this thief-in-chief. Those who refuse to disagree with God, must now be pressured into accepting the steal, under the guise of "being humble enough" to admit being wrong. How about "being humble enough" to keep agreeing with God after even believers and fellow leaders push for abandoning what He has clearly revealed? My Bible does not say to support or pray for criminal thieves just because it was the highest seat in the land. Those who gave up on going to the courts of heaven in order to now instead "rein in prophets" might consider that a more worthwhile assignment to get back to. 100 million Americans know that a grand theft has taken place. It is most definitely NOT the assignment of any Body of Christ "leadership group" to instruct that this be considered acceptable and "let's move on". There is no "moving on" from this moment. Justice either comes to roost in this season or 100% of this "leadership group" has to admit that their prayers, their marches, their fastings were altogether worthless. If Justice does not sweep in at this time, there is no foundation for ever motivating the Body of Christ to fast, pray, march, vote etc. The contending effort was unprecedented and worldwide surpassed 100 million people from almost every nation on the earth. Respectfully, "leadership group", maybe dig deeper and ask God the harder questions you are avoiding—instead of targeting the faithful prophets. Perhaps, you will be led to a more valuable assignment that is in keeping with God's agenda in our nation and the nations of the world. Why does your God-view allow for a criminal thief in power to be the answer from God after months of fasting and praying etc. etc.? Why would you allow a grand theft of the highest level to knock you off assignment? Why would you then blame shift—prophets!!? Did THEY inspire you to fast, pray, march, gather, vote or was it God? Are you afraid to approach God with your disappointment and so must project it elsewhere? Wrestle through that question and you might find yourself back on assignment. You need to know literally thousands in the prophetic community are still getting dreams and visions and audible voices from God on DJT officially back in power. Some of you can add that in the comment section so those who see this become aware that nameless and faceless prophetic voices are remaining faithful too.[119]

If you ever wanted an explicit picture of Trump idolatry, you have it here. Trump is depicted as "seated on a throne holding a golden scepter" with "a golden crown on his head" and with "a massive contingency [*sic*] of angels" in his support. And remember, this was allegedly Trump's PRESENT position, as of April 30, 2021. Who cares who is sitting in the White House? God has seated His man, Donald J. Trump, on a heavenly throne, royally crowned as well. Yes, if you are spiritual, you will see this too.

Indeed, "DJT was called and anointed by God to lead our nation and the world into a new era."[120] And how we do know this is the case? It's because tens of millions of Christians were praying for God's will to be done in the elections, and since God clearly wanted Trump to be the president, then to deny that Trump is currently president is to say that our prayers were worthless and that we are siding with grand theft.

Do you see how convoluted this thinking is? Do you see how it plays on the faith of well-meaning, sincere Christians? Do you see how effectively it demonizes those who recognize that Trump is *not* our president right now? And do you see how, in some upside-down way, the argument actually seems reasonable?

After all, Christians are "in this world but not of it," to use a biblical formulation (see John 17:16). We are citizens of an earthly country but also citizens of a heavenly country, and when push comes to shove, our ultimate allegiance is to our Lord, not to an earthly government (see Acts 4:19–20; 5:29). And often, our faith gets tested. So why should we be so easily moved now? Give this time. Wait and see. Soon enough, Donald Trump, the true president in God's sight, the chosen and anointed one, will be restored to office. On that day, the prophets will be vindicated and people like me will be put to shame.

That is the narrative that many bought into, and it seems that no passage of time will jar them back into reality. Another explanation will be concocted ("God *would have* restored Trump to office, but people like you hurt our faith" or "Trump decided to wait until 2024 in order to make the Democrats look even worse, even though he could have been restored at any time") or an even more convoluted "spiritual" explanation will be given ("Trump continues to rule over America from his heavenly throne") and reality will be denied once again.

This is a terribly dangerous deception, one that will ultimately lead to complete apostasy for some since these disappointed believers will reason, "If I was so sure that Trump would be reelected and if so many prophets assured us it would happen yet he did not return to office, maybe everything else I believe is false too."

This is what happens when we put too much trust in a man. This is what happens when we get caught up in a partisan political spirit. This is what happens when we give too much credence to prophets and prophetic ministry and ignore practical wisdom. This is what happens when we mistake fleshly enthusiasm for the voice of the Spirit. And this is why the failed (and false) Trump prophecies were a massive accident waiting to happen.

But how was it that so many prophets got things so wrong? Some of them actually had good track records in the past, giving accurate messages to individuals whom they had never met before or describing future events in detail before they took place. Some of them were known as good teachers of the Bible, people of integrity, not known to be greedy or corrupt. Yet so many of them wrongly prophesied that Trump would serve a second consecutive term. How did this happen?

CHAPTER EIGHT

The Genesis of False Prophecy

Writing for Ministry Watch on July 27, 2021, Christian reporter Steve Rabey began his article with these words: "Joe Biden is not the duly elected President of the United States. The 2020 election was stolen. Trump will soon be officially reinstated. Patriots need to buy weapons and prepare for a second civil war."

But this was not Rabey's opinion. Rather, he explained, "These are God's views on American politics, according to dozens of preachers who claim to be Christian prophets." Yes, researchers James Beverley and Gordon Melton "found that more than 150 prophets predicted Trump's victory last November, but only a handful have admitted they were wrong and apologized." As expressed by Prof. Beverley, who is affiliated with the Institute for the Study of American Religion in Texas and Tyndale University in Toronto, "Others have dug in and prophesied a return of Trump to the White House"[121]—and that does not mean by election in 2024 but rather by divine intervention well before then.

Rabey quoted Nebraska pastor Hank Kunneman, who received national attention (and derision) for his numerous Trump prophecies in 2020 and 2021, reiterating shortly before July 4, 2021, "Look to the skies of your 4th of July" for "signs of the freedom and the restored order that is coming to your nation, and it's coming fast." The prophecy, Rabey noted, "was made on a broadcast on Elijah Streams, a 200,000-subscriber streaming service from Steve Schultz's

Elijah List prophecy website, which serves as a clearinghouse for prophetic messages."

To quote the prophecy further, the Lord allegedly said through Pastor Kunneman, "Listen to the sound of My voice that shall be heard within your fireworks, for it shall be My fist that is cracking down! For I have declared that this shall mark an hour and a day of a shift that shall come to you, America."

Of course, July 4, 2021, came and went without incident. But this was nothing new. A number of pro-Trump prophets in spring 2021 issued a series of specific prophecies detailing what would happen within specific time frames, and those had proven false as well. Yet in many circles the popularity of these prophets did not wane at all. How could this be?

But it was not only Christian believers who were following these prophecies with interest. Anti-Trump, anti-conservative websites were following them too, and they were quick to post the videos once the predicted dates failed to come to pass,[122] including this one, originally posted online March 2021. It was later mocked by the Right Wing Watch (RWW) website on April 2, 2021. As summed up by Kyle Mantra, reporting for RWW,

> "President Trump won the election," Kunneman asserted. "So, for people to say, 'Well, people prophesied that he'd win,' he did win, and so we had a stolen election."
>
> "President Trump is not going anywhere," Kunneman added. "If you don't like President Trump, that's your problem because he's not done talking, and God's not done with him."
>
> Claiming that there "have been a lot of signs in the month of March" that the alleged voter fraud that supposedly stole the election from Trump will soon be exposed, Kunneman insisted that Christians must

remain faithful that he and the other "prophets" were right when they declared that Trump would serve a second term.

"I'm sensing very strongly by the signs that God has given ... that we are close to justice and righteousness being established," he said. "What we cannot do is quit, give up, point the finger, and then begin to think, 'Well, you know what? All of this was just a smoke-screen.' No, that's what the enemy wants because it's a sad day if all of God's messengers, prophets, intercessors, [and] Christians were somehow wrong and the fake news that we know has been fake news were the voice of truth. I don't think so."[123]

This brings further mockery to the gospel on a website that attacks conservative Christian ideology day and night.[124] Yet this was not an unmerited attack on our ideology. It was an attack that we deserved, an attack on our spiritual delusion.

But this is what happens when accountability is cast off and when prophecy marries patriotism and the gospel is wrapped in the American flag. This is what happens when the Holy Spirit is mistaken for a partisan political spirit. This is what happens when we confuse the election of a president with a spiritual awakening.

Were All of Them False Prophets?

The Bible has much to say about false prophets. They are wolves in sheep's clothing. They lead God's people into spiritual and moral apostasy. They speak in the names of other gods. They prophesy for financial gain. And when they speak in the name of the one true God, their words do not come to pass, since they speak out of their own hearts and minds rather than delivering a word from the Lord.[125]

But what about sincere Christian leaders with good track records, men and women who were not morally corrupt or greedy for gain and yet who became committed Trump prophets? How did so many good people get things so wrong? How is it that so many leaders who were not that politically involved in the past ended up delivering false prophecies about Trump? Rather than throw stones, let's try to understand. If so many people made such serious mistakes, there must be reasons why.

Loren Sanford was one of the few leaders who prophesied Trump's reelection and then repented with real humility, recognizing the damage he and others had done. As noted by Steve Rabey, Sandford attributed "the rise of partisan political prophecy to [a] host of problems within the prophetic community," including:

- a long-running lack of accountability for prophets;
- a growing number of preachers who have little or no theological training;
- prophets who have no connection to a local church, and thus remove the Holy Spirit's gift from its intended context;
- celebrity- and money-hungry prophets who compete for eyeballs, clicks, donations, and sales of books and DVDs by issuing ever more fantastical pronouncements;
- social media outlets that spread their words far and wide;
- prophetic conferences and events that titillate audiences with "sanctified psychic readings" that reinforce what they want to hear instead of what God is saying;
- and the most basic problem prophets have confronted for millennia. "There's a lot of confusion between what we really desire passionately, and what's the voice of the Lord," says Sandford, who supported Trump.[126]

In Sanford's view, then, the failed 2020 prophecies were an accident ready to happen. It was the culmination of years of abuse within the charismatic movement. The events surrounding the Trump presidency simply brought to the surface something that was already very wrong.

Digging deeper we can unearth additional factors that led to such widescale deception. One of those factors is the sin of presumption. This happens when we make false assumptions about the future—sometimes in pride or arrogance—based on our experiences in the past. In this case, well before 2016 some prophets were predicting a Trump presidency, much to the shock of their followers. Some immediately followed up saying, "Look, I don't like the man either! I just believe the Lord showed me that he would be the next president."

There were only a few such prophecies, but the words came at a very unexpected time, and, for the most part, the prophecies seemed to be unconnected to any type of partisan politics.[127] Once Trump was elected, it brought validation to these prophecies, which seemed so unlikely when they were originally delivered. And once Trump became a hero of evangelicals (of which charismatics are a subset), many other prophets came on board also prophesying Trump's reelection. So, in some cases, this was simply a matter of presumption.

Others were guilty of prophesying what people wanted to hear, bringing to mind the warning of Paul, who wrote: "For the time is coming when people will not endure sound teaching, but having itching ears they will accumulate for themselves teachers to suit their own passions, and will turn away from listening to the truth and wander off into myths" (2 Timothy 4:3–4). Today, some Christians accumulate for themselves "prophets" to suit their own passions, and when these "prophets" realize there is money to be made (or fame to be had) by "prophesying" what the people want to hear, they change their message accordingly. The outright charlatans— the real false prophets—do this knowingly and willfully.

The deceived leaders fall into a trap little by little, not realizing what they have done until they have crossed some very dangerous lines.

Centuries earlier, the prophet Micah rebuked the misleading prophets of his day, speaking against those who proclaim "Peace!" to those that feed them, but to those who don't give them something to eat, they launch a holy war (Micah 3:5). As paraphrased in *The Message*: "Here is God's Message to the prophets, the preachers who lie to my people: 'For as long as they're well paid and well fed, the prophets preach, "Isn't life wonderful! Peace to all!" But if you don't pay up and jump on their bandwagon, their "God bless you" turns into "God damn you." ' "

You might ask, "Does this mean that people just make up prophecies as they go? Is it that corrupt and that bad?" In some cases, the answer is yes, that's exactly what happens. I would not want to be in the shoes of those people on judgment day. In other cases, the prophets are self-deceived, believing that the thoughts of their own minds are really God's thoughts, mistaking their own feelings for divine inspiration.

The Lord addressed this very same thing more than twenty-five hundred years ago through the prophet Ezekiel, saying:

> The word of the LORD came to me: "Son of man, prophesy against the prophets of Israel, who are prophesying, and say to those *who prophesy from their own hearts*: 'Hear the word of the LORD!' Thus says the Lord GOD, Woe to the foolish prophets *who follow their own spirit, and have seen nothing!* . . . They have seen false visions and lying divinations. They say, 'Declares the LORD,' when *the* LORD *has not sent them*, and yet they expect him to fulfill their word. Have you not seen a false vision and uttered a lying divination, whenever you have said, 'Declares the LORD,' although I have not spoken?" (Ezekiel 13:1–3, 6–7, my emphasis)

A few years earlier, the prophet Jeremiah delivered a similar word of rebuke:

Thus says the LORD of hosts: "Do not listen to the words of the prophets who prophesy to you, filling you with vain hopes. They speak *visions of their own minds, not from the mouth of the* LORD. They say continually to those who despise the word of the LORD, 'It shall be well with you'; and to everyone who stubbornly follows his own heart, they say, 'No disaster shall come upon you.'" . . . I did not send the prophets, yet they ran; I did not speak to them, yet they prophesied. (Jeremiah 23:16–17, 21, my emphasis)

Again, in some cases, these people were (and are) outright charlatans. In other cases, they are sincere leaders who went astray, mistaking their thoughts for God's thoughts and their words for God's words, buoyed by the crowds, energized by their online followings, and assuming that the great increase in ministry finances was a sure sign of God's blessings. As someone once said, the problem with deception is that it is very deceiving.

Many pastors and Christian teachers fall into this very same error, but in a different way since they don't claim to be prophets. Instead, they only speak on certain portions of the Bible—the "feel good" parts of Scripture—never rebuking or correcting or calling out sin or confronting unrighteousness. In the process, they gain large followings or grow large churches. But their messages are little more than pep-talks, and they sound more like motivational speakers than preachers of the gospel. That's why, in the same book in which I addressed abuses in the prophetic movement, I also had a chapter titled "The Pep-Talk Prosperity Gospel."[128] This problem transcends prophetic ministry, and all of us who preach and teach the gospel must be careful not to fall into this trap.

Additional Reasons for the Failed Trump Prophecies

Others were guilty of unconsciously yielding to the power of the group, meaning that since other leaders were confidently prophesying a Trump victory, they felt the pressure to join in too. After all, they didn't want to appear unspiritual. They didn't want to miss what the Holy Spirit was saying. And surely if so many others were prophesying four more years for Trump, they should join in too.

Ironically, there is only one instance in the Bible where all the prophets said the same thing at the same time, guaranteeing a godless king (Ahab) a major military victory. Talk about being court prophets and telling the king what he wanted to hear. But this happened because Ahab had excluded the one and only prophet who would tell him the truth, which is why this king so hated him. (A few years earlier, the king's wife, Jezebel, had many of the true prophets killed. Others went into hiding, so there were not that many true prophetic voices around at that time.)

Another king, a godly king (Jehoshaphat), insisted on hearing from that excluded prophet, a man named Micaiah. So King Ahab sent for Micaiah, and the king's messenger gave the prophet this message: "Look, all the prophets are promising victory for the king. Be sure that you agree with them and promise success" (1 Kings 22:13 NLT). To his credit, and despite intimidation and threats, Micaiah refused to cave. He prophesied the truth to Ahab: you will die in battle today. Ahab, in turn, threw Micaiah into prison, then marched out to battle and was killed, just as the prophet declared. But note the power of the group and the harmony of the group: "They are all prophesying the same thing! You must join in too. Don't you dare dissent!"

Returning to the 2020 elections, consider things through this lens: (1) you personally wanted Trump to win; (2) you knew that millions of good Christians were praying for the elections; (3) one or two of your colleagues had the prophetic insight that Trump would win in 2016, even against all odds; (4) now, almost all of your colleagues were prophesying a second Trump victory; and (5) your followers, who are largely Trump voters, expected you to hear from the Lord too and give a prophecy about the elections. Can you see how easy it would be to simply repeat what the others are saying?

Back in Jeremiah's day, the Lord rebuked the false prophets "who steal my words from one another" and "who use their tongues and declare, 'declares the LORD' " (Jeremiah 23:30–31). So, one prophet claims to have a word from the Lord, and that word quickly spreads from prophet to prophet as they steal one another's words all while claiming to have heard the voice of the Lord for themselves. I wouldn't doubt that many of them actually believed they *were* hearing from the Lord. That's the nature of prophetic deception.

Others simply got caught up in a partisan political spirit, intoxicated by the power of having "their man" in the White House, equating a presidential victory with the advance of the gospel, viewing Trump as uniquely anointed by God, in which case his political opponents were of the devil. Indeed, Trump was perceived as the leader of the Jesus Team whereas Biden was the leader of the Satan Team. I'm exaggerating things just a bit to make a point, but such an argument sounded very appealing based on the contrasting political platforms of the two parties. "Biden wants to kill babies and Trump wants to save them!" Who could argue with that?

All this tied in with earlier, pre-2016 prophecies that likened Trump to King Cyrus, a non-Israelite, idol-worshiping leader whom God raised up to rebuild Jerusalem and release the Jewish people from exile in Babylon (see Isaiah 44–45). Those prophecies seemed to have credibility at the time, since Trump, too, was a spiritual outsider, obviously not a true Christian and hardly living in harmony with evangelical morality. Trump was a modern-day Cyrus!

This was all confirmed when Trump proved himself to be such a good friend to Israel, brokering unique peace treaties and even moving our embassy to Jerusalem. Commemorative coins were even minted in Israel, bearing the images of both Cyrus and Trump. And didn't the Lord say Cyrus was his anointed one (see Isaiah 45:1)? And isn't the Hebrew word for "anointed one" *mashiach*, from which we get the English word "messiah"? Did this mean that Trump, too, was God's anointed one? Was he, too, some kind of messianic figure who would save America?

As we saw in the last chapter, some of the prophets got caught up in this deception as well—and I call it a deception even if the pre-2016 "Trump is like Cyrus" prophecies were true, since the whole point of those prophecies was to say, "Just as God used a highly unlikely outsider to bless Israel twenty-five hundred years ago, He will do the same today with Trump, doing good for the Church and for Israel." That and that alone was the prophetic message, rather than deducing that in a special way, Donald Trump is God's anointed, and to be in harmony with God, you must support Donald Trump. That's how so many were deceived and misled, going from reluctantly supporting Trump in 2016 to guaranteeing his victory in the Lord's name in 2020. This is the epitome of a partisan political prophetic spirit.

Yet There Is More to This Story Than Meets the Eye

Not everyone was caught up in a partisan political spirit. Some prophetic voices simply veered into another lane, venturing into areas outside of their calling, similar to a sports commentator offering medical opinions or to a street preacher delivering a lecture on quantum physics. In this case, these sincere men and women tried to function as spiritual prognosticators—almost like Christian fortune tellers—telling us what we could expect in the months and years ahead.

Unfortunately, many of them didn't learn the lesson from their mistaken prophecies about the diminishing of COVID-19 (which was supposed to happen by mid-April 2020). Instead, they continued to make political predictions for the 2020 elections. Yet these same leaders could stand in a room with five hundred people and describe in detail what was happening in the lives of some of the individuals there, demonstrating God's love for them and His personal interest in their well-being. They could walk into a church they had never attended before and deliver a shockingly accurate prophetic word about the current state of that congregation. But when it came to predicting the end of COVID or the winner of the 2020 elections, they were wrong on both counts.

Why? They stepped out of their proper lane of ministry. They moved outside of their calling. They yielded to the pressure of "Tell us what's coming next." In the end, doing their best to hear something when God wasn't speaking, they heard what they wanted to hear or what others wanted them to hear. Some of them even had dreams that seemed to confirm the prophecies they were receiving, but quite obviously, none of it was really from the Lord.

This doesn't mean that they succumbed to some form of Trump idolatry or prophesied for financial gain or fell into a partisan political spirit. It simply means they assumed that, as prophets, they should know the future. And that assumption led to presumption since the Lord had clearly not revealed these things to them.

It's even possible—if we want to examine every possible option—that some of these prophets simply got their timing wrong, predicting a Trump victory in 2020 when it will actually happen in 2024. And lest that seems far-fetched to you, remember that the biblical prophets experienced this very same thing, delivering prophecies and recording them, only to wonder why the words didn't come to pass. It was only later, the Bible tells us in 1 Peter 1:10–12, that they understood that the prophecies were not for their own day but for hundreds of years later.

In fact, one of the most famous Trump prophets, fireman Mark Taylor, felt sure that Trump was going to be our next president back in 2012, when Barack Obama was elected to his second term, only to realize that his prophecy was for 2016. (You don't have to believe that any of this is true, of course. You can dismiss it all as guesswork mingled with charismatic terminology or even write it all off as demonic deception. I'm simply giving you a contemporary example of mistaken timing. For the record, Taylor wrongly prophesied Trump's reelection in 2020.)[129]

So, if Donald Trump is alive and well in 2024 and if he wins a second term as president, then some of these prophets could say, "That's what we saw coming! We just got the timing wrong." The problem is that you don't prophesy in hindsight, and if you're not sure about the timing of something, then don't announce the timing. Otherwise, you end up with egg on your face, you sow confusion in the body, and you make a public mockery of the Spirit.

What is interesting, though, is that many prophetic leaders did not prophesy Trump's victory, but we never heard from them since they had nothing definitive to say. I spoke with an international prophetic leader with a network of four thousand prophets, and he told me that only one of them claimed to hear a definitive word that Trump would win in 2020. Another internationally respected leader told me that in her network of about seventy-five prophetic voices only a few prophesied a Trump victory, so they decided not to publish anything as a group.[130]

Even more interesting is the fact that other leaders, not known as prophets, felt the Lord showed them that Biden would win, an outcome they did not want to see. One of them, a lifelong friend of mine now based in Israel, messaged me in September 2020, saying that he felt the Lord showed him that Biden would win because the church was looking to Trump in an idolatrous way. Not sure what to do with the message, he sent this word to several of us whom he looked to for accountability.

We counseled him to keep the word to himself until after the elections, lest anyone think he was trying to influence people's votes. Then, if he was right, he could share this afterward, and we would verify it. That's what he did. He let people know what the Lord had showed him after Biden's victory—and he received a mountain load of hatred and vitriol in response. This is quite telling. It looks like he hit a nerve.[131]

But he was not alone in receiving that same message. Other leaders came to me after the elections, saying that they had sensed the very same thing, namely that Trump would be removed because the Church made him into an idol and because of his failure to humble himself. But they were hesitant to say anything because of the overwhelming pro-Trump momentum among the most prominent, outspoken prophets. "Who am I to differ with them?" they thought.

This also revealed the existence of what some of us have called the "cult of the prophets," as if they were an elite spiritual guild specially called and anointed, never to be questioned. Again and again in the aftermath of the 2020 elections, I heard followers of the leading Trump prophets say, "How dare you challenge their words. They are prophets of God." This, too, is a very serious deception since prophets today are no different than pastors or teachers or evangelists. All need accountability, and all need the others.

A Prophetic Warning from January 2018

Jeremiah Johnson, who I mentioned in the last chapter, received the most attention for his Trump prophecies, beginning in 2015 and right through 2021 in the aftermath of his apology for wrongly prophesying Trump's reelection. Describing what happened in June 2015, he noted that, "At the time, I had no previous knowledge of Donald Trump whatsoever or any interest in politics." Yet to his great surprise, he received this prophetic message, which went completely viral once published online:

"Trump shall become My trumpet to the American people, for he possesses qualities that are even hard to find in My people these days. Trump does not fear man nor will he allow deception and lies to go unnoticed. I am going to use him to expose darkness and perversion in America like never before, but you must understand that he is like a bull in a china shop. Many will want to throw him away because he will disturb their sense of peace and tranquility, but you must listen through the bantering to discover the truth that I will speak through him. I will use the wealth that I have given him to expose and launch investigations searching for the truth. Just as I raised up Cyrus to fulfill My purposes and plans, so have I raised up Trump to fulfill my purposes and plans prior to the 2016 election. You must listen to the trumpet very closely for he will sound the alarm and many will be blessed because of his compassion and mercy. Though many see the outward pride and arrogance, I have given him the tender heart of a father that wants to lend a helping hand to the poor and the needy, to the foreigner and the stranger."[132]

Some of this word, to be sure, sounds very odd—in particular, the last lines. But all my friends who worked closely with Trump told me that, behind the hard, harsh, and even ugly, public exterior was a man who really did care, a man who really did want to help the poor and the needy. Either way, that was the message Jeremiah received, and it was shared around the world.

Then, just two years into Trump's first term, he received this word of warning, which he also published and disseminated. It was largely rejected by those who received his 2015 pro-Trump message with joy. Jeremiah explains:

In early January of 2018, two years into Trump's presidency, I was on a fast and received an open vision of Donald Trump's right hand that began to turn into an IRON FIST. God spoke to me and said, "Trump's grip is going to tighten while the liberal agenda loses its grip." I saw the liberal agenda in America gasping for breath as the Trump agenda (the iron fist) squeezes and suffocates its opponents. I saw desperation, wild accusation, and startling trepidation descend upon Washington. Then I began to see something that both surprised me and caused me to pause. The iron fist of Donald Trump was too much for the American people to bear. The pressure and strength of his grip while at first was reassuring, in the end, it brought great unnecessary destruction. I felt an alarm go off deep within my spirit. God said, "I have raised Donald Trump up for four years as a battering ram and trumpet in this nation, but without a serious sanctification and softening of his heart and words, ***there will be great trouble and danger that will mark his run for a second term***. Even those who were once for him, will see the error of his ways and begin to cry out for his soul. Do not be deceived by the wealth and change that Donald has and will bring to America, for I am after far more than the gifts I have irrevocably given him, ***I must have his heart so that I can order His steps.***"

The following night after receiving this word, I had a prophetic dream where I saw Donald Trump crawling around on the White House lawn eating grass and acting like an animal. Immediately I cried out to the Lord in the dream and said, "God, shall Donald Trump become like Nebuchadnezzar? Shall he become so consumed with his success that he begins to credit his accomplishments to his own strength and power? Will you remove sovereignty from his life?" God spoke to me and said, "***Donald Trump is in great danger of becoming like Nebuchadnezzar in the years ahead. He will have great success, but the Church must pray for humility and the Daniel Company to arise. Just like Nebuchadnezzar, if Donald breaks away from his sins by doing righteously and showing mercy to the poor, I will prolong his prosperity***." (Dan 4:27)

I woke up from the prophetic dream with a tremendous burden upon my heart. To be honest, I could not believe what I just received. Could Donald Trump have been raised up by God Himself like a Cyrus and bring necessary change to America, but through his own pride, arrogance, and forsaking of the poor end as a type of Nebuchadnezzar? The answer is: ABSOLUTELY. The truth is that Donald Trump desperately needs our prayers more than many care to realize. ***The truth is that many in the Church are guilty of idolizing and worshipping Donald Trump as the savior of America***.

While I do believe that Donald Trump could win a second term, I also sense strongly that there is potential great danger and trouble ahead for America if he is re-elected.[133]

I believe this was a true message from the Lord, a genuine warning about: (1) the dangers of Donald Trump's style of leadership, (2) the consequences of his failure to humble himself and repent, and (3) a rebuke to the many Christians who were "guilty of idolizing and worshipping Donald Trump as the savior of America." The closer we got to November 2020, the more accurate this word seemed to be.

Yet researcher James Beverley, cited above, told me personally that when he compiled every Trump prophecy he could find for his book *God's Man in the White House* (published in 2020), along with every relevant article among prophetic voices, Jeremiah was the only one to speak anything negative about Trump or issue these kinds of warnings.[134]

Unfortunately, Jeremiah himself got caught up in the partisan politics of 2020, also misinterpreting a dream he had, because of which he, too, wrongly prophesied Trump's victory. As he wrote on January 7, 2020, "I was wrong, I am deeply sorry, and I ask for your forgiveness." He continued, "I specifically want to apologize to any believer in whom I have now caused potential doubt concerning the voice of God and His ability to speak to His people. As a human being, I missed what God was saying; however, rest assured, God Himself is NOT a liar and His written Word should always be the foundation and source of our lives as Christians."[135]

But he had been forewarned in January 2018. He simply lost sight of this warning in the intensity of the events of 2020, events which knocked many a good person off his or her game.

Recovering Our True Prophetic Calling

In October 2018, Destiny Image published my book *Donald Trump Is Not My Savior: An Evangelical Leader Speaks His Mind About the Man He Supports as President*. In the first chapter of the book, I asked whether our relationship with Trump was a match made in heaven or a marriage with hell. In short, the answer was "still to be determined."

The last chapter, "Where Do We Go from Here?", laid out seven key action points if we were to navigate the Trump presidency successfully. We'll look at these points in the last chapter of this book, but number six was this: "Sometimes, we must function as the president's loyal opposition." I referenced a Jewish scholar named Yochanan Muffs who wrote a profound article in 1980 titled "His Majesty's Loyal Opposition: A Study in Prophetic Intercession."[136] I noted that:

> Prof. Muffs argued that "Prophecy is a dialectical tension between passive transmission of divine anger and active intercession in the name of prophetic love." He added, "The life of Moses is a vivid illustration of the prophet as intercessor. The stories of the Exodus are marked by periodic eruptions of divine anger which are soothed by the wise intercession of Moses."
>
> Muffs' point is that God relied on the prophets to intercede, to plead the case of their people, to appeal for mercy, to ask for a respite, to oppose the divine decree of judgment. And, Muffs notes, "when the dialogue between mercy and anger is silent, there arises an imbalance of divine emotion."
>
> You ask, "But what does that have to do with evangelicals and President Trump (or, for that matter, believing Christians and any president)?"
>
> Simply this: At times, our calling is to oppose the president, with respect and honor and love. At times, being loyal means disagreeing. At times, being a true friend involves conflict, since no one needs a bunch of yes men—in particular, the President of the United States.[137]

Had our contemporary prophets been more interested in hearing what the Lord was saying *about* the Trump presidency and *about* our relationship to Trump as followers of Jesus, rather than primarily prophesying about the 2020 elections and speaking glowing words about him while demonizing his political opponents, things might look very different in America today. And had those prophets focused more on the state of the Church than on the outcome of the elections, pointing out the rampant carnality and divisions in our midst, we might not find ourselves where we do today.

To be sure, prophetic ministry is multifaceted and prophetic words can sometimes be complex and even mysterious. But the moment prophecy becomes subservient to partisan politics it loses its effectiveness, it compromises its accuracy, and eventually it does much more harm than good.[138]

In this context, the old dictum of A. G. Gardiner is worth repeating: "When a prophet is accepted and deified, his message is lost. The prophet is only useful so long as he is stoned as a public nuisance, calling us to repentance, disturbing our comfortable routines, breaking our respectable idols, shattering our sacred conventions."[139] Enough said.

CHAPTER NINE

Enter QAnon

Sometime in the year 2018, people began to talk to me about a pedophile ring, a really large and powerful ring, one that was engaged in all kinds of crimes against children, including sex trafficking and even murder. But it was mentioned to me as common knowledge, as if everyone was familiar with it, leading me to wonder, "What am I missing here?"

As the months went on, the talk became more specific. This pedophile ring was connected to the Clintons. And the Obamas. And Joe Biden. And other Democratic leaders. And it was absolutely massive. Not only so, but Donald Trump was about to expose it. That's one of the main reasons the attack against him was so severe. He was the man who could bring this cabal down, and the powers that be wanted him out. That's what all the buzz was about.

These theories can be traced back directly to 2016 and the infamous Pizzagate scandal. As explained in *Esquire Magazine,*

> It all started in early November 2016, when [Hillary] Clinton campaign manager John Podesta's email was hacked and the messages were published by Wikileaks. One of the emails, according to *The New York Times,* was between Podesta and James Alefantis, the owner of D.C. pizzeria Comet Ping Pong. The message discussed Alefantis hosting a possible fundraiser for Clinton.

Users of the website 4Chan began speculating about the links between Comet Ping Pong and the Democratic Party, according to the BBC, with one particularly vile connection burbling to the surface: the pizzeria is the headquarters of a child trafficking ring led by Clinton and Podesta.

And so, "The conspiracy theory that prominent members of the Democratic Party are somehow involved in a global child-trafficking ring took root on far-right conservative websites."[140]

I had read about Pizzagate in 2016 and was familiar with the allegations against the Clintons and others. I simply didn't realize how many people, especially born-again Christians, believed the charges to be true. But this was only the beginning, and soon enough, even more bizarre theories began to circulate, all coalescing around the allegedly top-secret information being released online by someone known only as Q, the founder of what became known as QAnon.

I even had a ministerial colleague tell me that he was 100 percent sure that Hillary Clinton had raped and killed children. He saw the video for himself! This was just one of many, completely fictional theories he embraced, every one of them straight out of QAnon. Yet he also insisted that he knew very little about QAnon, despite embracing all of QAnon's talking points.

This seemed to be very common. People were believing completely unfounded conspiracy theories which were getting wackier and wilder by the day, with Trump as the savior figure in all of them, yet they had no idea everything they believed was straight out of QAnon, virtually word for word. To ask the question again, How on earth did this happen?

The Origins of Q and QAnon

In his book *The QAnon Deception: Everything You Need to Know about the World's Most Dangerous Conspiracy Theory*, research scholar James Beverley noted that:

In 2020 Q has become increasingly recognized as more than just the 17th letter of the English alphabet. The indication that something more is going on with Q is proven by various realities. There are major markets selling Q shirts, Q hats, Q decals, and Q coffee mugs. Flags are now emblazoned with Q and there are also phone cases with Q on the cover. There are also Q tote bags, and even pet hoodies with Q front and center.33 On the academic level, there are a now a whole slew of books with Q in the title or on the cover. As well, at Trump rallies his fans are proudly waving signs with the letter Q on them.[141]

Beverley even released a compilation in 2021 titled *The QAnon Resource Guide: 2400 Linked News Reports, Articles & Opinion Pieces*.[142] This was quite a hot topic, one that refused to go away even after Trump's defeat. How did it become so prominent? And how did these theories become so widespread?

In answer to the question Where did it all start? BBC News explained on January 6, 2020 (as part of its reporting related to the storming of the Capitol), "In October 2017, an anonymous user put a series of posts on the message board 4chan [which is an anything goes message board known as being part of the darker part of the internet]. The user signed off as 'Q' and claimed to have a level of US security approval known as 'Q clearance'. These messages became known as 'Q drops' or 'breadcrumbs', often written in cryptic language peppered with slogans, pledges and pro-Trump themes."[143]

Soon enough, others began to join in, also claiming to have inside information, and QAnon was born. As the *Wall Street Journal* explains, QAnon is

a far right-wing, loosely organized network and community of believers who embrace a range of unsubstantiated beliefs. These views center around the idea that a cabal of Satan-worshipping pedophiles—mainly consisting of what they see as elitist Democrats, politicians, journalists, entertainment moguls and other institutional figures—have long controlled much of the so-called deep state government, which they say seeks to undermine President Trump, mostly with aid of media and entertainment outlets.[144]

Or, in the words of the BBC:

At its heart, QAnon is a wide-ranging, completely unfounded theory that says that President Trump is waging a secret war against elite Satan-worshipping paedophiles in government, business and the media.

QAnon believers have speculated that this fight will lead to a day of reckoning where prominent people such as former presidential candidate Hillary Clinton will be arrested and executed.[145]

As bizarre as all this sounds, millions of people bought into these theories, some quite fervently, and many still believe them today, despite the fact that none of the predicted events have taken place. (Does this sound familiar now?)

To give you an idea of just how farfetched these QAnon posts became, consider Prof. Beverley's list of "ten theories tied directly or indirectly to Q and QAnon":

- JFK Jr. is still alive and living as a guy named Vincent Fucsa.[146]
- Barack Obama is part of the Satanic cabal.
- Michelle Obama is male.
- Donald Trump is a time traveler.
- Mother Teresa was a child trafficker.
- John McCain was executed for treason.
- Queen Elizabeth II is part of the child trafficking network.
- George Floyd is still alive.
- North Korea's dictator is working in sync with Trump.
- COVID-19 panic is generated by Democrats.[147]

You might be scratching your head as you read this list not believing that anyone in his or her right mind could ever think these theories were true. (Even if you strongly differed with the Democratic handling of COVID-19.) The truth is that millions of people believed some (or even all) of these theories. In fact, when I invited Prof. Beverley on to my radio show to talk about Q, I received a flood of angry, hateful, even outraged comments from professing followers of Jesus.[148] How dare we question Q!

Some of the responses on the AskDrBrown Facebook page included these:

- Elvira: I was going to unfollow you as its obvious you are a globalist puppet. But then I thought about that old saying keep your friends close and your enemies closer. So I'm going to continue following ad its good to know all of the globalist minions.
- Gary: Sorry Dr. Brown but you sound like the lying world system. You would have been in the crowd yelling "crucify Him", you would have been on the sides of the 10 spies report rebuking Joshua and Caleb. Afraid?

- Cat: You, Dr. Brown are obviously a wolf in sheep's clothing.....!!!
- JF: False teacher run from this guy he's part of the iluminati. I block trolls.

As I remarked in the aftermath of the broadcast, if I ever needed proof that QAnon had become a cult, I got all the proof I needed that day. The unwavering loyalty of the followers was deeply disturbing, as if they had been corporately brainwashed. And whereas my listeners are used to me tackling controversial subjects, often asking me to have another guest on who will challenge my views, when it came to questioning Q, they were absolutely indignant. How dare I bring on an anti-QAnon guest. I must *immediately* rectify this or else they would never listen again. This was clearly cultlike.

They instantly dismissed Prof. Beverley as an outright liar who was completely ignorant of the facts and claimed that I was part of the Deep State, intentionally working to cover up the truth. Who were we to challenge the claim that Hillary Clinton was not only involved in sex-trafficking but actually murdered *and ate* the children herself? How dare we question that both the Pope and the Dalai Lama were some of the global elites involved in this sex-trafficking scheme. I kid you not.

What was scary was that there seemed to be no way to penetrate this conspiratorial fortress, since the more facts we presented, the more this was taken as proof of the conspiracy. "That's how deep the cover up is!" I was told.

It reminds me of a story involving one of my closest friends, Scott V. He once received a phone call early in the morning, waking him out of a sound sleep. (He lived near the West Coast; the caller lived on the East Coast.) When my friend answered the phone, it was his elderly grandfather, who said, "I need to renew my prescription," thinking he had called the local Walgreens pharmacy.

Realizing that his grandfather had dialed the wrong number, my friend replied, "Grandpa, this is Scott. You called me by mistake." His grandfather replied, "What are you doing at Walgreens?" That's an illustration of what we're dealing with when we try to interact with QAnon believers.

What makes things all the more pathetic is that while QAnon is absolutely right in standing against the very real, absolutely horrific, child-trafficking industry, QAnon's spreading of baseless conspiracy theories has actually undermined the work of those who are fighting against this evil. (A number of my ministry school grads have been working in America and overseas to combat this foul industry and to rescue and rehabilitate the children who have been abused. Not one of these grads entertain any of the QAnon, Democratic-led, pedophile theories.)

During our interview, Prof. Beverley drew attention to an open letter signed by almost one hundred organizations involved in fighting against sex-trafficking. The letter, which is quoted in his book, was emphatic and decisive "Anybody— political committee, public office holder, candidate, or media outlet—who lends any credibility to QAnon conspiracies related to human trafficking actively harms the fight against human trafficking. Indeed, any political committee, candidate, public office holder or media that does not expressly condemn QAnon and actively debunk the lies should be held accountable."[149]

And how did some QAnon believers respond to this open letter? According to Prof. Beverley, this was proof that these organizations had also been bought out by the Deep State. Put another way, "What are you doing at Walgreens?"

What Gave QAnon so Much Credence

It's easy to look at the wackiest QAnon theories and wonder how anyone could believe such nonsense. But at the root of the Q conspiracy is a deep concern about the direction in which America is going and a deep distrust in some of the nation's major institutions, including the mainstream media and the political system. The more "they" tried to take down Trump, most notoriously with the false "Russia collusion" charges, the more that Q's theories appeared to be real.

"You see," we were told, "things are happening just as Q predicted. Just wait and see. Biden will be exposed, the military will take over, and Trump will be back. It's about to happen!" Plus, who among us is not utterly revolted at the thought of child abuse and pedophilia and the trafficking of children? Who would not want all of that exposed?

As Beverley explained, "The good guys are the patriots in the U.S. military and their global partners who turned to Donald Trump and asked him to run for President. After his victory, the cabal (including top figures in the FBI and Justice) sought to destroy Trump. This has led to 'a dramatic covert war of biblical proportions, literally the fight for earth, between the forces of good and evil.' "[150] The lines had been drawn, and there was only one righteous side, the side of Donald Trump.

Beverley explained further that the

QAnon material is a mixture of realization of society ills and utopian hopes for a better world. This is captured in one quotation from the *Invitation* book [a major, pro-Q book]. "While a lot is improving, it still puzzles many that most of these known criminals are still free. Especially higher ups like the Hillary Clinton, the Bushes and Obama. That is coming in the next chapter of the story. That's why we have Q. The good guys, with control over the NSA, began the Q intelligence dissemination program to invoke an online grassroots movement called 'The Great Awakening.'"[151]

Ironically, while many of us have been praying for another Great Awakening for many years, believing it was America's only hope (this was actually the title of my 2021 book *Revival Or We Die: A Great Awakening Is Our Only Hope*), other Christians were saying, "Yes, we need a Great Awakening, and it is coming very soon"—except they were referring to the Q "Great Awakening." This only added to the confusion.

Let's also remember that QAnon was not birthed in a vacuum. We live in the internet age when conspiracy theories spread like wildfire in a moment of time, and when someone like Alex Jones, who does expose some left-wing lunacy while also espousing his own conspiracy theories, can have an audience of millions.

Yet there is something especially distressing when it comes to evangelical Christians and QAnon, since we of all people seemed to be especially prone to believing this nonsense. What happened to our discernment? What happened to being sober-minded? What happened to being lovers of truth?

In the aftermath of the Biden inauguration on January 20, the light went on for many QAnon devotees, as evidenced by these headlines:

- "'We've been had': Biden inauguration has QAnon followers confused" (*National Post*, January 20, 2021). The subtitle read, "In one group with more than 18,400 members, QAnon believers were split between those still urging others to 'trust the plan' and those saying they felt betrayed."[152]
- "'We All Got Played': QAnon Followers Implode After Big Moment Never Comes" (*Forbes*, January 20, 2021)[153]

As the *Forbes* story stated, "As Joe Biden was sworn in as president, QAnon followers finally saw their hope for the 'storm'—when President Donald Trump would bring down the 'deep state' and expose a far-reaching child-sex-trafficking ring—disappear, leaving followers of the unhinged conspiracy theory in despair and searching for answers, while one of the most prominent adherents gave up." As a result, "QAnon adherents appeared to have fractured into two groups on popular far-right message boards Wednesday, with some real-izing their crackpot conspiracy theory was a fraud, while others tried to somehow keep the flame of the Crazy Candle alive."[154]

Yet among those keeping that "Crazy Candle" alive were many conservative Christians, including both evangelicals and Catholics, as documented by stories well into 2022.[155] How is it that, while many others recognized that they had "been played" and that the whole QAnon conspiracy was based on myths, these Christian believers were still hanging on? The title of an American Enterprise Institute survey in spring of 2021 said it all: "Evangelicals more likely to believe QAnon conspiracy."[156] What a shameful headline.

I do recognize that many of the websites reporting on this slant clearly to the left. But there is no denying that there is much truth to what is being reported. The real question is: Why?

On February 21, 2021, NPR ran a story titled "Disinformation Fuels A White Evangelical Movement. It Led 1 Virginia Pastor To Quit."[157] On March 4, 2021, the *FiveThirtyEight* website carried this headline: "Why QAnon Has Attracted So Many White Evangelicals."[158] The story began with these words:

One week after his first drop, Q was already quoting scripture. "The LORD is my shepherd, I lack nothing," Q posted on the imageboard site 4chan. The line was from Psalm 23, possibly the most well-known of the 150 psalms, and a beacon of hope for Christians going through challenging times. Is it any wonder that the fringe conspiracy theory QAnon has attracted true believers in every sense of the word?

On April 27, 2021, the *Daily Beast*, another Left-leaning website, ran this headline: "Why So Many Evangelicals Are Susceptible to QAnon Craziness." It also made this claim, "The connection between white conservative evangelicals and conspiracy theories goes back at least a century."[159] Similarly, *Newsweek* stated that, "One-Quarter of White Evangelicals Believe QAnon 'Storm' Is Coming to 'Restore Rightful Leaders'."[160]

According to Jason Springs, posting on *Contending Minorities* June 16, 2021:

Rather than an aberration, the fascination with conspiracies at the heart of Trump-era White evangelical Christian nationalism is symptomatic of a distinctively modern manifestation of evangelicalism's obsession with end-time prophecies. These form a surging and resurging current throughout late twentieth and twenty-first century evangelicalism. Confronted by an ever more rapidly changing socio-political context, and now inextricably intertwined with Republican Party politics, end-time apocalypticism and messianism have come to infuse evangelical approaches to contemporary politics and culture. Caught in the siren-song of Trump and QAnon conspiracy ideology, this fixation has leapt from the folk theology pages of popular Christian fiction and populism-inflected evangelical church pews, into voting booths, political rallies and activism, and onto the lawn of the U.S. Capitol at the January 6th, 2021 insurrection. Together, apocalypticism and messianism form a recurring dynamic, pattern, and logic that drives the latest resurrection of

White evangelical nationalism—a dynamic, pattern, and logic I describe as "zombie nationalism."[161]

Springs obviously painted with a broad brush, especially with the emphasis on *white*. At the same time, he definitely hit some nails on the head. The predicted QAnon "storm" fit very well into a much larger, even bigger-than-life, perfect storm, one in which Trump and Christian conservatives found themselves in an apocalyptic battle for the soul of America. Only Trump could be trusted to do the right thing and save the nation (and the world) from disaster.

As expressed on December 13, 2020, by David French, a thoughtful, Christian conservative who himself is a frequent target of other thoughtful, Christian conservatives:[162]

> This is a grievous and dangerous time for American Christianity. The frenzy and the fury of the post-election period has laid bare the sheer idolatry and fanaticism of Christian Trumpism.
>
> A significant segment of the Christian public has fallen for conspiracy theories, has mixed nationalism with the Christian gospel, has substituted a bizarre mysticism for reason and evidence, and rages in fear and anger against their political opponents — all in the name of preserving Donald Trump's power.[163]

While this clearly does not speak of many Christian conservatives who supported Trump, it definitely speaks of many others. I have witnessed it with my own eyes, this book has documented it, and the QAnon deception was the ugly icing on the cake. The passage of time, as we get further and further away from the 2020 elections, does not change this reality. Something was dreadfully wrong.

And once again, in the midst of this, Trump knew how to play into the mistrust, claiming months before the elections,

"The only way we're going to lose this election is if the election is rigged."[164] As a close friend exclaimed to me upon hearing this when he first uttered the words, "Can you see what he's doing? He's setting things up! This way, even if he loses, he can claim that the whole thing was fraudulent. And because his most loyal followers believe him and him alone, dismissing everything else as fake news, they'll believe that he really did win the election, no matter what the outcome." Talk about an accurate prediction.

Yet even as late as October 2021, when Trump held a large rally in Iowa, he could spend considerable time claiming the election was stolen, and rather than losing the crowd, he inspired the crowd.[165] He even went as far as saying, "If we don't solve the Presidential Election Fraud of 2020 (which we have thoroughly and conclusively documented), Republicans will not be voting '22 or '24. It is the single most important thing for Republicans to do."[166, 167]

In the months following Biden's inauguration, the rift between Right and Left grew even deeper, with Democratic policies becoming more extreme and dangerous, from vaccine mandates and the teaching of radical race theories in our schools and draconian lockdowns to attacks on Christian liberties and legal assaults on pro-life bills and the pushing of the so-called Equality Act. The perfect storm was being recreated, and once again, Trump could emerge as the man to save the day.

And be assured that these conspiracy theories are not simply going to disappear, as confirmed by a talk given in late October 2021 by the popular Christian actor Jim Caviezel, the man who played Jesus in Mel Gibson's *The Passion of the Christ*. Speaking at a conference called "For God and Country Patriot Double Down"—dubbed "a QAnon conference" by the secular media—Caviezel said, "We must fight for that authentic freedom and live, my friends." And he added, "By God, we must live, and with the Holy Spirit as your shield and Christ as your sword may you join Saint Michael and all the other angels in defending God and sending Lucifer and his henchmen straight back to hell where they belong."

He also said this, with direct reference to QAnon: "We are headed into the storm of all storms. Yes, the Storm is upon us." As explained by the *Washington Examiner*,

> "The Storm" references a hypothetical event when former president Donald Trump would arrest members of a Satanic cabal that is controlling the world through a deep state – this hypothetical cabal is believed by QAnon members to include an assortment of media and political personalities, including former Secretary of State Hillary Clinton and former President Barack Obama.[168]

Yes, old myths die hard.

Will we learn from our mistakes this time, or will 2022 and 2024 look like a repeat of 2020 (in terms of our fleshly attitudes and political obsession)? Or will we put things in their proper perspective, voting for the candidate we feel would best represent us (and for many, that candidate will still be Trump), but doing so without getting caught up in partisan politics, without putting too much hope in a person or a party, and without compromising our own integrity and witness in the process?

Moving Forward with Integrity and Truth

On December 30, 2020, in the aftermath of my tackling the Q controversies, Colleen commented on Facebook:

> "Well said Dr Brown... QAnon has become a major source of deception within the Church. It is demonic at its core because those who believe it think they're

defending what's right, but are actually taking God &
His authority completely out of the equation. Good
on you for calling it out!!!"

Amy emailed us, saying:

Thank you for exposing the truth about Trump/
QAnon! The way you've taken a stand in love with
just calm facts is inspiring and I'm grateful to know
I'm not alone in having seen this "phenomenon" swal-
lowing the church.

I moved from California to Kansas last year. Little
did I know I would find a whole new level of deception in America's heartland. I've spent the last year
researching and attempting to show members of my
congregation the lies and deceit spread by this "Trump
as Messiah" movement. Mostly to no avail.

I'm truly grateful for your work and your willing-
ness to call evil what it is.

And David posted:

"I'll say it again, saying this to your audience takes
courage. There are many people in churches dedicated
to these lies, and by simply telling them the truth, you
are enraging many of them to the point that you've
lost a hearing with them. You have my admiration."

But how could we not call this out, when the deception
was so blatant and obvious? How could we not speak the
truth? This was not so much a matter of courage. It was a
matter of basic human decency.

A man named Paul wrote to us, saying:

I want to thank you for helping set me free from the Cult of Trump. You have reminded many thousands of Christians that we serve a jealous God. And that He will broker no substitutions. You have been a firebrand on the subject. You called it early on. Again, thank you.

I had a case of what I call "Reverse Trump Derangement Syndrome". I fell into it because of his stance on Israel, abortion, etc. In retrospect his rallies revealed cult-like mob delusion of his followers. Of which I was one.

This happened to some very fine people, and, on a certain level, it is understandable given the stakes at hand. But the question, once again, is simply this: Have we learned our lessons?

Bethany wrote this to our ministry:

I was one that was deceived. Not by Qanon, but I prayed faithfully with [a well-known evangelical leader], which led me to watch [a very popular Christian YouTube channel that hosted many pro-Trump, conspiracy theory interviews].

I did not share or even comment on any of the videos I watched, but just remained prayerful.

I was one that was waiting and watching til the 20th [or 2021], but now that it has passed, I know they weren't hearing from God. I will not be watching or listening to any of them from now on.

Your voice in this has been painful, but also soothing.

My heart is for Jesus and His will, even when I don't understand.

And "G" wrote this:

There is enough hard evidence now for us to conclude that the most powerful voices in America advocating Deep State siege narratives, Nationalistic ideas and rabid Qanon conspiracies are those who profess the name of Christ. These poisonous ideas may have been birthed in the dark underbelly of anonymous discussion forums, but they have been given power, parsonage and a wide pulpit by the Church of Jesus Christ.

Outsiders like myself (a former Evangelical) will have little to no effect confronting these rank deceptions among the faithful. But they will listen to YOU. The issue is very serious. The repercussions are potentially lethal. And it's impact on the future of the Church in America, catastrophic. I wish you success.[169]

Addressing these issues was, in my mind, a matter of simple decency. Nothing heroic, nothing courageous, and nothing particularly noble. Just one leader shouting out to my brothers and sisters, "Get your eyes back on the Lord and do not be deceived!" Nothing more than that.

In fact, if there was anything that compelled me to speak, it was love, especially when our ministry received emails that started with this:

Dear Dr. Michel Brown

Me and some other church members are in a very difficult situation.

My pastor is believing Qanon and other conspiracy theories, also preaching it in the church, what to do?

I'm writing to you from Europe and I'm asking you sincerely a question which I hope you have some wisdom to share. I listened to your show just now on YouTube about "Debunking the March 4 Conspiracy Theories." I've been listening to all other shows as well regarding Trump prophecies, Qanon and other similar topics recently.

Yet the writer, whom we'll call "B," explained that although he has always submitted to his pastor, a missionary to his country for decades and a man whom he describes as "sweet," he is not allowed to broach this subject at all. He writes, "We had prayer meetings (for two weeks every day during the election time and praying for the elections and specifically for Trump). Also there were leaders who started to preach weird things about the name 'Trump' having a prophetic meaning etc." When he posted some of my videos to his Facebook page, he got a call from his pastor wanting to talk to him about other subjects. The pastor quickly changed the subject to talk "about Trump being re-elected, about the military being ready and other stuff."

What was he to do? And what were his friends to do? How could we not call this out? How could we not address this? How could we possibly function as shepherds of God's flock without confronting such serious deception? And how did the Lord feel about this when His own sheep were being deceived and abused?

In a January 11, 2021, article titled "A Jesus I Do Not Know: Christians and the Capitol Riot," Methodist leader Dr. David F. Watson wrote:

Jesus—the real Jesus—does not bow at the altar of politics. He does not require the assistance of the kingdoms of this world. He transcends all governments, states, and borders. He cannot be held captive by any political agenda. He is not an ideological wax nose. Jesus—the real Jesus—is Lord of all. And attempts to remake him in our image, no matter how sincere our intentions, are affronts to his lordship. We do not honor him by parading his image in displays of political showmanship. We do not honor his cross by distorting its meaning for political gain, nor do we honor his name by co-opting it in the service of some other cause. Jesus is the cause, and he is too holy, too righteous, too perfect to serve as a spokesman for our this-worldly enterprises. We are not his masters. He is ours, and he abides no rivals.[170]

We do well to heed these words and to get our focus back where it belongs: on the real Jesus of the Bible. He alone can save and deliver, and He alone is worthy of our absolute trust and loyalty. He alone will never fail or disappoint. May we reset our priorities today so that we can be wise tomorrow.

The storms around us will only increase in intensity, and the deceptions will only grow deeper. May we walk as children of light with our faith founded on a rock. This way, we will never be shaken or misled.

CHAPTER TEN

The Fatal Error of Wrapping the Gospel in the American Flag

Writing in his 1984 book, *The Great Evangelical Disaster*, Francis Schaeffer warned that "we must stand against those who would naively baptize all in the past and that would wrap Christianity in the country's flag."[171] More fully, he explained that "there is the danger of confusing Christianity with the country. In this area," he continued, "I have stressed first that we must not wrap Christianity in our country's flag, and second that we must protest the notion of 'manifest destiny' that would permit our nation to do anything it chooses. We are responsible for all that we do and all that God has given to us, and if we trample on his great gifts we will one day know his judgment."[172]

What, exactly, did Schaeffer mean? First, he meant that, as American believers, we cannot whitewash our past as if, for most of our history, we were a wonderful, pristine, holy, Christian nation. Second, he meant that we must recognize that it is one thing to be an American, which has to do with our nationality and earthly citizenship, while it is another thing to be a Christian, which has to do with our relationship with God and heavenly citizenship. We must not confuse the two since you can be an American without being a Christian and you can be a Christian without being an American. Third, Schaeffer argued, we must reject the idea that America is so specially called by God that we have a guaranteed, glorious, future promised to us. To the contrary, if we continue in sin, we will be judged like any other nation.

Those are serious warnings from Schaeffer, and they are certainly applicable today. That's why when I pray for our nation I prefer to say, "Lord, Your kingdom come to America!" rather than say, "God bless America!" Of course, I want the Lord to bless us not curse us. Absolutely! But when we pray, "Lord, Your kingdom come to America," we're saying, "Lord, come to our nation and grant us repentance of our many sins so that You can change us and bless us." When we pray, "God bless America," we often mean, "God, make our great nation bigger and stronger and better!" There is little thought of repentance and little recognition of our sin and guilt when we simply say, "God bless America!"

That's also why I have mixed feelings when I see a large crowd at one of our political rallies chanting, "USA! USA! USA!" On the one hand, I feel proud to be an American, knowing the good our country has done around the world and knowing that we have so many outstanding qualities. In numerous significant ways America is an amazing country, and I understand why people from around the world send their children to study in our universities or relocate here themselves. On the other hand, I think of more than 60 million babies that we have aborted. I think of our high homicide rates. I think of the breakdown of our families. I think of how we try to push LGBTQ activism on other countries. I think of how we lead the world in producing and exporting pornography. I think of the deep divisions that are tearing us apart. Suddenly, the chant of, "USA! USA! USA!" sounds a little hollow, and I feel more shame than pride.

Yet all too often, we have this notion that God must be with us because, after all, we are a Christian nation, called to be a city set on a hill, founded on biblical principles, and with a destiny to bless the world.[173] Surely the Lord is standing with us against our enemies. Surely He will prosper us and grant us victory. Surely, as we return to our Christian roots, the Lord will bless us in incredible ways.

That's how many conservative Christians think. But it is not entirely wrong. There is truth mixed in with the error.

Thinking Honestly about Our Origins

Think about it for a moment. The Roman Empire did not have Christian origins nor did it have Christian sympathies. To the contrary, Rome ruthlessly persecuted the early followers of Jesus and was complicit in the Lord's crucifixion. It is no surprise then that the goal of the first Christians was not to expand the Roman Empire or make Rome even greater. Their goal was the Great Commission—to go and make disciples of all the nations—and their primary identity was found in Christ, not in the country in which they happened to live.

It's the same with countries like China today. While the Christians there might love their country, they understand that China was not birthed as a Christian nation, and the national leadership is anything but Christian. The Chinese government wants to crush and destroy the Church, and the believers know that they are citizens of another, heavenly kingdom, even while living here on earth. There is no confusion about where their ultimate loyalties lie.

But when it comes to America, things can get a little confusing. After all, we reason, wasn't America founded as a Christian nation? Didn't the Pilgrims flee here to escape religious persecution in England? And wasn't the Mayflower Compact, our earliest, founding document, dating back to 1620, explicitly Christian in tone and purpose? Here's the actual text of the Compact:

> In the name of God, Amen. We whose names are underwritten, the loyal subjects of our dread Sovereign

Lord King James, by the Grace of God of Great Britain, France, and Ireland King, Defender of the Faith, etc.

Having undertaken for the Glory of God and advancement of the Christian Faith and Honour of our King and Country, a Voyage to plant the First Colony in the Northern Parts of Virginia, do by these presents solemnly and mutually in the presence of God and one of another, Covenant and Combine ourselves together in a Civil Body Politic, for our better ordering and preservation and furtherance of the ends aforesaid; and by virtue hereof to enact, constitute and frame such just and equal Laws, Ordinances, Acts, Constitutions and Offices from time to time, as shall be thought most meet and convenient for the general good of the Colony, unto which we promise all due submission and obedience. In witness whereof we have hereunder subscribed our names at Cape Cod, the 11th of November, in the year of the reign of our Sovereign Lord King James, of England, France and Ireland the eighteenth, and of Scotland the fifty-fourth. Anno Domini 1620.[174]

And what about the Old Deluder Act of 1647? It was a law passed by the leaders of the colony of Massachusetts to ensure that children received a proper education *so that they would be able to read the Bible*, thus making them into good citizens. As for the Old Deluder, that was none other than Satan himself. (It was actually called Ye olde deluder Satan Act.)"[175] In the past, the organized Church had kept the Bible from English-speaking Christians, not allowing it to be translated into the language of the people, even persecuting and killing those who undertook such work. In the colonies, the leaders recognized that Satan would try to keep the Bible from their people by illiteracy. That's why it was essential to teach the children to read so that they could be literate in the Scriptures. That sounds pretty Christian to me!

Similarly, in order to graduate from Harvard College, founded in 1636, with the most basic degree in Arts (not Theology—that came later), the student had to be able "logically to explain the Holy Scriptures, both of the Old and New Testaments" and "be blameless in life and character." Among the Rules and Precepts of Harvard to be observed by the students were these: "Let every Student be plainly instructed, and earnestly pressed to consider well, the main end of his life and studies is, to know God and Jesus Christ which is eternal life"; and, "Every one shall so exercise himself in reading the Scriptures twice a day, that he shall be ready to give such an account of his proficiency therein, both in Theoretical observations of Language and Logic, and in practical and spiritual truths."[176] Harvard was actually founded with the stated purpose to train a literate clergy.

Yet Harvard did not stand alone in having such overtly Christian foundations. To the contrary, almost all of our first schools of higher learning were explicitly Christian.

For further evidence of the Christian roots of America, consider the original charters of our first colonies. Stephen McDowell cites these representative examples:

- The First Charter of Massachusetts (1629) states the desire that all the inhabitants would "be so religiously, peaceably, and civilly governed, as their good life and orderly conversation may win and incite the natives of country to the knowledge and obedience of the only true God and Savior of mankind, and the Christian faith, which in Our royal intention and the adventurers' free profession, is the principal end of this plantation."
- Adopted January 14, 1639, the Fundamental Orders of Connecticut began with the inhabitants covenanting

together under God "to maintain and preserve the liberty and purity of the gospel of our Lord Jesus which we now profess."

- The Charter of Rhode Island (1663) mentioned their intentions of "godlie edifieing themselves, and one another, in the holie Christian ffaith and worshipp" and their desire for the "conversione of the poore ignorant Indian natives."

- In 1682 the Great Law of Pennsylvania was enacted revealing the desire of Penn and the inhabitants of the colony to establish "laws as shall best preserve true Christian and civil liberty, in opposition to all unchristian, licentious, and unjust practices, (whereby God may have his due, Caesar his due, and the people their due)."[177]

Fast-forward to the Revolutionary War when some of our Founding Fathers, like Samuel Adams, were outspoken and unashamed Christians, while many pastors stood on the front lines of the call to revolt against England.[178] Even our iconic Liberty Bell contains a quote from Leviticus 25:10: "Proclaim liberty throughout all the land unto all the inhabitants thereof." In fact, it was the Bible itself that was used as a textbook for generations of American students, right into the early twentieth century.

Surely, we have every right to think of America as a Christian nation, at least in its origins and in the profession of faith of the great majority of our citizens, right? Surely, it is understandable that, as followers of Jesus, we want to preserve our Christian heritage, isn't it? And so, to "make America great again" means to restore America to its Christian roots—at least, that's the logic involved.

In the Introduction to Benjamin F. Morris's thousand-page volume, *Christian Life and Character of the Civil*

Institutions of the United States, Byron Sunderland wrote in 1863:

> This is a Christian nation, first in name, and secondly because of the many and mighty elements of a pure Christianity which have given it character and shaped its destiny from the beginning. It is pre-eminently the land of the Bible, of the Christian Church, and of the Christian Sabbath. It is the land of great and extensive and oft-repeated revivals of a spiritual religion— the land of a free conscience and of free speech—the land of noble charities and of manifold and earnest efforts for the elevation and welfare of the human race. The chief security and glory of the United States of America has been, is now, and will be forever, the prevalence and domination of the Christian Faith.[179]

This was his perspective roughly 150 years ago, much closer to the events in question than we are today. As for Morris's volume, it is primarily a massive compilation of primary documents, indicating the degree to which our roots were clearly Christian. Yet, already in 1863, Sunderland could also write this:

> We have abandoned, in a great measure, the faith and practice of our ancestors, in putting aside from their lawful supremacy the Christian ordinances and doctrines. The natural result is, that we have corrupted our ways in all the circles of society and in all the pursuits of life. We have become as a field rank with the growth of all the vices and heaped with the pollution of mighty crimes. The rigid training of former times through family government, discipline, and instruction has been greatly relaxed, if not in many cases wholly neglected. Indeed, there are multitudes

of parents in the land who from physical and moral causes are totally unfit to have the care of the children to whom they have given birth: so that a generation of human beings is growing up in one of the most favored regions of the globe, whose preparation for the responsibilities of their age and mission has been sadly at fault, and whose precocity in levity, mischief, and insubordination already equals the vitiating examples that are set before them. The education of the nation is going forward with rapid strides, but it is in a lamentable degree under the auspices of immorality and irreligion, alike in the high and the low places of the community. The unblushing venality and brazen wickedness of a large portion of the conductors of the public press and of the public men of the country have strongly tended to demoralize the nation, to undermine the foundations and destroy the influence of Christian discipline, and to turn the mind and heart of many to infidelity and licentiousness.[180]

The reality, of course, is that America, even from its very beginnings, has been a mixture of fine Christian elements along with sinful worldly elements, including the terrible practice of slavery, which was also part of America's earliest history. And what of our treatment of the Native Americans? Do they view America's "Christian" past with a sense of pride and joy? And does "MAGA" mean the same thing to an African American as it means to an American of European descent?

That's also why we have needed serious spiritual awakenings during the course of our history, beginning with the First Great Awakening in the 1730–1740s. We have had frequent periods of backsliding, rationalism, worldliness, and dead, formalistic religion, as Sunderland acknowledges as well. (He also wrote, "Our wrongs to the Indian and the African, continued from the beginning, have brutalized the temper,

162

darkened the understanding, and perverted the judgment of the nation in regard to the plainest principles of common humanity and justice.")[181]

America, like every other nation on earth, is part of what the Bible calls the world as opposed to being part of the kingdom of God. Yet within every country there are followers of Jesus, whether their numbers are large or small, and it is the followers of Jesus who are part of the kingdom of God, meaning that they live under the rule and reign of God. The rest of the world is part of another kingdom. 1 John 5:19 says, "We know that we are from God, and the whole world lies in the power of the evil one" (1 John 5:19). In other words, God looks down on the earth and sees the saved and the lost, the believers and the unbelievers, those who are part of His family and those who are not. As for the nations of the earth, they are all mixed with both saved and lost in their midst. But there is not a single nation on the planet, including America, that lives fully under the Lord's rule, with Him as the King and final authority, nor will that take place until Jesus returns and sets up His kingdom on earth.

Of course, more than three thousand years ago, God called Israel to be a priestly kingdom living directly under His rule. But we know how that ended up. As for the modern state of Israel, while I am convinced that my Jewish people have been regathered to their ancient homeland by the Lord in fulfillment of biblical prophecy, I can't imagine that anyone would claim that contemporary Israel is a priestly nation governed by God. Not a chance.

Now, I personally believe that to the extent that we return to our Christian roots in America we will be blessed. But that is simply because God's ways are best and living by His principles brings blessing rather than cursing. As Proverbs 14:34 states "Righteousness exalts a nation, but sin is a reproach to any people." This is a universal principle for all nations. Put another way, this is not about America recovering her alleged divine calling to lead the world in righteousness. Rather, it is a matter of saying, "What made us great was honoring the Lord. To the extent we do that, we can be even greater. To the extent we do not, we will destroy ourselves, if not come under the active judgment of God."

So, this is anything but wrapping the gospel in the flag or confusing Christianity with country. It is saying, "We have an amazing heritage. Let's return to that and live it out today. Otherwise, we are in dire straits." Yet all too often we get things confused here. As one of the callers to my radio show observed, "There is a difference between the MAGA spirit and the Holy Spirit." Yet, in the height of 2020 election fever, it was all too easy to blur the distinction between the two.

Consider things from the perspective of that pivotal year 2020. You understand perfectly well that you are a Christian first and an American second, relating to the Lord in one way and to the president in a very different way. And so, while you honor and respect the Constitution, you do not study it daily, you do not memorize its contents, and you do not carry it wherever you go. In sharp contrast, you recognize the Bible as God's Word, you study it daily, you memorize its contents, and it is always with you, now in an app on your cell phone.

As for the church you attend, the focus was on Jesus, on worship, on Bible teaching, on reaching your communities. In fact, months could go by without any mention of anything political at all or without special prayer for America. At least, that was the pattern before the mid-2010s.

The mid-2010s changed everything. Some of your most important biblical values started to come under increasing attack. You lost your job because you pushed back against your company's aggressive LGBTQ agenda. You were mortified by the "Shout Your Abortion" movement. Your kids came home from school, telling you how their teachers mocked their beliefs. And if the Equality Act ever became law, it would essentially strip religious liberties from the nation.

Surely, as a believer, you could not sit idly by. Surely, this was one of the moments when faith and politics intersected. And surely, it was the Democrats and the liberals and the leftists who were driving this anti-God agenda while it was the Republicans, led by Trump, who were fighting against it. As for America as a whole, we had departed so far from our Christian roots that, barring divine intervention, we would soon be destroyed.

Surely this was an urgent hour, and surely it was time to act. "Let us pray for our elections and let us rally behind Donald Trump! The fate of America and the Church in America are directly tied to the outcome of these elections, and the cause of Christ is integrally joined together with the cause of the nation!" In this way, quite innocently and quite understandably, the gospel became wrapped in the American flag. The two had now become one.

In her book *Red State Christians*, Angela Decker claimed that, in response to the perceived spiritual and moral decline of our nation,

Red State Christians have turned toward the flag, feeling their patriotic fervor and nostalgic desire for a more Christian America (where kids used to pray in school). This desire to turn back the clock is more about national identity than Christian identity, though the two are inextricably tied together for many Red State Christians. They want to be the ones who get to define what America is, and for them, it must be conservative, and it must be Christian. Otherwise the country—and their Christian faith—will utterly collapse.[182]

Indeed, she opined, "Red State Christians consider America and American Christianity under siege, resulting in a defensive pushback. Churches today must defend not just

Jesus but also America. The American flag and the Christian flag are posted side by side in sanctuaries across the country, often directly in front of the cross."[183] Thus, patriotism is equated with Christian commitment, and allegiance to the nation equated with allegiance to God.

She added,

> Two years into Trump's presidency, the Pew Research Council released a new religious typology to categorize American Christians. Among the 39 percent considered highly religious, 12 percent were called "God and Country Christians," for whom American conservative values and national Christianity are most important. You can see this throughout the early twenty-first century at Southern Baptist churches across America, where even Christmas and Easter are subsumed by a sort of civic religion that worships God, Guns, and Country (really, the military), lifting up Veterans Day, Memorial Day, and the Fourth of July to the same place of honor as religious high holy days.[184]

Thinking back again to the 2020 elections (or, as things currently stand, to the 2022 or 2024 elections), the argument would sound like this: "You're not going to tell me that God is with the Democrats are you? They're demoncrats if you ask me—pro-abortion, pro-homosexual, pro-open borders, pro-socialism. And the more they govern our country, the more they destroy our country, taking away the hope of future generations and trampling on our Christian foundations. There is blood on their hands, but there will not be blood on my hands. I'm voting Republican (or in 2020, Trump)."

The argument might continue, "If America falls, the world will suffer. Islamic terror will rise. Russia will get more aggressive. Middle East peace will be threatened. Iran might even get a nuclear bomb and try to blow up Israel or even attack

America. And China will try to dominate the globe. That's why I'm voting Republican (or, Trump). It's my Christian duty to do so, and if you can't vote Republican (or, Trump), don't tell me that you're a Christian. And if you're ashamed of our great country, then you're ashamed of our God." In short, MAGA is not just a patriotic theme. It is a gospel theme.

Now, I actually agree with a lot of this argument, which is why I have voted Republican for many years now. It comes down to issues and policies, and as a follower of Jesus, I agree with Republican policies over Democratic policies, overwhelmingly so. I also recognize that Republican leaders seem much more concerned with protecting our religious freedoms than do their Democratic counterparts.

That's why I explained in a September 2019 article titled "The Demonization of the Democrat Party" that

> The Democrat Party continues to grow spiritually darker to the point of actually proclaiming itself the party of the religiously non-affiliated. Is it any surprise?
>
> Back in 2012, the *Washington Post* reported that the Democrats were under fire for removing "God" from their national platform.
>
> This was not missed by Paul Ryan, then a Republican presidential candidate, who stated on Fox News, "I guess I would just put the onus and the burden on them to explain why they did all this, these purges of God."
>
> And was it a coincidence that, the same year, the Democrats also failed to affirm Jerusalem as Israel's capital?
>
> To put this in perspective, the *Post* observed that, "God is mentioned 12 times in the 2012 GOP platform. The 2008 Democratic platform made one reference to God: the 'God-given potential' of working

people. The 2004 platform had numerous references to God."

How times have changed.

Two years ago, in 2017, Selena Zito claimed in the *New York Post* that, "The Democratic Party has a God problem."

Remembering what happened in 2012, when it was widely reported that the Democrats "booed God" (during the platform hearings), Zito argued that the Democrats have since "pushed away religious voters not simply by ignoring them but by actively repelling them with accusations of bigotry and backwardness."

And, she added, "Unless they change that, Democrats haven't got a prayer of solving their God problem."

As of today, I wouldn't be holding my breath.

The DNC has now issued a resolution stating that "religiously unaffiliated Americans overwhelmingly share the Democratic Party's values, with 70% voting for Democrats in 2018, 80% supporting same-sex marriage, and 61% saying immigrants make American society stronger."

Yes, the Democratic Party is the party of the religiously unaffiliated, and this is now seen as something to celebrate. "If you have no religious affiliation, we're the party for you!"

Not surprisingly, this fairly substantial group, which is growing by the year, holds to strongly liberal social views, especially when it comes to abortion and same-sex "marriage." And this, in particular, is something praised by the Democrats. "If you support LGBT activism and stand for abortion, we're the party for you!"

As noted by a Pew Forum poll, "About three-quarters of white evangelical Protestants (77%) think abortion should be illegal in all or most cases.

"By contrast, 83% of religiously unaffiliated Americans say abortion should be legal in all or most cases, as do nearly two-thirds of black Protestants (64%), six-in-ten white mainline Protestants (60%) and a slim majority of Catholics (56%)."

This is a strikingly high number: 83 percent. It looks like lack of religious affiliation deeply affects one's views of the sanctity of life, beginning in the womb.

The DNC resolution states that "the nonreligious have often been subjected to unfair bias and exclusion in American society, particularly in the areas of politics and policymaking where assumptions of religiosity have long predominated."

This, of course, is ironic, since there has been an increasing attack on religious beliefs in America in recent decades, from the courts to the universities and beyond. Are the non-religious really being "subjected to unfair bias and exclusion in American society, particularly in the areas of politics and policymaking?"

The resolution also states that "those most loudly claiming that morals, values, and patriotism must be defined by their particular religious views have used those religious views, with misplaced claims of 'religious liberty,' to justify public policy that has threatened the civil rights and liberties of many Americans, including but not limited to the LGBT community, women, and ethnic and religious/nonreligious minorities."

So, in contrast with conservative evangelicals, who are branded as religious hypocrites and who are abusing their religious power, it is the religiously non-affiliated who hold to ethical values and truly care about all Americans.

Of course, it is good strategy for the Democrats to make such an explicit appeal to this substantial voting bloc. And it appears that the values of the religiously non-affiliated are much closer to the those of the DNC than the RNC. And, without question, there is some hypocrisy among those of us on the conservative evangelical side, which the DNC wants to highlight. (No group has a monopoly on hypocrisy. It affects all groups on all sides.)

But it is still quite enlightening to see how lack of religious affiliation (which does not theoretically mean lack of faith but simply lack of affiliation) does impact one's worldview, as it appears that lack of religious affiliation means lack of connection to biblical mores.

Still, not everyone on the Democrat side thinks that the DNC's resolution was wise. According to Michael Wear, who previously served as a faith adviser to President Obama, the DNC's resolution is "stupid on a fundamental level that transcends electoral politics."

Given that the resolution will be used as further evidence that the Democrat Party is the God-less party, Wear could well be right.

What is undeniable, though, is this. The militantly pro-abortion, pro-LGBT activism party is the party of those without religious affiliation.[185]

So, it could easily be argued that: (1) the Democratic Party, based on its platform, is the anti-God party; (2) the Republican Party, based on its platform, is the pro-God party; and (3) because God wants to bless America, to be a patriotic, Christian American, you must vote Republican. Unfortunately, the argument gives too much credit to the Republican Party, which is why in September 2012 I wrote the article "Is the Republican Party the Party of God?" in which I noted that,

> The Democratic Party Platform contains just one reference to "God," and the inclusion of that single reference was famously booed by many delegates at the Democratic convention. In contrast, the Republican Party Platform contains 12 references to "God," and candidate Romney has emphatically stated, "I will not take God out of the name of our platform. I will not take God off our coins and I will not take God out of my heart. We're a nation that's bestowed by God." Does this make the GOP the party of God?

> The Democratic Platform certainly stands in stark contrast with the Republican Platform. The former is radically pro-abortion, endorses same-sex "marriage," and is decidedly weak on Israel. The latter is strongly pro-life, in favor of natural, organic marriage, and unashamedly pro-Israel.

> All this is readily seen in Liberty Counsel's Voter's Guide, which contrasts 10 categories in both platforms: Abortion and Human Life; Family Values; First Amendment, Liberty, and Responsibility; ObamaCare; Gun Rights; Fiscal Reform; Israel as an Ally; Government Oversight; Judiciary; Word Use Comparisons.

> . . . But that does not mean that the Republican party is the party of God. Not by a long shot.

> Both parties have more than their share of cronyism, compromise (if not outright corruption), ungodly alliances, hypocrisy, blind spots, and poor role models. It would be a terrible mistake to invoke some kind of divine sanctity on the Republicans. (For the record, it would also be a terrible mistake to think that there are no godly Democrats out there.)

To be perfectly clear, as a religious conservative, I strongly support the GOP Platform when it comes to family, life, and Israel. And I find it interesting that individuals, religious organizations, and political parties which invoke God and the Bible as authorities tend to be pro-life, pro-traditional family, and pro-Israel (which does not necessarily mean anti-Palestinian). In contrast, individuals, religious organizations, and political parties which either marginalize God and the Bible or reject the plain sense of the Scriptures tend to be pro-abortion, in favor of same-sex "marriage," and anti-Israel (or, at least, not strongly pro-Israel).

And I do understand why conservative pundits have referred to the "godless Democrats" and why conservative politicians have runs ads highlighting the Democratic "booing of God." But even if many (or most) Democrats are "godless," that does not mean that the Republicans, for the most part, are godly, nor should we look at them as the Party of God. (For the conservative Christians reading this, do you think God would appoint a Mormon to head up his party?)

Let's not forget how many Republican candidates have used "God language" to win the votes of conservative Christians (especially evangelicals) only to disappoint those very voters once in office.

Let's not forget that marriage was redefined in New York State because four Republican senators caved in. (It's true that the bill was driven and supported by Democrats, but the Republicans certainly failed to hold the line.)

Let's not forget that the Republican Party of Massachusetts has not embraced the national platform as its own.

And let's not forget the fundamental error we make when we exaggerate the goodness and godliness of a large and diverse political party.

Without a doubt, the Republican Platform is far closer to conservative Judeo-Christian values than is the Democratic Platform, but let's not get carried away. The only true, political "party of God" is sitting in heaven right now. Here on earth, the political scene is mixed, and the ones calling themselves the "party of God" are groups like Hezbollah. (In case you didn't know, that's what Hezbollah means in Arabic.)[186]

That's why we must be very careful when it comes to blurring the distinctions between the kingdom of God and any nation (or party on earth). The one is perfect and pure, headed by God Himself. All other kingdoms and nations and organizations and parties and movements are flawed and a mixture of good and bad at best. That means that the kingdom of God versus the kingdom of Satan is not directly parallel to Republicans versus Democrats. Rather, both the kingdom of God and the kingdom of Satan intersect with both the Republican and Democratic parties.

It's About Returning to Our Heritage

Others, however, would not put the emphasis on Republicans versus Democrats as much as on America returning to her Christian heritage. As expressed by Christian author and prayer leader Dutch Sheets early in the presidency of Barack Obama:

Through the intentional distorting and rewriting of our history by those who do not want us to be a Christian nation, it can be truly said that most Americans have no understanding of our God-given destiny and heritage. Sadly, the younger the age, the more this is true. The next logical step in this attempt to take over America and change it forever is now in effect—to remove God from every area of American life except church on Sunday. I am not an alarmist but the fruit of this unfolding plan has been horrifying:

- 65% of my grandparents' generation were true, committed Christians (born again, believed the Bible, attended worship regularly, etc.).
- 35% of my parents' generation were/are true, committed Christians.
- 15% of my generation are true, committed Christians.
- 4% of teenagers today are true, committed Christians (or will remain so after they leave home).

Then, after contrasting President Obama's statement that America was not a Christian nation with President Reagan declaring 1983 the Year of the Bible, Sheets wrote, "We can and will reverse this abandoning of God and our roots! The way this will occur—indeed, the only hope for America—is another great awakening (a powerful, sweeping revival) and reformation (a true and lasting transformation of our society and culture). This is my new mission statement: 'Awakening in Our Day, Reformation in Our Lifetime!' " [187]

As for this new mission statement of Dutch Sheets, I affirm it wholeheartedly. In fact, I share it. I would simply emphasize that, while the party in power can influence the direction of the nation, it is up to the Church to lead the way—not by taking over and enforcing our faith but by living out our faith, which begins with corporate renewal and repentance, with returning to God and His Word and with spreading the light of the gospel from coast to coast. And all that can take place under a Democratic administration just as much as under a Republican administration. In fact, we tend to pray for revival with greater desperation when we have an unfriendly president in power, often taking our foot off the gas and allowing our fervor to wane when we have a friendly president in power. This, too, is a dangerous if not fatal mistake.

Either way, whoever is in office, we need to remember the Church transcends the state, and the state, including our own nation, can turn against the Church, bringing heavy persecution. Yet the Church can still grow and thrive. And the state, including our own nation, can choose to abandon God, yet that will just embolden us to preach the gospel all the more clearly and loudly and publicly. Put another way, the state can turn on us, but it cannot stop us. That's because there's a difference between the cross and the flag, between the Bible and the Constitution, between the Lord Jesus and whoever our president might be.

The Church that Jesus is building will endure forever. America, as powerful as our nation is today, is a relative newcomer to the world stage and before long might fade from power and split into a number of smaller countries. Who knows for sure? But what we do know is that every day around the world, God's kingdom is advancing, and it is our calling as followers of Jesus to advance that kingdom wherever we live.

To quote Schaeffer one last time:

> In the Old Testament there was a theocracy commanded by God. In the New Testament, with the church being made up of Jews and Gentiles, and spreading over all the known world from India to Spain in one generation, the church was its own entity. There is no New Testament basis for a linking of church and state until Christ, the King returns. The whole "Constantine mentality" from the fourth century up to our day was a mistake. Constantine, as

the Roman Emperor, in 313 ended the persecution of Christians. Unfortunately, the support he gave to the church led by 381 to the enforcing of Christianity, by Theodosius I, as the official state religion. Making Christianity the official state religion opened the way for confusion up till our own day. There have been times of very good government when this interrelationship of church and state has been present. But through the centuries it has caused great confusion between loyalty to the state and loyalty to Christ, between patriotism and being a Christian.

We must not confuse the Kingdom of God with our country. To say it another way: "We should not wrap Christianity in our national flag."

None of this, however, changes the fact that the United States was founded upon a Christian consensus, nor that we today should bring Judeo-Christian principles into play in regard to government. But that is very different from a theocracy in name or in fact.[188]

We'll dig into this more deeply in the next three chapters, first exploring the relationship between Church and state (also looking back at Constantine) and further examining why politics and religion don't make for a good mix.

CHAPTER ELEVEN

Why Politics and Religion
Make for a Toxic Mix

In a February 1981 interview for *Parade Magazine*, and with reference to Rev. Jerry Falwell, leader of the Moral Majority, Dr. Billy Graham, said,

> I told him to preach the Gospel. That's our calling. I want to preserve the purity of the Gospel and the freedom of religion in America. I don't want to see religious bigotry in any form. Liberals organized in the '60s, and conservatives certainly have a right to organize in the '80s, but it would disturb me if there was a wedding between the religious fundamentalists and the political right. The hard right has no interest in religion except to manipulate it.[189]

Was he right? Or did he overstate things, perhaps drastically? The best way to answer that is to ask another question: What, exactly, did Dr. Graham mean when he spoke of "a wedding between the religious fundamentalists and the political right"?

As stated earlier, there is no question that Christians should be involved in politics since we are called to be the salt of the earth and the light of the world (see Matthew 5:13–16). This means that as God's people living in this world we are called to set a standard of morality and equity and compassion and kindness and justice. Put another way, as expressed by Dr. Martin Luther King Jr., "There was a time when the church was very powerful, in the time when the early Christians rejoiced at being deemed worthy to suffer for what they believed. In those days the church was not merely a thermometer that recorded the ideas and principles of popular opinion; it was a thermostat that transformed the mores of society."[190]

To quote Dr. King again, "The church must be reminded that it is not the master or the servant of the state, but rather the conscience of the state. It must be the guide and the critic of the state, and never its tool. If the church does not recapture its prophetic zeal, it will become an irrelevant social club without moral or spiritual authority."[191] This is a high and lofty calling, one which we often miss as we go to one extreme or the other. Sometimes we get so absorbed with politics that we lose our spiritual perspective. Other times we get so fed up with the politics of this world that we simply abandon the political scene entirely. That, too, is a grave mistake. If we abandon politics, someone else will fill the void that we left, someone with a very different agenda than our own, which means suffering and pain and destruction for the nation.

In short, if we abandon politics entirely, we cease to be a moral witness. We cease to speak truth to power. We cease to plead for justice for the oppressed and downtrodden. We cease to stand against governmental tyranny. We cease to hold our leaders accountable. We cease to advocate for freedom of religion, speech, and conscience, and we cease to stand up for the rights of "the least of these" (Matthew 25:45). (In past generations, "the least of these" in America would have been African slaves; today, it is the unborn and the victims of human trafficking.)

When we live in a democratic republic like the United States, if we give up our right to vote, we hand the nation over to those who disagree with, if not despise, our values. As a result, we will forfeit our right to preach the gospel and to live by biblical values, even in our own homes and schools and congregations. Consequently, the very freedom of religion that Dr. Graham wanted to preserve will be lost.

But there is a major difference between having a healthy, God-honoring, uncompromising involvement in politics with Christians also running for office and serving as judges and working as lobbyists and having an unhealthy union between politics and religion. That's because, on a certain level, they simply do not mix, let alone make for a good marriage. Either politics pollutes religion, defiling the purity of the gospel with its carnality, partisan power plays, political gamesmanship, and mixed priorities, or religion distorts politics, using the power of the government to force Christian values on a nation.

Either way, the New Testament faith cannot be *married* to politics or a political party without disastrous results, and in the end, rather than simply having the gospel of Jesus, we have the gospel plus something else. (We discussed this in more detail in chapter 2.) The Christian faith says: Bless those who curse you. Love your enemies. Lay down your life to help your neighbor. Politics says: Run attack ads to win. Demonize your opponent. Divide and conquer. The contrasts are large and obvious, like the contrasts between Jesus and Trump (or, Jesus and Obama or Bush or Biden or Reagan or Clinton).

When we deeply identify with a party or candidate, we add unnecessary baggage to our gospel witness, greatly complicating matters. When people associate us with a political leader rather than with the Lord, and we try to talk to them about the state of their souls, they reject our message because of our political leanings. Of course, people will also reject the gospel message because of our moral stands. But there's a difference between being identified as pro-life, for example, and being identified as pro-Trump (or any other candidate). In the first case we are standing against the slaughter of the unborn in the womb, which we can do categorically and without apology. In the second case, we are casting our lot with a flawed human being, and his or her failings now become ours. Again, the differences are great.

Certainly, most every Christian would agree that God is neither a Republican nor a Democrat. But all too often, in practice as well as in attitude, we act as if He *were* either Republican or Democrat. His cause is the party's cause (and vice versa). A vote for one party means a victory for the kingdom of God. It is us (meaning, Christians and one particular party) versus them (meaning, nonbelievers and the other political party). This overstates reality and is displeasing to the Lord. As believers we are *in* this world, but we are not *of* this world (see John 17:16 and 1 John 2:15–17)—and that applies to the world of politics too.

We must never forget that the political arm of our work will always be fleshly. It will always be a mixture of believers and nonbelievers. It will always be corrupted by power and personal ambition and greed. That's why we must never put our full trust in the political system or a party or a candidate. Politics has its place, but it is *not* the kingdom of God. To the extent we get in bed with it, we are making a deal with the devil. Really now, if the church itself has its share of fleshly corruption, how much more the world of politics?[192]

Lessons from the Church Under Caesar

We do well to think back to the situation of the first-century church, living in the Roman Empire and subject to the Roman emperor, meaning men like Caligula (AD 37–41) and Nero (AD 54–68). According to one history website, "Caligula was Rome's most tyrannical emperor. His reign from AD 37–41 is filled with murder and debauchery, to levels even his infamous nephew Nero could not reach. The great-great grandson of Julius Caesar certainly left his mark by his possible madness and definitely horrific acts."[193]

Another website states, "Historical accounts of Caligula may vary, but nearly all historians agreed on one dark fact: this deranged emperor placed very little value on human life. In one twisted story, Caligula was supposedly meant to sacrifice a bull to the gods by hitting it over the head with a huge mallet. At the last minute, Caligula had an even worse idea—he turned and struck the priest instead."[194] This was the leader of the empire.

As for Nero, where do we start? According to the historian Tacitus, to stop the rumor that he had set Rome on fire, Emperor Nero "falsely charged with guilt, and punished with the most fearful tortures, the persons commonly called Christians, who were [generally] hated for their enormities. . . . Accordingly first those were arrested who confessed they were Christians; next on their information, a vast multitude were convicted, not so much on the charge of burning the city, as of 'hating the human race.'" (Yet these early Christians were called "haters.") Tacitus continues: "In their very deaths they were made the subjects of sport: for they were covered with the hides of wild beasts, and worried to death by dogs, or nailed to crosses, or set fire to, and when the day waned, burned to serve for the evening lights."[195] Picture this happening in your city to your friends and family members.

Yet it was during the reigns of Caligula and Nero, among others, that the early church thrived. It was during these times of intense, unspeakable cruelty and persecution, that the gospel message flourished and grew. And it was while the demented, murderous Nero was emperor that Paul wrote these words: "Let every person be subject to the governing authorities. For there is no authority except from God, and those that exist have been instituted by God" (Romans 13:1).

Of course, Paul did not call for unqualified submission to governing authorities, as in cases where the authorities command you to do evil. Accordingly, if you were a Christian living in Hitler's Germany and were commanded to turn in any Jews you knew, the right thing would be disobedience—disobedience to man but obedience to God. We always submit to the highest authority.

But that's not what I want to focus on here. Instead, I want to draw our attention to the attitude of believers under a dictatorial regime. You could not vote. You could not take legal action against the government. You could not protest (unless you want to be killed in the process). You could not change "the system." Such matters were out of your hands.

But you could do something much more powerful. You could spread the gospel. You could advance God's counter-cultural, spiritual kingdom. You could liberate people's hearts and minds. You could bring healing and redemption. You could be an agent of eternal change. You could challenge the system from the ground up. And that's what these early believers did, turning their world upside-down.

The ultimate battle is a spiritual battle, and that battle can be waged regardless of what kind of government we're under. In fact, it is often during the hardest times that the church grows the most. Just look at the explosive growth of the church in Communist China over the last seventy to eighty years.[196] Or consider the church in Muslim Iran, which is growing as rapidly as any church in the world.[197] The church often does much better under persecution than under prosperity.

That's why it doesn't surprise me that the most precious, devoted Christians I have met in the world are often Christians under persecution. Conversely, it doesn't surprise me that, quite often, the most complacent Christians I've met have been Christians in the midst of abundant prosperity. That's why the church became much more compromised and worldly once Constantine Christianized the Roman Empire. With the good came the bad. Governmental backing produced a foreign mixture as the Church became an appendage of a still-worldly empire. Freedom and prosperity are gifts that can be easily abused.

It's true, of course, that at different times in history (including recently), radical Islam has virtually wiped out entire Christian populations in some parts of the world. And it's true that no one in their right mind would want to bequeath brutal persecution and mass killing on the generations to come. To repeat: we must guard the freedoms and liberties God has given us here in America. But let's also be realistic. Just as Donald Trump is not Jesus, Joe Biden is not the devil. Neither is he Nero. Biden may support gay "marriage" and transgender activism, but Nero "castrated a boy named Sporus to make him womanlike, and then married him in a traditional ceremony, which included a bridal veil and a dowry, according to the Roman historian and biographer Suetonius (circa AD 69)."[198] And I do not believe for a moment that Biden would call for Christians to be set on fire and burned alive to illuminate the night. Please!

So, while we work hard to preserve our freedoms and push back against those who seek to take them from us, we must never put our trust in the arm of flesh. Here in America, we should get involved in the political system as much as we are called to and have the opportunity to do so. But our trust is placed elsewhere. The invisible kingdom is advancing, and no power in heaven or on earth can stop it. Peter and Paul and a host of other first-century Christians, all killed for their faith, would add their hearty amen.

Can Christians Handle Political Power?

This is the perennial question going back to Constantine in the fourth century of this era. How much power can Christians handle? Put another way, are we better off when we are the persecuted minority or the empowered majority?

One of my friends, who lived in Israel for sixteen years, was speaking with an Iranian Christian leader. He asked him, "Would you like to go back to the days of the Shah when Christians had full religious liberty?" The Iranian friend replied, "Absolutely not. The Church is thriving now under Islamic persecution and growing like never before. We're actually praying for more persecution."

Yet in past centuries, the Church in parts of the Middle East and Northern Africa was almost entirely wiped out by fierce Islamic persecution. Historian John Phillip Jenkins wrote a whole book on the subject titled *The Lost History of Christianity: The Thousand-Year Golden Age of the Church in the Middle East, Africa, and Asia—and How It Died*. Certainly for those Christians persecution brought more death than growth. But perhaps we're looking at this in too extreme forms rather than asking some more basic, practical questions. What about here in America? Does the Church do better with persecution (as limited as it may comparatively be) or with prosperity? Do we pray more, witness more, and work harder for change when we have hostile administrations in power or friendly administrations in power? Do we look to God more when the government is against us and look to Him less when the government is for us?

Going back to the days of Constantine, Gene Edward Veith wrote:

> The Edict of Milan in A.D. 313 legalized Christianity. Toleration of this new faith in Rome was not a gradual development. It happened suddenly, right after some of the most brutal persecutions of Christians. Soon, Roman officials were kissing the broken hands of Christian confessors whom they had tortured. Quickly, paganism faded as the official religion of the Roman Empire, only to be replaced by the Christian Church. Christianity, once despised and persecuted, emerged from the catacombs in triumph. Whereupon its problems really began.[199]

The great Methodist leader John Wesley saw things in similar terms, stating in one of his sermons that

> Persecution never did, never could, give any lasting wound to genuine Christianity. But the greatest it ever received, the grand blow which was struck at the very root of that humble, gentle, patient love, which is the fulfilling of the Christian law, the whole essence of true religion, was struck in the fourth century by Constantine the Great, when he called himself a Christian, and poured in a flood of riches, honours, and power upon the Christians; more especially upon the Clergy.[200]

And it was largely downhill from there, according to Wesley.

Veith went on to explain that with

> the legalization of the Church, Christianity under Constantine began to exert a positive moral influence upon a Rome that had become decadent." Yes, "women were terribly oppressed and misused under paganism, and it was Christianity that liberated them. . . . . The bloody spectator sport of watching gladiators kill each other was halted. Provision was made to care for widows and orphans, the sick and the poor."[201]

Isn't this positive, a cause for rejoicing rather than mourning? The real issue in Veith's view was this: "But not only did the church begin to influence the culture; the culture began to influence the church."[202] That has been the challenge ever since (really, as long as God has singled out a people for Himself on the earth): will the people of God change the culture, or will the culture change the people of God?

Wesley encountered a similar difficulty when preaching the gospel to drunkards and gamblers and others who were irresponsible with their money. When they were truly converted, they became hardworking and responsible. As a result, they began to make more money and became more worldly and less spiritual. As Wesley remarked toward the end of his life, "I fear, wherever riches have increased (exceeding few are the exceptions), the essence of religion, the mind that was in Christ, has decreased in the same proportion. Therefore, do I not see how it is possible, in the nature of things, for any revival of true religion to continue long."[203]

On the other hand, financial provision can be a great blessing from God. We can help the poor and needy. We can support world missions. We can engage in all kinds of humanitarian efforts. We can provide for our own families. We can lend and give without having to borrow or beg. This is certainly positive. What, then, is the solution?

Some Christian leaders have argued that for all of Wesley's brilliance he missed the simple answer here, namely stewardship. If we could learn to be good stewards, we could be trusted with more money. Then, rather than money dominating our lives, it would simply be a tool in the service of others. Could it be the same thing when it comes to political power?

On the one hand, it is a fatal mistake to put our trust in a political leader (or even a political system), as if our help or deliverance could come from that leader (or system), or as if the political realm could advance righteousness or change hearts. During the Trump administration, this is something I addressed time and again.[204] On the other hand, we are instructed to pray for the salvation of our leaders (see 1 Timothy 2:1–4), meaning that having a godly leader is better than having an ungodly leader. And isn't it positive when the gospel spreads through a country, resulting in more genuine conversions and a higher percentage of the population following the Lord? How could that not be good?

Yet it seems that whenever we do have a sympathetic president, we tend to rely on that person to do our job. We also give the larger society the impression that we are trying to "take over" and impose our values by legal fiat. Worse still, as I've stated previously, we often become better known for our association with that leader than for association with the Lord. What then should we do?

First, pastors and leaders must continually emphasize the priority of the gospel, keeping our focus on being disciples and making disciples. That can never change, regardless of who controls the government. The Great Commission must always come first.

Second, we must never cease praying for revival and awakening, never cease preaching repentance, and never cease addressing the moral evils of the day. Surely change in these areas must come from the grass roots up.

Third, we must be known as servants in our communities, as those who lead the way in doing good, as people who care. Let us be known for our love.

Fourth, to the extent Christian leaders have open doors to minister to political leaders, they should try to influence them behind closed doors rather than on a stage for the world to see. Billy Graham had access to numerous presidents but was largely perceived as being nonpartisan. When the world sees us as an appendage to a political party, we have compromised our testimony.

Fifth, we should pray for political leaders who can model gospel principles in their conduct. They can be fearless, strong, uncompromising, and firm without being nasty and mean-spirited. They can be gracious and decent human beings without being wimps. This, too, can have a positive impact on the larger culture.

Rediscovering the Third Way of the Early Christians

In his book *Resilient Faith*, Professor Gerald Sittser gives a survey of early Christian history, explaining the different ways Emperor Constantine was viewed by subsequent Church leaders. He notes that the Church historian Eusebius "honored God for his goodness. But he honored Constantine, too, as God's good and godly leader."[205] Eusebius wrote, "In every city the victorious emperor published decrees full of humanity and laws that gave proof of munificence and true piety." Indeed, Sittser explains, "It was a new day for Christianity and empire, for the two had become one. God had established his rule within history; Constantine was his chosen servant."

To quote Eusebius again, "Thus all tyranny had been purged away, and the kingdom that was theirs was preserved securely and without question for Constantine and his sons alone. They, having made it their first task to wipe the world clean from hatred of God, rejoiced in the blessings that He had conferred upon them, and, by the things they did for all men to see, displayed love of virtue and love of God, devotion and thankfulness to the Almighty."[206]

Lest this seem shortsighted, remember that Eusebius died in AD 339, meaning less than twenty years after Constantine declared himself a Christian. Consequently, Sittser writes,

> We can hardly fault Eusebius for his euphoria, considering the terrible persecution Christians suffered under Constantine's predecessor, Diocletian.
>
> Still, there is a problem with Eusebius's view of history all the same. It is easy to write history in light of the winners, especially if Christians attribute the victory to God. But what happens if, a generation or two later, they lose? Eusebius did not live long enough to witness the demise of the empire: the rise of Arian

emperors who closed down orthodox churches and exiled orthodox bishops; the invasion of tribal groups that overran the western half of the empire; the massive decline of cities; the rise of the Arabs (and their new religion, Islam), who conquered more than half of the Mediterranean world; the strain between eastern and western churches, which later divided into Orthodox and Roman.[207]

Even more importantly, Eusebius did not live to see the worst effects of the Christianizing of the Roman Empire, including: (1) the creation of a class of Christians in name only (in the past, under persecution, such pseudo-Christians were much harder to find); (2) the idea that the Christian faith could be commanded or coerced; (3) the rise of Christendom, meaning, a Christian political system often unrelated to the New Testament faith; (4) the creation of a cultural Christianity; (5) the idea that we can have some kind of heaven here on earth; and (6) the image of the sword displacing the image of the cross. Once we were the downtrodden and persecuted; now we were the ruling class![208]

Sittser advises us to look back to a late second-century letter written by an unknown Christian disciple to a Roman leader named Diognetus. The Roman leader wanted to better understand this relatively new faith, so the disciple contrasted it the way of the Roman Empire (which he called the first way) and the way of Judaism (which he called the second way), portraying the Christian faith as a third way. He wrote:

> For the Christians are distinguished from other men neither by country, nor language, nor the customs which they observe. For they neither inhabit cities of their own, nor employ a peculiar form of speech, nor lead a life which is marked out by any singularity. The course of conduct which they follow has not been

devised by any speculation or deliberation of inquisitive men; nor do they, like some, proclaim themselves the advocates of any merely human doctrines. But, inhabiting Greek as well as barbarian cities, according as the lot of each of them has determined, and following the customs of the natives in respect to clothing, food, and the rest of their ordinary conduct, they display to us their wonderful and confessedly striking method of life.

They dwell in their own countries, but simply as sojourners. As citizens, they share in all things with others, and yet endure all things as if foreigners. Every foreign land is to them as their native country, and every land of their birth as a land of strangers. They marry, as do all [others]; they beget children; but they do not destroy their offspring. They have a common table, but not a common bed. They are in the flesh, but they do not live after the flesh. They pass their days on earth, but they are citizens of heaven. They obey the prescribed laws, and at the same time surpass the laws by their lives. They love all men, and are persecuted by all. They are unknown and condemned; they are put to death, and restored to life.

They are poor, yet make many rich; they are in lack of all things, and yet abound in all; they are dishonoured, and yet in their very dishonour are glorified. They are evil spoken of, and yet are justified; they are reviled, and bless; they are insulted, and repay the insult with honour; they do good, yet are punished as evil-doers. When punished, they rejoice as if quickened into life; they are assailed by the Jews as foreigners, and are persecuted by the Greeks; yet those who hate them are unable to assign any reason for their hatred.[209]

Here in America, where Christianity has been dominant since the founding of our first colonies, where our coins have proclaimed In God We Trust since 1864 and our Pledge of Allegiance has described America as "one nation under God" since 1954, where virtually every president in our history has been a professing Christian of sorts,[210] where, as recently as 2011, America had the largest number of professing Christians of any nation on the planet,[211] and where, until fairly recently, there was little state-sponsored opposition to our faith, it is all too easy to lose sight of the degree to which, as Christians, we are just passing through this world. It is all too easy, as we have emphasized repeatedly in this book, to equate political victories with the advancement of the kingdom of God and to equate political power with spiritual power. It is all too easy to merge Christian faith with American culture. It is all too easy to lose sight of this third way.

Someone once said, "What began as a movement in Jerusalem became a philosophy in Greece, a monument in Rome, a culture in Europe, and an enterprise in America."[212] While not speaking here of political issues, the point of this quote is well taken, namely that from country to country and kingdom to kingdom, the church has often taken on the culture of the surrounding society, becoming conformed to the image of the world rather than calling the world to become conformed to the image of God. And so it is here in America. We know how to make everything Christian, and we know how to sell it. We know how to produce a bigger and better Christianity (that's the American way!). We know how to tailor make the gospel to suit the sinner rather calling the sinner to die to self and follow Jesus. (Put another way, we know how build up the sinner's ego rather than call the sinner to repent.) In short, we have learned how to merchandize Jesus and market the gospel, promising a better life—including financial prosperity, physical health, and loads of popularity—to which all will respond quickly, as long as this special offer lasts.

As a result, we have cheapened the gospel, we have demeaned our Lord, we have misled the world, and we have lost our distinctives. Who needs a "gospel" like this? When it comes to politics, we have often become appendages to political parties (different groups of Christians have done this with both Democrats and Republicans), putting our hope in political solutions more than gospel solutions and giving more energy to winning elections than to winning the lost. And, when we have been entrusted with political power on the highest levels, we have often forgotten our call to serve and love, enjoying our moment in the sun.

A Lesson from India

I have had the privilege of traveling to India twenty-seven times since 1993, missing my trips the last two years because of COVID but otherwise visiting there every year to serve the Christian believers. On my first trip, my wife, Nancy, and some of our close friends joined me. We were introduced to about seventy-five orphans who lived in two small homes, one for boys and the other for girls. They slept on the floor, and each had one set of clothes. But they were fed three meals a day and were getting a solid education as well as a robust spiritual grounding.

When we saw these precious kids, the first thought Nancy and I had (along with another couple with us) was adoption. Why don't we adopt one of these precious children and bring them to America where they can live in relative luxury and enjoy the many benefits our country has to offer?

We quickly concluded that this would be the worst thing we could do for them since, in India, these kids were being raised without TV and movies, without peer pressure and obsession with the latest fashion, without our cultural narcissism and our many addictions to entertainment and technology and sports. And that's why they were so amazingly content and even happy. They were being loved and cared for. They were being raised in a beautiful Christian environment. They were learning the most important of Christian values. And they were getting a good education that would prepare them for a blessed future.

That being said, I am truly and deeply thankful for the amazing blessings we do have here in America, and I'm glad that, when our daughters were growing up, they could sleep on comfortable beds at home with their mom and dad. At the same time, I realize that living here in our great country can also be challenging as we have our unique set of minefields to navigate.

Can we enjoy prosperity while maintaining the same level of commitment as our persecuted brothers and sisters? Can we live with plenty while walking in discipline and self-denial? Can we be part of the dominant political power while still being servants of all? Can we be active politically without losing sight of our higher calling, namely to know Jesus and make Him known? Can we be in this world without being of this world, living as loyal citizens of an earthly kingdom without losing the perspective that, first and foremost, we are citizens of a heavenly kingdom? Can we show solidarity with good political leaders without compromising our morality or spirituality?

In short, can we be better known for our spiritual affiliation than for our political affiliation, for our devotion to Jesus than our vote for a candidate? Can we live just the same under Caesar as under Constantine? Can we emulate that third way—not the American way and not the way of other religions and cultures, but the gospel way—while remaining fully engaged in the country we call home here on earth, namely the United States of America?

It is a challenging task, but it must be done. Do we really have any other choice?

CHAPTER TWELVE

Is the Church Called to Take Over Society?

"Rulership is in our genes, dominion is in our makeup. We were designed to rule the earth."[213] What comes to mind when you hear these words? For some, this is a powerful spiritual concept, expressing that in Jesus we are overcomers and victors, that no earthly power or demonic power can stand against us, that the authority God gave Adam at creation—namely the authority to rule over the animal kingdom—now belongs to us in a spiritual sense. And when Jesus returns and sets up His kingdom on the earth, we will rule and reign with Him.

For others, it means that, as God's children, leadership is in our DNA, which in turn means that we should get actively involved in every sphere of society, from business to media and from education to politics, believing that the Lord would use us to bring positive change to each of these different cultural spheres. Let us show the world that there is a better way, God's way, and let us demonstrate practically that the wisdom of the Word really works.

Still others relate to these words in a much more literal way, understanding them to mean that the Church is called to take over the world, as expressed by Rousas John Rushdoony (1916–2001):

[O]ur responsibility is to exercise dominion which means to declare where sovereignty resides and to declare God's sovereign world; the word of dominion, to every area of life and thought. And we are promised that when we go forth in terms of that word the commission tells us, the commission to Joshua, which our Lord summarizes then later, that if we go in the power of this word and faithfulness to it wherever the soul of your feet shall tread that shall be your ground. Let's plant our feet on the face of all the earth and claim it for Jesus Christ.[214]

Similarly, Pat Robertson said,

God's plan is for His people, ladies and gentlemen, to take dominion. . . . What is dominion? Well, dominion is Lordship. He wants His people to reign and rule with Him. . . but He's waiting for us to . . . extend His dominion. . . . And the Lord says, "I'm going to let you redeem society. There'll be a reformation. . . . We are not going to stand for those coercive utopians in the Supreme Court and in Washington ruling over us any more. We're not gonna stand for it. We are going to say, 'we want freedom in this country, and we want power. . . .' "[215]

Focusing on the concept of taking America back, D. James Kennedy said, "Our job is to reclaim America for Christ, whatever the cost. As the vice regents of God, we are to exercise godly dominion and influence over our neighborhoods, our schools, our government, our literature and arts, our sports arenas, our entertainment media, our news media, our scientific endeavors—in short, over every aspect and institution of human society."[216]

To be sure, none of these leaders advocated a forceful, let alone military, takeover of America, let alone of the whole world, in Jesus' name. Absolutely not! But they did clearly teach that, as followers of Jesus and using His spiritual authority, we were to take dominion over every area of society until the world became Christianized, which is why this teaching is known as dominionism.

Of course, some on the left will cry, "Dominionism!" the moment a Christian leader gets involved in politics or speaks about the Christian heritage of America or seeks to bring about cultural change.[217] Others on the Left go even further, and the moment Christian conservatives speak out about their faith and values, they shout, "Separation of Church and State! You sound just like the Islamic extremists!" Thus, we are demonized simply for holding to biblical values.

For example, in May 2012, Rev. Billy Graham, then ninety-three years-old, took out full-page ads in newspapers throughout North Carolina addressing the upcoming vote on the definition of marriage. The ads featured a large picture of Rev. Graham and carried his own words: "At 93, I never thought we would have to debate the definition of marriage. The Bible is clear—God's definition of marriage is between a man and a woman. I want to urge my fellow North Carolinians to vote FOR the marriage amendment on Tuesday, May 8. God bless you as you vote."

Wayne Besen, a confrontational gay activist, took strong exception to these ads, writing,

> I'm a little confused here, because I thought we lived in America. Yet, Graham is now trying to jam his own church's rules and doctrine down my throat. The last time I checked, I never signed up for the Billy Graham Evangelistic Association. (BGEA). I don't even like his church, yet he thinks I should be forced against my will to live by its rules.
>
> Do we now make our civil laws based upon Christian Sharia? Do we all have to follow his version of the Bible or be punished by government? And if this

is the case, are we really a free country? Are we really much different than Iran, or is it only by a matter of degrees or a matter of time until these so-called "Christian Supremacists" get their paws on all of our laws?[218]

Christian Sharia? Christian Supremacists? Are you kidding me? But Besen was not the only one to throw around such accusations. Already in May 2005, John McCandlish Phillips, formerly a Pulitzer Prize–winning *New York Times* reporter, pointed out how newspapers like the *Washington Post* and the *Times* told their readers that evangelicals and traditional Catholics were engaging in a jihad against America. Phillips noted that, days before his article was published

> Frank Rich, an often acute, broadly knowledgeable and witty cultural observer, sweepingly informed us that, under the effects of "the God racket" as now pursued in Washington, "government, culture, science, medicine and the rule of law are all under threat from an emboldened religious minority out to remake America according to its dogma." He went on to tell Times readers that GOP zealots in Congress and the White House have edged our country over into "a full-scale jihad."[219]

By 2010, Markos Moulitsas, founder of the strongly Left-leaning Daily Kos website, had written an entire book on the subject. The title said it all: *American Taliban: How War, Sex, Sin, and Power Bind Jihadists and the Radical Right.* This, then, is a reminder that activists on the Left, especially on the extreme Left, will slander and malign those of us who advocate for biblical morality, even though we work within our American system of government peacefully and legally seeking to change individual hearts and minds. Simply stated, our method is to live out our faith, to share the gospel with others, to pray, to debate the issues in the public square, to vote, and to lobby. What could be more American than that?

On the other hand, there *is* a Christian teaching today that *does* emphasize the Church's alleged calling to take over the world based on the account in Genesis where God said at the time of creation, "Let us make man in our image, after our likeness. And let them have dominion over the fish of the sea and over the birds of the heavens and over the livestock and over all the earth and over every creeping thing that creeps on the earth" (Genesis 1:26). This verse is then tied in with the commission that Jesus gave to His disciples after His resurrection, saying, "All authority in heaven and on earth has been given to me. Go therefore and make disciples of all nations, baptizing them in the name of the Father and of the Son and of the Holy Spirit, teaching them to observe all that I have commanded you. And behold, I am with you always, to the end of the age" (Matthew 28:18–20).

So, a commission to subdue the animal kingdom and rule over it, given by God to the human race at creation, is reinterpreted to mean that the Church is supposed to rule over all peoples and nations and institutions and governments. And a commission to spread the gospel throughout the world, given by Jesus to His disciples, is understood to mean that we should Christianize whole nations (as opposed to leading individuals within each nation to Christ).[220] Yet past Christian leaders who foresaw the Christianizing of the world did not see this as a matter of dominion. Their vision was very different.

The Old Postmillennialism

Some of the greatest Christian leaders in American history, including Jonathan Edwards (1703–1758) and Charles Finney (1792–1875), believed in the doctrine of postmillennialism, which teaches that the whole world will become

Christian, ushering in God's kingdom here on earth, after which Jesus will return. And they both believed that the great revival movements they witnessed in America (in the days of Edwards, the First Great Awakening; in the days of Finney, the Second Great Awakening) had the potential of bringing America (and the world) into this millennial kingdom.

As expressed by Edwards in the early 1740s,

> It is not unlikely that this work of God's Spirit, so extraordinary and wonderful, is the dawning, or, at least, a prelude of that glorious work of God, so often foretold in Scripture, which, in the progress and issue of it, shall renew the world of mankind. If we consider how long since the things foretold as what should precede this great event, have been accomplished; and how long this event has been expected by the church of God, and thought to be nigh by the most eminent men of God in the church; and withal consider what the state of things now is, and has for a considerable time been, in the church of God, and the world of mankind; we cannot reasonably think otherwise, than that the beginning of this great work of God must be near. And there are many things that make it probable that this work will begin in America.[221]

As for Finney, in 1835 he said, "if the church will do her duty, the Millennium may come in this country in three years."[222] And what, exactly, would that look like? In the words of Horace Bushnell (1802–1876), "The wilderness shall bud and blossom as the rose before us [alluding to Isaiah 35]; and we will not cease, till a christian nation throws up its temples of worship on every hill and plain; till knowledge, virtue and religion, blending their dignity and their healthful power, have filled out our great country with a manly and happy race of people, and the lands of a complete christian commonwealth are seen to span the continent."[223]

And what was the fruit of this teaching? According to the Christian History Institute, and with specific reference to Finney, "This led in the years before the Civil War to unprecedented evangelical social and religious reform: temperance, antislavery, peace, women's rights, education, as well as dramatic expansion in home and foreign mission work."[224] That sounds pretty good to me.

Finney was actually convinced that the belief that the church could usher in the millennium was crucial for positive social change. Otherwise, Finney argued, if Christians believed that the world would only get worse before Jesus returned, at which time He would establish His kingdom on the earth (the belief called premillennialism, held to by many evangelicals today), this would impede social transformation. Still, Finney was very clear in his priorities: the gospel must come first, including evangelism and revival; social change must come second. To reverse the process could be deadly. Literally.

That's why in 1835 he wrote a letter to his staunch antislavery colleague Theodore Weld who came to faith through Finney's ministry, urging him to reconsider his methods and to put changing of hearts first and the abolition of slavery second. He wrote:

> Br.[other] Weld, is it not true, at least do you not fear it is, that we are in our present course going fast into a civil war? Will not our present movements in abolition result in that? ... How can we save our country and affect the speedy abolition of slavery? This is my answer.... If abolition can be made an appendage of a general revival of religion, all is well. I fear no other form of carrying this question will save our country or the liberty or soul of the slave....

Abolitionism has drunk up the spirit of some of the most efficient moral men and is fast doing so to the rest, and many of our abolition brethren seem satisfied with nothing less than this. This I have been trying to resist from the beginning as I have all along fore-seen that should that take place, the church and world, ecclesiastical and state leaders, will become embroiled in one common infernal squabble that will roll a wave of blood over the land. The causes now operating are, in my view, as certain to lead to this result as a cause is to produce its effect, unless the publick mind can be engrossed with the subject of salvation and make abolition an appendage.[225]

Looking back through the lens of history, Finney's warning was chillingly prophetic as "ecclesiastical and state leaders" did indeed become "embroiled in one common infernal squabble" that rolled "a wave of blood over the land." There is a lesson for us here today.

There Is a Difference Between Taking Ground and Taking Over

Although I do not believe that the Bible teaches postmil-lennialism, when rightly understood, it is not a dangerous doctrine. It simply proclaims the triumph of the gospel, expecting the whole world to be converted to the Christian faith as the message of Jesus gains more and more ground in every sphere until the whole earth is filled with the knowledge of the glory of God (see Matthew 13:31–33).

Again, I do not believe this is what the Bible teaches, but it is very different than the idea that the Church will somehow take over the society. That is a very dangerous teaching, one that can lead to the twisting of our message and all kinds of toxic mixtures, including the fusion of the gospel with politics and the reliance on coercion to execute God's will, as if the Christian faith could be imposed.

Some Christian leaders, like Pastor Bill Johnson, believe that the Church will change the world through service not through coercion. "Our assignment is to see the dominion of God realized into people's lives," he wrote. "It is not an overpowering control, it is a life-giving, liberating experience with the almighty God, who is an ultimate, perfect Father who loves to bring liberty and freedom to His people."[226]

But not all Christian leaders emphasize the idea of societal transformation through service. Back in August 2011, Michelle Goldberg wrote,

> With Tim Pawlenty out of the presidential race, it is now fairly clear that the GOP candidate will either be Mitt Romney or someone who makes George W. Bush look like Tom Paine. Of the three most plausible candidates for the Republican nomination, two are deeply associated with a theocratic strain of Christian fundamentalism known as Dominionism. If you want to understand Michele Bachmann and Rick Perry, understanding Dominionism isn't optional.
>
> Put simply, Dominionism means that Christians have a God-given right to rule all earthly institutions. Originating among some of America's most radical theocrats, it's long had an influence on religious-right education and political organizing. But because it seems so *outré,* getting ordinary people to take it seriously can be difficult. Most writers, myself included, who explore it have been called paranoid. In a contemptuous 2006 First Things review of several books, including Kevin Phillips' *American Theocracy,* and my own *Kingdom Coming: The Rise of Christian Nationalism,* conservative columnist Ross Douthat

wrote, "the fear of theocracy has become a defining panic of the Bush era."

Now, however, we have the most theocratic Republican field in American history, and suddenly, the concept of Dominionism is reaching mainstream audiences.[227]

How much more would Goldberg say today, "I told you this was coming!"

To be clear, I believe that Goldberg greatly overstated her case, also misunderstanding the viewpoints of some of those she critiqued. At the same time, there *are* Christians who hold to these views, even in ways that are much more innocent than ominous, simply because these Christians believe that they will "take over" through loving conversion rather than forced coercion. To quote Pastor Bill Johnson again:

We have been given authority over this planet. It was first given to us in the commission God gave to mankind in Genesis (see Gen. 1:28-29) and was then restored to us by Jesus after His resurrection (see Matt. 28:18). But Kingdom authority is different than is typically understood by many believers. It is the authority to set people free from torment and disease, to destroy the works of darkness. It is the authority to move the resources of Heaven through creative expression to meet human need. It is the authority to bring Heaven to earth. It is the authority to serve.

As with most Kingdom principles, the truths of humanity's dominion and authority are dangerous in the hands of those who desire to rule over others. These concepts seem to validate some people's selfishness. But when these truths are expressed through the humble servant, the world is rocked to its core. Becoming servants to this world is the key to open the doors of possibility that are generally thought of as closed or forbidden.[228]

Still, any talk about "taking over" can easily be understood, as Pastor Johnson himself acknowledges, which is why it is understandable that many nonbelievers see such expressions as a real threat. It's also easy to understand how professing Christians can shift their emphasis from reaching the lost and making disciples to seeking to occupy positions of power and influence. As explained by Brad Christerson in 2018, "[Dominionism] is not so much about proselytizing to unbelievers as it is about transforming society through placing Christian believers in powerful positions in all sectors of society."[229] As the learned Christian author George Grant once explained: "Christians have an obligation, a mandate, a commission, a holy responsibility to reclaim the land for Jesus Christ—to have dominion in civil structures."[230]

Of course, there is nothing wrong with Christians running for office or working their way up to high-level positions in the business world or in academia or media or entertainment. Why shouldn't they seek to do this, setting examples of honesty and integrity and compassion and wisdom along the way? Conversely, why should Christians leave all the influential positions in society to nonbelievers, especially to those who are hostile to our faith? To give one example, how did it help the nation, let alone the Church, when our schools of higher learning departed from their Christian foundations and became hotbeds of radical secularism?

The issue, again, is emphasis, and we make a serious mistake if we think we can bring about major societal change from the top down. It will always be the reverse, as God changes the hearts of people, and those people then go and change the society.[231]

Some would argue that the New Testament uses the word *ekklesia* (the Messiah's congregation, wrongly translated as "church" in our English Bibles), in the sense of "the ruling governing council," as if the Church had authority over the government. But that is based on a misunderstanding of the primary Greek usage in the New Testament and is not accepted by any major New Testament Greek dictionary.[232]

Is it possible that having genuine followers of Jesus in high places will help to change the hearts of the people? Of course. And is it possible that having these solid believers in places of societal influence will bring about the betterment of the country as a whole? Absolutely. And again, it's not a question of either evangelism or social involvement. It is a question of priorities, and we must always put the gospel message first and social action second; we must put prayer first and politics second (and by that I don't mean that most of our prayers should be directed toward political outcomes).

Yet this is where we have gotten deeply off track in recent years, as if by electing the right president (or congressperson or others) we could fundamentally change the nation. To the contrary, if we are not fulfilling our role as salt and light in the society, the more we push a political agenda, the more the society will resist that agenda and become embittered to our message. In the end, rather than advance the cause of Christ in the land, we will hurt it.

Digging Deeper into Dominionism

According to Frederick Clarkson,

> Dominionism is the theocratic idea that, regardless of theological view, means, or timetable, says that Christians are called by God to exercise dominion over every aspect of society by taking control of political and cultural institutions.
>
> Analyst Chip Berlet and I have suggested that there is a dominionist spectrum running from soft to hard

as a way of making some broad distinctions among dominionists without getting mired in theological minutiae. But we also agree that:

1. Dominionists celebrate Christian nationalism in that they believe that the United States once was and should once again be, a Christian nation. In this way, they deny the Enlightenment roots of American democracy.
2. Dominionists promote religious supremacy, insofar as they generally do not respect the equality of other religions, or even other versions of Christianity.
3. Dominionists endorse theocratic visions, insofar as they believe that the Ten Commandments, or "biblical law," should be the foundation of American law, and that the US Constitution should be seen as a vehicle for implementing biblical principles.

Of course, Christian nationalism takes a distinct form in the United States, but dominionism in all of its variants has a vision for all nations.[233]

Obviously, as followers of Jesus, we advocate for righteous causes, including standing for the life of the unborn, and we support God's definition of family and do what we can to change both hearts and laws. But how far do we go in our legislative initiatives? What would happen if we had even more control? Would we also enforce penalties for not attending church or for working on Sunday, as some of the American colonies did?

Consider this, from "The Laws of Virginia" (1610–1611):

Every man and woman duly, twice a day upon the first tolling of the bell, shall upon the working days repair unto the church to hear divine service upon pain of losing his or her day's allowance for the first omission, for the second to be whipped, and for the third to be condemned to the galleys for six months. Likewise, no man or woman shall dare to violate or break the Sabbath by any gaming, public or private abroad or at home, but duly sanctify and observe the same, both himself and his family, by preparing themselves at home with private prayer that they may be the better fitted for the public, according to the commandments of God and the orders of our church. As also every man and woman shall repair in the morning to the divine service and sermons preached upon the Sabbath day in the afternoon to divine service and catechizing, upon pain for the first fault to lose their provision and allowance for the whole week following, for the second to lose the said allowance and also to be whipped, and for the third to suffer death.[234]

Does anyone think we should enforce laws like this again in America? Is that what it means to "take America back for God"? Is this part of making America great again? If we wouldn't go this far, how far would we go? Would we ban sports on Sunday? Would be bring out the whipping post for those who slept in on Sunday morning? Would we impose these same laws on Jews and Muslims and Hindus and atheists?

It was because of laws like this that America, unlike some of the colonies, was not established as a theocracy, although we had strong biblical roots. That's also why someone like Thomas Jefferson, who was hardly an evangelical believer, could play such a major role in our early history. And that's why one of the chapters in my 2017 book *Saving a Sick America: A Prescription for Moral and Cultural Transformation* was titled "The Bible, Not a Theocracy, Is the Answer." But not everyone sees things this way.

Theonomy Makes a Comeback

Writing for the Gospel Coalition on March 31, 2021, Andrew T. Walker asked,

> Have you noticed this vision of Christianity in the public square that seems muscular, confident, even brashly triumphalist? It is tired of Christianity's never-ending losses in the culture war. It rightly criticizes the decadence, perversion, and irrational norms of secularism and understands that under the guise of "neutrality," secularism has become the functional god of this age. The only way for cultural sanity to be restored is for Christians to truly grasp the lordship of Jesus Christ and unapologetically assert his authority over every part of life, even government.
>
> This vision may seem new if you're younger than 40, but it is not. What we're seeing is the rebirth of Christian Reconstruction or its more applied form, Theonomy.[235]

What exactly is a theonomy? As explained by Walker, Theonomy "seeks to apply the civil law of the Mosaic covenant to contemporary civil government. . . . Theonomy as a theological program believes that civil law should follow the example of Israel's civil and judicial laws under the Mosaic covenant."[236] So, as much as possible, Old Testament law—meaning, the laws of the Sinai Covenant—should be instituted in America.

He continues, in somewhat technical language,

Though the jurisdictions of church and government remain separate in Theonomy, both are under God's authority for civil righteousness, which is enclosed in the Old Testament. Thus, Old Testament penology [referring to the system of punishment for crime] remains especially relevant to solve moral and criminal wrongdoings today.

The hermeneutic [meaning, system of biblical interpretation] used to make such an application assumes the abiding authority of the Mosaic law and would lead to executing people for a multitude of sins and crimes in our contemporary context.

Thus, he concludes, "Theonomy should be repudiated as an evangelical framework for understanding the mission of the church and the relationship between civil and sacred, eternal authority and spiritual authority." And, when it comes to the Great Commission and making disciples of the nations, he writes,

We are not discipling nations for the sake of political hegemony. Satan would be content with a moral nation animated by the values of civil religion if those values eclipse the scandal of the cross. We are discipling nations to glorify Christ and to see obedience in every domain of life. Yes, that includes those who occupy government. But just government is not the object of our mission; it is a byproduct of transformed consciences adhering to the natural law, not submitting to the Mosaic law.[237]

As for why we advocate for just and righteous laws, it is not simply because these laws are found in the Bible. Rather, as explained by philosopher J. Budziszewski, "Government enforces those parts of the divine law that are also included in the natural law, such as the prohibition of murder."[238] So we are informed by Scripture, which gives us a heart for the unborn and for the poor and the needy. But we do not push for laws because "the Bible tells us so." We advocate for those laws because they are right and for the common good.

What About the Seven Mountains Mandate?

Still, the question remains, how, exactly, *should* we influence the culture? This is where the Seven Mountains Mandate comes in to play. Have you heard about it? Some consider it to be a commonsense application of biblical principles while others think it is a dangerous and heretical philosophy of ministry. Which is it?

The Generals International website offers a positive assessment, offering some historical background as well:

> In 1975, Bill Bright, founder of Campus Crusade and Loren Cunningham, founder of Youth With a Mission (YWAM), developed a God-given, world-changing strategy. Their mandate: Bring Godly change to a nation by reaching its seven spheres, or mountains, of societal influence.
>
> They concluded that in order to truly transform any nation with the Gospel of Jesus Christ, these seven facets of society must be reached: Religion, Family, Education, Government, Media, Arts & Entertainment and Business.[239]

In other words, be strategic in your gospel outreach and don't just reach individuals. Influence the culture with the gospel as well.

The Got Questions website paints a decidedly negative picture:

The seven mountain mandate or the seven mountain prophecy is an anti-biblical and damaging movement that has gained a following in some Charismatic and Pentecostal churches. Those who follow the seven mountain mandate believe that, in order for Christ to return to earth, the church must take control of the seven major spheres of influence in society for the glory of Christ. Once the world has been made subject to the kingdom of God, Jesus will return and rule the world.[240]

What are we to make of this?[241]

Again, I do not believe that "the church must take control of the seven major spheres of influence in society" before Jesus can return. Absolutely, categorically not. There is far too much in the Bible that speaks of rebellion and darkness and satanic activity at the end of this age, side by side with glorious spiritual harvest and outpouring. The whole world will certainly not become Christian before Jesus returns.

More importantly, and in keeping with the emphasis of this chapter, it is certainly dangerous to think that in order to usher in the Second Coming the church must "take over" the world. This would actually be contrary to the spirit of the Founders of our nation, who emphasized that "Congress shall make no law respecting an establishment of religion, or prohibiting the free exercise thereof; or abridging the freedom of speech, or of the press; or the right of the people peaceably to assemble, and to petition the Government for a redress of grievances."[242]

Normally, we do not put the emphasis on the opening words of that famous statement, since there is no chance today of Congress imposing a national religion on America. But that was very important to our Founders. There would be no state-imposed Church of America like there had been a Church of England. That would not be the American way.

But the vast majority of leaders I know who emphasize the Seven Mountains are not trying to establish the Church of America. Instead, they talk about these Seven Mountains for two reasons. First, they believe we should not abandon these crucial areas of society. Rather, we should be salt and light in the midst of them. Why let the world dominate our universities, many of which were founded as Christian colleges? Why let nonbelievers dictate the curriculum for our children in elementary school? Are Christians not called to teach and lead in the public school system, as well as in Christian schools?

Why let the world control the airwaves? Shouldn't we do our best to get our message out as well? And why give up any involvement in the government and politics? After all, if it's right to pray for kings and rulers to become Christians, it's right for Christians to run for office. If we constantly complain about what's wrong with our world, shouldn't we do our best to make things better?

Second, evangelism is often much more effective when the surrounding cultural atmosphere is less hostile to Christians. This, I believe, was one of the major issues for Bill Bright and Loren Cunningham. Martin Luther King Jr., expressed this when he said, "The Christian gospel is a two-way road. On the one hand, it seeks to change the souls of men, and thereby unite them with God; on the other hand, it seeks to change the environmental conditions of men so the soul will have a chance after it is changed."[243] Not only so, but when there is less hostility to the Christian message, there is often more openness to receive it. And there is certainly more ability to get the message out.

To the extent that this is what is meant by the Seven Mountain Mandate, we should embrace it. And to the extent that Seven Mountains means seeing every area of life and culture as a mission field, we should embrace that as well.

In the words of Loren Cunningham:

Therefore, we can be missionaries, where the word 'missionary' means 'one sent', and one sent of Jesus, if you're a lawyer in a legal office, *you* are sent of God. You're sent to be his missionary, or if you're in Hollywood, or you're working as a dentist, or you're working as a doctor, everything you can do for the glory of God. You may be in the area of foodservices. The Bible says in Zach 14:20 that even the cooking pots will be called 'holy' to the Lord. That's foodservices. Or transportation. Everything from a bus driver to an airplane pilot or to a car dealer or whatever it is, it says even the veils of horses will be called holy to the Lord.[244]

At the same time, we should reject any kind of talk of a Christian "takeover." It is misleading. It is potentially dangerous. It gives the impression that the Christian faith can be forced on a nation (at least legislatively). And it is contrary to the spirit of the cross.

To be sure, men like Rushdoony stated plainly that "Godly men are not revolutionists: the Lord's way is regeneration, not revolution."[245] So, to repeat, he was absolutely not advocating for some type of militaristic takeover—God forbid—and he clearly understood the spiritual nature of the gospel. As he wrote, "The Christian theonomic society will only come about as each man governs himself under God and governs his particular sphere. And only so will we take back government from the state and put it in the hands of Christians."[246]

Yet he also wrote,

The creation mandate was precisely the requirement that man subdue the earth and exercise dominion over it. There is not one word of Scripture to indicate or imply that this mandate ever was revoked. There is every word of Scripture to declare that this mandate must and shall be fulfilled. Those who attempt to break it shall themselves be broken."[247]

And this: "We are very much in need now of Christian pioneers. This means a people who are zealous to grow and to exercise dominion in Christ."[248]

With human nature being what it is, it is all too easy for us to try to take matters into our own hands, thinking we can "Christianize" America by exercising the dominion God has given us, thinking, "We are called to rule the nations! We will impose our rule in America too! Thank God for a man like Trump (or whoever the latest icon might be) who will help us lead the way." How far this is from the gospel of Jesus!

Some Insights from Francis Schaeffer and John Whitehead

In the summer of 2006, Christian attorney John W. Whitehead, founder of the Rutherford Institute and known as a champion of civil and religious liberties, published a lengthy article in *Liberty* magazine titled "The Rise of Dominionism and the Christian Right." In fact, a number of the quotes cited in this chapter are taken directly from Whitehead's important article. He explained,

Unlike Rushdoony, who exhorted Christians to take over the world for Christ through political means, Francis Schaeffer (1912-1984), a Presbyterian minister and apologist, called for a return to true Christian spirituality through social activism. At no time did Schaeffer advocate a Christian theocracy. In fact, Schaeffer's book *A Christian Manifesto* (1981) embraced the idea of "freedom for all and especially freedom for all religion. That was the original purpose of the First Amendment."

Whitehead continued,

Although Schaeffer rightly pointed out that the separation of church and state in America is often used to silence the Christian church, he disagreed vocally with Rushdoony's dominionist ideas. Schaeffer wrote:

"[A]s we stand for religious freedom today, we need to realize that this must include a general religious freedom from the control of the state for all religion. It will not mean just freedom for those who are Christians. It is then up to Christians to show that Christianity is the Truth of total reality in the open marketplace of freedom."

In Schaeffer's mind, a truly Christian America would be an America in which all peoples of all faiths could live in freedom. Yet, Whitehead observed,

This also means, as Francis Schaeffer noted in *A Christian Manifesto*, that Christians must avoid joining forces with the government and arguing a theocratic position. "We must not confuse the Kingdom of God with our country," Schaeffer writes. "To say it another way, 'We should not wrap Christianity in our national flag.'" Indeed, by fusing Christianity with politics, one will only succeed in cheapening religion, robbing it of its spiritual vitality and thus destroying true Christianity. Rather than taking over the country and the world, as Dominionists suggest, Schaeffer advocated Christian involvement in all areas of life. To quote Schaeffer, "[O]ur culture, society, government and law are in the condition they are in, *not because of a conspiracy, but because the church has forsaken its duty to be the salt of the culture* [italics supplied by Whitehead]. It is the church's duty (as well as its privilege) to do now what it should have been doing all the time—to use the freedom we do have to be that salt of the culture."

And then these important conclusions:

Thus, the activism of the true Christian flows from a sense of loving care for what God has created. This means the Christian has a responsibility to assist in preserving both freedom and order—indeed, to work for justice—while keeping in mind one's fallen nature, spiritual priorities, and the limitations of the political process.

However, as we speak of political involvement and activism, we must be mindful that *our problems are not political or cultural, but spiritual.* The present state of Western culture and the declining value of human life generally are mere *symptoms* of a deeper problem. That problem is moral and spiritual decay.

No matter what Dominionists believe, the present spiritual problems we face will not be changed through the political system. Therefore, unless there is a *spiritual reformation*, there will be little alteration in the present course of society. If the hearts of people are not changed, then further moral, and thus cultural and societal, decay is to be expected.[249]

I could not have said it better.

Yet this is exactly how so many of us got so far off track in the last election cycle, bringing to a head a wrong emphasis that was gaining ground in our midst over a period of years. We put our *emphasis* on political change more than spiritual change, on legislative action more than spiritual action, on reversing negative societal trends by our votes more than by our voices. In short, we fought in the flesh rather in the Spirit.

And that, a hundred times out of a hundred, is a recipe for disaster.

CHAPTER THIRTEEN

Christian Nationalism, the Coming Civil War and the Call to Take Up Arms

On December 13, 2020, Christian author and speaker Beth Moore ignited an internet firestorm when she tweeted, "I do not believe these are days for mincing words. I'm 63 1/2 years old & I have never seen anything in these United States of America I found more astonishingly seductive & dangerous to the saints of God than Trumpism. This Christian nationalism is not of God. Move back from it."[250]

But, what, exactly, did she mean by Trumpism and Christian nationalism? It would appear that by Trumpism, Moore was referring to a cultlike devotion to Trump in which he became the political savior of conservative Christians. But Christian nationalism can be harder to define. It could be representing something healthy and positive for some Christians but representing something dangerous and negative for other Christians. In the case of Moore, it was obviously a negative term, the merging together of right-wing politics, Christian theology, and a militant patriotism. "Move back from it," she urged her fellow Bible-believing Christians.

In chapter 1, I pointed to a January 11, 2021, article in the *New York Times* which claimed that, "A potent mix of grievance and religious fervor has turbocharged the support among Trump loyalists, many of whom describe themselves as participants in a kind of holy war."[251] This was Christian nationalism at its worst. As expressed by an alt-right leader at the December 12, 2020, Jericho March prayer rally in DC: "God is about to do something. This is our city ... We are the government of America."[252] Or in the words of Alex Jones at the same rally: "America is awakening! Humanity is awakening! And Jesus Christ is King! ... God gave us Donald Trump."[253]

The battle for Trump was the battle for America, and the battle for America was the battle for the Church. This was a threefold cord that was not easily broken, with the strong call for Christian values (which I deeply affirm) becoming inextricably linked with partisan politics, a super-charged patriotism, and one particular candidate. As I've said before (see chapter 11), this makes for a toxic mix.

Writing in the *Washington Post* on March 26, 2018, Andrew L. Whitehead, Joseph O. Baker, and Samuel L. Perry noted that "A porn actress says she had sex with Donald Trump, only a few months after his wife gave birth to a son. A former Playboy model says she had an affair with him, too. And yet according to a Pew Research Center poll conducted March 7-14, both white mainline and evangelical Protestants continue to approve of Trump as president at higher levels than other religious groups." This led them to ask,

> Why are white Christians sticking so closely to President Trump, despite these claims of sexual indiscretions? And why are religious individuals and groups that previously decried sexual impropriety among political leaders suddenly willing to give Trump a "mulligan" on his infidelity?
>
> Our new study points to a different answer than others have offered. Voters' religious tenets aren't what is behind Trump support; rather, it's Christian nationalism – their view of the United States as a fundamentally Christian nation.[254]

And, since America was founded as a Christian nation and has been a Christian nation throughout its history (obviously, it was not Muslim or Hindu or Buddhist or Jewish or atheist), it must remain a Christian nation, by any means necessary. Many of those who stormed the Capitol on January 6, 2021, would concur.

So on the one hand Christian nationalism can simply be defined as "an ideology that idealizes and advocates a fusion of American civic life with a particular type of Christian identity and culture." This could be either good or bad. On the other hand, Christian nationalism, at its worst, can be defined as "political idolatry dressed up as religious orthodoxy" (Philip Gorski).[255] As Andrew Whitehead and Samuel Perry wrote, in keeping with some Christian nationalist beliefs, some think that "God requires the faithful to wage wars for good." This, they argue, "is entirely consistent with Philip Gorski's observation that Christian nationalism has historically been used to justify bloody conquests, often taking the form of imperialist and jingoist projects under the banner of God's blessing and mandate for his people."[256]

Not So!

But not everyone accepts this view of Christian nationalism, with some conservative thinkers arguing that, more than anything else, the Left is using the term as a weapon against conservative Christian values. This was pointed out by John Zmirak, a conservative Catholic and an incisive cultural commentator. He argued *for* the use of the term "Christian nationalist," claiming that "to a certain type of bourgeois, comfortable Christian . . . [i]f you care about what happens to the country where you and your kids and grandkids will live? Then you're abandoning citizenship in heaven. If you're loyal to a politician like Trump who tried to protect you? You're committing 'idolatry.' "

He continued, "If you aren't content to be subjugated to third-class citizenship in an anti-Christian, viciously race-baiting country where new Islamist immigrants strut around demanding sharia? Then you're a dangerous 'Christian Nationalist.' Are you unwilling to pervert Christianity into a philosophy of craven surrender, a renunciation of basic rights no one would demand of any other group? Then expect to have that epithet hurled at you."[257] Consequently, in Zmirak's view we should actually embrace this term rather than renounce it.

He even penned a December 26, 2020, article titled "Why I'm a Christian Nationalist and You Should Be Too," in which he referenced an interview he did with Robert Oscar Lopez, an ex-gay Christian who is not afraid to take on the corrupt culture and the compromised church. Zmirak wrote:

> [Lopez] said that servile, squishy Christians clearly wanted to call the Trump coalition something extremely damaging, such as "White Nationalist." "But they just saw too many people of color, like me, visibly supporting the president, to get away with that. So they coined this ridiculous term, 'Christian Nationalist,' hoping people would have the same reaction," Robert said.
>
> The Church's open enemies are slavering over this. As I wrote the other day:

> Already, the "secularist" faction of the Democrat party is equating orthodox Christians with white supremacists. And demanding that we be carefully monitored as potential sources of "terrorism." NBC is following the Southern Poverty Law Center in smearing our ministries as "hate groups" that shouldn't get neutral benefits like PPP loans.

The term of abuse getting used by those who want the FBI monitoring biblically faithful churches (instead of, I dunno, Islamist mosques) as likely hotbeds for terrorism? "Christian Nationalist."[258]

Zmirak and Lopez, then, addressed the leftist strategy of equating Christian conservatives with white supremacist, nationalist terrorists, grouping us all together under the term "Christian nationalist." (And note that he wrote this less than two weeks before the storming of the Capitol, at which point the Left could now point to the real threat posed by these "Christian nationalists," as I explained in chapter 1.)

Thus, Zmirak argued:

I think instead we should go with "Christian Nationalist," and explain in calm detail exactly what we mean. What's so poisonous about Nationalism, anyway? As Israeli scholar Yoram Hazony explains in his brilliant work of original political philosophy, *The Virtue of Nationalism*, it's a concept with a mostly noble pedigree. (American nationalists saved the Union. Zionists established Israel. Polish nationalists brought down Communism.) Yes it has been abused, but what word hasn't? Jim Jones called himself a "reverend," but we didn't drop that word. Hitler and Stalin both claimed to be "socialists"; the socialists of Norway didn't cringe and rename themselves.[259]

Similarly, my good friend Dr. Joseph Mattera, another top conservative Christian thinker, noted that "most of the recent concerns about the rise of Christian nationalism are coming from the radical Left. This is primarily because most Evangelicals support President Trump's policies. The radical Left utilizes a lens of interpretation skewed against anything for what Conservative Evangelicals stand."

He also wrote,

> I am willing to die for my nation. I believe the United States of American is the greatest nation on the earth despite all its flaws and sins. Hence, I am a patriot. I support our right to have a strong military, and I believe God had a special plan for the nation from its very inception. I would love to see the United States build its laws upon the Scriptures' standard of morality and justice. I am strongly pro-life and pro-biblical marriage. I also advance a biblical worldview in many of my teachings.
>
> These beliefs do not make me a Christian nationalist.[260]

Similarly, when responding to Beth Moore's tweet, I wrote:

> Are you a Christian nationalist simply because you love and appreciate America? No.
>
> Are you a Christian nationalist simply because you are patriotic and serve in the military? No.
>
> Are you a Christian nationalist simply because you believe Trump was better for America than Biden? No.
>
> Are you a Christian nationalist simply because you believe there was electoral fraud and are doing your best to fight for a free and fair election? No.
>
> Are you a Christian nationalist simply because you believe that America must protect our religious liberties? No.
>
> Are you a Christian nationalist simply because you believe that God raised up America for special purposes in order to bless and help the world? No.

I continued:

But you *are* a Christian nationalist if you confuse loyalty to your country with loyalty to the kingdom of God.

You *are* a Christian nationalist if you wrap the gospel in an American flag.

You *are* a Christian nationalist if you "merge Christian and American identities" . . .

As defined by Pastor Jeremie Beller, "Christian nationalism is the intertwining of the Kingdom of God with the kingdoms of men. In the American context, it is often displayed by describing America through language reserved for the Kingdom of God. . . . The marriage between patriotism and righteousness further blurs the line between the Kingdom of God and the kingdoms of the world."[261]

Getting into even more depth, Dr. Mattera listed these distinctions between the kingdom of God and Christian nationalism:

1. The Kingdom of God focuses on the advancement of the Gospel. Nationalism focuses on the advancement of the politics of the nation.
2. The Kingdom of God produces loyalty to Christ above all else. Nationalism produces loyalty to the nation above all else.
3. The Kingdom of God produces martyrs for the cause of Christ. Nationalism produces citizens who are willing to die for their nation.
4. The Kingdom of God raises the banner of Jesus above all else. Nationalism raises the national flag above all else.
5. The Kingdom of God promotes the interests of God above the world. Nationalism promotes the interests of the nation above the Kingdom.

6. The Kingdom of God views the world with a biblical lens. Nationalism views the world with a geo/political lens.[262]
7. The Kingdom of God is dependent upon neither an earthly kingdom nor an earthly ruler. Nationalism is dependent upon both the ideology of a nation and its ruler.
8. Followers of the Kingdom of God are passionate about a Christ-centered global awakening. Adherents of nationalism are passionate about an ideological awakening.
9. Christ-followers are primarily identified with the Kingdom of God. Nationalists mostly derive their identity from their nation.[263]

He also pointed to the rise of a deeply twisted, pro-Hitler, Christian nationalism in the days of Nazi Germany, writing, "In the mid-20th century, we witnessed Christian nationalists turn a blind eye to the 3rd Reich when most of the German churches aligned themselves with Hitler. If it happened once, it can and will continue to happen again, especially to a non-discerning church."[264]

So, while we might be loyal, country-loving patriots, we are Jesus-first, not America-first, in our orientation. There *is* a difference between the two. And that's one reason why I recommend that we *not* embrace the term "Christian nationalism." It has way too much social baggage, and it is fundamentally flawed—unless you believe that America has been raised up by God out of all nations on the planet, called to be a uniquely Christian nation just as Israel was called by God to be *the* chosen nation in the ancient world. For many reasons, I do not, including the fact that the Bible gives not the slightest hint of other "chosen nations" being raised up by God for the purpose of world redemption. Instead, He raised up Israel to bring the knowledge of God and the Messiah to the world, and now, out of all peoples and nations, He is building His *ekklesia*—His Church (or, messianic community). Let's be careful not to blur the lines.

Are We Merging Our Loyalties?

I tweeted on December 13, 2020: "As a Trump voter, I must say candidly that it is very troubling to see many American Christians far more mobilized for Trump than they have ever been mobilized for Jesus."[265] Put another way, when shouts of "Jesus! Jesus!" merge with shouts of "Trump! Trump!" something is deeply and profoundly wrong. As I explained,

> The problem is that the differences between being Christians who love America and Christian national- ists are often subtle, since we have many shared values (such as being pro-life).
>
> Many sincere believers would also ask, "Should we just stand back and let our country be destroyed? Should we let democracy be crushed forever? Should we simply hand over our nation to corrupt leaders? Should we not stand up and fight for what is right?"
>
> Certainly not. We should fight *for* what is right and *against* what is wrong.
>
> But the cause of Trump is not the cause of Christ, nor is the battle for the Senate a battle for the kingdom of God.
>
> America, like every other nation on the planet, is part of the world system (or, in New Testament terms, part of "the world"). It is not the kingdom of God, nor is it a special manifestation of the kingdom of God. In fact, God's kingdom values are often diametrically opposed to the values of our country.

In sum, and as stated throughout this book,

> To equate America with God's kingdom or to merge the cross with the flag is to make a terrible and dangerous mistake. And that is the error of Christian nationalism.
>
> The irony of all this is that if we would be kingdom-minded people first and foremost, we would bring the most blessing to America. If we would look at America as our mission field rather than our spiritual refuge, we would help our nation fulfill whatever plans the Lord has for us. And if we would exalt Jesus infinitely more than any political leader, we would best serve our country (and our leaders).[266]

In keeping with this mindset, on December 28, 2020, I wrote an article titled "Why I Reject the 'Christian Nationalist' Label." A major point of the article was to address how the term "Christian nationalist" was understood today. Was it a positive term that we should embrace or a negative term that we should reject? Was it even a term worth fighting over? I noted that my "conservative colleagues are certainly right to critique those who claim that, for Christian followers of Trump, Christian nationalism is the religion of white supremacy."

I added, that, "I, too, have rejected that equation, making clear that for the vast majority of white, Christian conservative, Trump supporters, our vote for him was not a vote to preserve a white America.[267] Yet to the extent that the gospel is merged with patriotism and loyalty to Jesus is conflated with support for America, we are in error."

Was this, then, simply a matter of semantics? I answered, "Perhaps for some it is. But, since the term 'Christian nationalism' is already fraught with so much baggage and can be so easily misunderstood, why not simply identify as a 'Jesus-loving American'?"

I then explained that in the Bible, the prophets were some-times of being anti-patriotic.

That's because, rather than joining with the nation-alistic prophets, they spoke of impending judgment unless repentance came first. On some occasions, they even told the Israelite kings to submit to foreign leaders, since God was chastising the nation. What could seem less patriotic than that? Yet it was because they truly loved their country that they felt the need to speak.

It is the same with many of us today who strongly reject the language of Christian nationalism. Our love for God and country, which moves us to speak unpop-ular words, can be misconstrued as a lack of patrio-tism. So be it.

In the same way, when the prophets renounced idolatry in any form, they were not applauded by their idolatrous nation. Yet it was zeal for God and love for their nation that drove them.

It is that same zeal for God and love of country that moved some of us to speak up in the aftermath of the elections, as we saw a dangerous spike in Trumpism (meaning, an unhealthy looking to Trump as some kind of political messiah).

Did we do this to gain the approval of Never Trumpers or to appease a potential Biden administra-tion? The suggestion is as laughable as it is ludicrous.

Speaking for myself, this reflected a position I have held to for decades in terms of Christians putting too much trust in a political leader. And it is a position I often addressed as a Trump supporter.

Perhaps there is room for some self-examination on the fervent pro-Trump side? Perhaps the concerns some of us are raising are not based on "squishy compromise" or a desire to find the "mushy middle" but rather on sober spiritual reflection?[268]

As for me, "as a preacher of the gospel first and a cultural-political commentator second," my priorities were clear: first and foremost, I see America as a nation needing to be saved, a nation needing to repent, a nation in need of God, a nation that is part of "the world." And I see us, the believers, as a remnant within the nation, living in this world and yet not of this world.

My perspective was also shaped by the fact that I am a Jewish follower of Jesus. That's because Jews, generally speaking, have not fared well in countries where a zealous Christianity ruled, just as they have not fared well in countries where a zealous Islam ruled. Jewish failure to conform to the spiritual and cultural norms brought all kinds of reprisals, sometimes culminating in exile. That's one reason why many Jewish voters in America fear the religious Christian Right, even irrationally. They wonder what would happen if Christian conservatives "took over" the nation. Which of our values would we impose? This is similar to the way Christians feel in India, historically a Hindu nation, when they hear Hindu leaders proclaim, "India is a Hindu nation, and we must preserve our Hindu legacy at all costs!"[269] That is *not* good news for the Indian Christians (or Indian Muslims for that matter.)

Getting Some Historical Perspective

Writing in a special issue of the journal *Religion*, Ethan Goodnight claimed that there were four historical pillars supporting the idea that America was formed as a Christian nation (a concept he then goes on to critique). He stated:

> As historian Steven Green has recently explained, the establishment in the early Republic of the Pilgrims as American's religious forbearers forms the first of what may be termed the four key pillars of Christian nationalism. The second pillar was constructed by the Christian nationalist movement through the composition of countless hagiographies of the supposedly great Christian leaders of the newly founded nation, the Founding Fathers. Working their same interpretive magic on America's heritage of religious and political liberty, second-generation Americans identified the third pillar, American common law tradition, as having emerged from Christian principles. The success of these three pillars was credited to and codified in the fourth pillar: Divine Providence guiding the nation. Taken together, these four pillars form the backbone of Christian nationalism in the early Republic.[270]

So, the Pilgrims, who were devout Christians were the nation's earliest founders. Then, the Founding Fathers were reconstructed by early historians, making them all into great Christian leaders. Next, second-generation Americans argued that the laws of the nation were Christian in origin. Finally, Christian writers and thinkers in our nation looked back at our history and declared that we had been founded and raised by Divine Providence. God Himself had a plan for America, a unique plan among other nations. In short, we were called by God to be a Christian nation.

Other scholars challenge the idea that America was ever a Christian nation. Historian Sam Haselby pointed out that when our nation was founded, the great majority of Christians worldwide were Catholic while the American colonies were "deeply, profoundly anti-Catholic." Consequently, he writes:

> Claiming that people moved by deep prejudice against most of [the] world's Christians wanted to form a "Christian nation" makes no sense. The problem cannot be solved by simply devolving to "Protestant nation." Britain was known as the sword and shield of Protestantism, set against a hostile Catholic Continent. In what form of Protestantism, exactly, did the United States rise up in rebellion against the 18th-century world's standard-bearer of Protestantism? Possible answers quickly begin to look rather sectarian, rendering any understanding of "*Christian* nation" into something very narrow, perhaps some kind of provincial country denomination.[271]

At best, then, America represented a specific, minority branch of Christianity, one that rejected the Protestantism of the Church of England and the Catholicism of the majority of the world's professing Christians. On the other hand, Haselby points out that it was the America of Jefferson and Madison that ultimately prevailed, one that emphasized freedom of religion for all. Not only so, but of "the 27 grievances against the British Crown that the Declaration puts forward, not one concerns religion. Likewise, the Constitution merely recognizes 'freedom of religion'; it doesn't endorse Christianity—it doesn't even mention it. These omissions present today's Christian nationalists with a real awkwardness."[272]

According to political scientist and professor Kenneth Wald, "The U.S. Constitution follows a classic liberal model in separating citizenship and religion. Rather than rooting citizenship in blood or religion, the American system eliminates ethnic particularity as a condition for full membership in the political community." Thus, he explains, "American

Jewish communities in the late 18th centuries [*sic*] celebrated the Constitution's prohibition on religious tests in Article VI as their Magna Carta. Despite the passage of centuries, they have remained deeply attached to the idea of a secular state, believing that it accounts for their integration in what some have described as the 'Kingdom of Kindness.' " [273] But are Christian nationalists today advocating that "Kingdom of Kindness"?

Kristin Kobes Du Mez notes that for Don Jacobson, whose Multnomah Press has published the writings of some of the best-known evangelicals,

> a growing discomfort with Christian nationalism led him to distance himself from the movement he helped foster. After studying more closely the history of Native Americans and accounts of imperial conquest, he could no longer sustain the idea of America as an anointed nation. If you believe that America is God's chosen nation, you need to fight for it and against others, he realized. But once you abandon that notion, other values begin to shift as well. Without Christian nationalism, evangelical militarism makes little sense.[274]

Can we really make the claim, then, that America has always been a Christian nation, at least in the way that Christian nationalists seem to think? Or, even if our country had strong Christian roots (which can hardly be denied), does that mean anything today when America is so diverse both religiously and culturally? Most importantly, how is it helpful to identify as a Christian nationalist today?

The Real Danger of Christian Nationalism

Again, I recognize that there is a healthy debate over the term "Christian nationalism," since not everyone uses it in the same way. For some on the Left, it is a convenient way to demonize conservative Christians who are strong patriots (especially if they voted for Trump). "You are dangerous Christian nationalists and diabolical white supremacists!" For some on the Right, it is a positive term, but in a healthy, balanced way, something to be embraced not rejected. "I love Jesus and my country, which has a wonderful Christian heritage." For others, who are further to the Right, it really is a dangerous term, one that could easily lead to bloodshed, including a Christian call to take up arms against the government. "Enough is enough! This nation is a Christian nation, and it's time that we retake it, by force if necessary." This latter view of Christian nationalism is why, for many conservative Christians in America today, being a follower of Jesus means being macho. And tough. And brash. And loud. And armed. And abrasive—especially if you're a preacher of the gospel. "You don't want to mess with me! I'm a man of God, and I'm not backing down!" As expressed by Du Mez, "Evangelical masculinity serves as the foundation of a God-and-country Christian nationalism."[275]

To be sure, we have had more than our share of sentimentalized, soft, overly emotional versions of the "Christian" faith that totally lack in backbone and conviction and courage and vitality. Away with those corrupt versions as well![276] But the last thing we want to do is replace those faulty versions of the New Testament faith with a call for spiritual triumphalism and gospel machismo, where the call to swing your fists (or take up arms) sounds more Christian than the call to fall to your knees and serve others. The former is seen as a sign of strength and resolve, the latter a sign of weakness and surrender.

According to Angela Decker, Christian nationalists are "desperate to reclaim the idea that America was a uniquely and especially Christian nation, where your culture—your positions on social issues, your views on gun control and abortion—were much more important than your grasp of theology or your understanding of grace, death, and resurrection."[277] She pointed to the example of Pastor Dean Inserra who stated, "I think there are two kinds of Trump supporters in the SBC [Southern Baptist Convention, the nation's largest evangelical organization]. . . . One type, they didn't want Hillary Clinton because of abortion and because of the Supreme Court; the other type is a nationalistic voter. I don't think they're racist, but American patriotism has become so linked to GOP politics, and [the SBC] has so intertwined that with what it means to be a Christian, that they almost can't question anything about the GOP nominee or about Trump." And, he claimed, "If you bring a missionary from India one week to a Southern Baptist church and the next week you bring a veteran, there's no question who's going to get the bigger applause."[278]

Denker added,

The near-deification of the American military in many conservative churches is a sign of growing Christian Nationalism and its influence on the local church, in some ways further isolating the military from everyday Americans. During this time when World War II and Vietnam War veterans are aging and many Americans don't have a family member on active duty, the worship of military members can lead to a misunderstanding of what it's really like to serve. As Trump selected several generals to serve in his Cabinet and on his staff ("my generals," he called them), the appearance of military support for Trump and the intertwining of nationalism and a "Christian America" increased conservative Christian support for Trump. In fact, support for America as a Christian nation may become the most prominent lesson many American Christians learn in church, rather than a focus on the gospel, on forgiveness, or even on Jesus's death and resurrection.[279]

But is she right? To be candid, I find some of these critiques to be over-the-top, generalized, and exaggerated. Having preached in evangelical churches for almost fifty years, I have never once encountered a congregation in which "support for America as a Christian nation" was emphasized more than the gospel, more than forgiveness or the Lord's death and resurrection. But that doesn't mean that the concerns of Denker and Du Mez and Inserra and Jacobson are not valid. They certainly are valid, since in all too many circles there has been an unhealthy mingling of the gospel and American politics, the very seduction spoken of in the title of this book.

Worse still, this unhealthy mixture has also been marked by increasing calls to prepare for battle, meaning literal physical battle, as in a military conflict. As reported on January 18, 2021, "A west-central Minnesota pastor has unleashed a flurry of praise and condemnation after posting a Facebook video telling citizens to be ready to 'arm up' and saying that he expects President Donald Trump to enact martial law."[280]

And he was not alone. As reported by *Newsweek* on September 14, 2020, "Conservative evangelical pastor Rick Joyner has urged Christians to 'mobilize' to fight a civil war against left-wing activists." In his own words, "We're in time for war. We need to recognize that. We need to mobilize. We need to get ready." He also referred to "our civil war," saying that, in a dream, he had seen that "militias would pop up like mushrooms" and that these militias would be backed by God. To quote him again: "Jesus himself said, 'There's gonna be a time when you need to sell your coat and buy a sword.' Now that was a physical weapon of their day, and we're in that time here. We need to realize that."[281]

Again, on March 16, 2021, *Newsweek* wrote that, "MorningStar Ministries founder and pastor, Rick Joyner, pleaded with the 'true disciples of Christ' in America to rise up and prepare for war with the 'evil' forces which he baselessly claimed 'stole' the November election from former President Donald Trump." He said, "It will be a civil war and it's going to be increasingly worse with the increasing time it takes for Americans to stand up and push back against this evil that has taken over our land." He continued, "You know, there's a time for peace and a time for war it says in [Book of the Bible] Ecclesiastes, well, we're not headed towards peace right now, we're headed towards conflict of war. And we need to prepare for it. We need to put out the word that people need to be prepared."[282]

Indeed, as it is written in Ecclesiastes 3:8, there's "a time to love, and a time to hate; a time of war, and a time of peace." Now, Joyner argued, we are coming into that time of war, just as America did in the nineteenth century when we had our first Civil War. The second is near at hand.

As noted by journalist and Christian media leader Steven Strang, "Joyner has spoken frequently and with much specificity about the inevitability of another civil war, which he calls the 'second American revolution,' for at least the past decade. He has been trumpeting this idea because of a dramatic vision he received in 1987."[283] To be sure, many of us who heard Joyner (who is a personal friend) speak about this coming conflict in years past understood him to be speaking in spiritual terms only: America will be deeply divided morally and spiritually in the days to come. But clearly he means more than that today, speaking of a literal, militarized, civil war.

As quoted by Strang (who is also a personal friend), Joyner said, "Until a couple of years ago, I would have used the word *possible*. But I don't anymore. I think it's inevitable," he said of this civil war. "Some of my friends who thought I was crazy back in 2018 when I started saying, 'It's coming,' they now say, 'No, it's here.' They think we're already in it. I'm talking about pretty high-ranking military people. They think we've already entered a phase of it."[284]

Yet it is not only conservative Christians who feel that another civil war could be at hand. As noted in a March 2019 article on the Boston University website,

> A recent *Washington Post* headline says: "In America, talk turns to something not spoken of for 150 years: Civil war." The story references, among others, Stanford University historian Victor Davis Hanson, who asked in a *National Review* essay last summer: "How, when, and why has the United States now arrived at the brink of a veritable civil war?" Another Washington Post story reports how Iowa Republican Congressman Steve King recently posted a meme warning that red states have "8 trillion bullets" in the event of a civil war. And a poll conducted last June by Rasmussen Reports found that 31 percent of probable US voters surveyed believe "it's likely that the United States will experience a second civil war sometime in the next five years."[285]

Even as I worked on the first draft of this chapter in September 2021, tensions were reaching a fever pitch over the subject of abortion, with the Texas Heartbeat Bill becoming law, with the real possibility that the Supreme Court could overturn *Roe v. Wade*, and with the House of Representatives passing the most extreme pro-abortion bill in our nation's history, a bill that would effectively undermine all pro-life legislation throughout America. Could it be that a real civil war is at hand?[286] And could it be that Christians should be prepared to fight in this war, not just spiritually and ideologically but with guns and bullets and bombs?

It's not enough, we are told, that there is an all-out war on our religious freedoms. Soon, we are warned, the government will be coming for our guns. And once it disarms us, it's over. That's why the Democrats, who are attempting to take over our lives, either by legislation or executive order, must be resisted. That's why their election stealing must be exposed. It's the last chance to preserve our liberties, and armed Christians could well be the last line of defense.

This Is Where Things Get Very Dangerous

This is very dangerous talk. As Cameron Hilditch wrote on December 18, 2020, in the *National Review*, with reference to the rhetoric at the Jericho March,

> We have to reckon with the nontrivial chance that someone out there will take these men seriously. When you reach for language like this while addressing an audience of politically enraged people, you're courting the possibility of violence. After all, who doesn't want to be the first one to take up arms against the Nazis, or to take up the mantle of liberty from George Washington?

As for the Jericho March event itself, he described it as, "A toxic ideological cocktail of grievance, paranoia, and self-exculpatory rage . . . a protest staged . . . by the president's most devoted Evangelical Christian supporters."[287] Or, in the words of Julia Duin, a seasoned religion reporter and herself a committed Christian, the Jericho March was

> a mix of evangelical Protestants, Catholics and Messianic Jews claimed that President Trump had

indeed won the election (but it was stolen) and that somehow, miraculously, God would see to it that he, not Joe Biden, will be inaugurated next month. This might require use of military force or militias.

Every religion reporter should have watched this rally; if not all of it, at least in part to see the most poisonous marriage of religion and politics I've seen in 40-plus years on the beat.[288]

And not a word of this is overstated.

Do you see how deeply troubling this is, even if you are very concerned, like I am, about the direction the Democratic Party is trying to take us? Even if, like many others, you see the handwriting on the wall of government overreach with the COVID crackdowns and mandates? Even if, like still others, you believe the elections were stolen? And even if you are alarmed at the attacks on the Second Amendment? Even with all this, can you see why this type of militaristic rhetoric is so dangerous?

As Rod Dreher noted in his detailed recounting of the Jericho March (which I quoted in chapter 1), "Another speaker, a man wearing a black cowboy hat, called on Trump to 'invoke the Insurrection Act' to 'drop the hammer' on 'traitors.' He said that Trump should know that the 'militia' is with him. 'Let's get it on now, while [Trump] is still the commander in chief,' said the speaker."[289] This is as dangerous as it is unchristian.

And note that Christians in other countries, in the midst of severe persecution, even government-sponsored persecution, do not form killing squads to wipe out their attackers. As John Allen wrote in his important book on the worldwide war against Christians, "The last thing the world needs is a contemporary version of the Crusader armies of yore, armed with AK-47 assault rifles and rocket-propelled grenades."[290]

Calmer Heads Must Prevail, Or Else

Jonathan Den Hartog, a historian of the American Revolution, wrote that,

> In early 1776, with the Revolutionary War ramping up, Peter Muhlenberg was serving as an Anglican minister in Virginia. One Sunday morning, he announced his text from Ecclesiastes 3, "There is a time for everything, and a season for every activity under the heavens." When he completed his homily, he announced, "This is the time of war." He threw off his black minister's robes to reveal a military uniform underneath. He strode out of the sanctuary and called for a recruitment table to be set up outside the church. He soon marched off with the regiment that was raised.
>
> In 1780, Presbyterian James Caldwell was serving as both a chaplain and a quartermaster with the army in New Jersey. During a battle at Springfield, the soldiers were running low on the paper necessary to seat their musket balls on their black powder. Caldwell rode off to a local church and grabbed the hymnals, which featured the songs of Isaac Watts (such as "Joy to the World" and "When I Survey the Wondrous Cross"). He galloped back to the troops and began tearing out pages for the soldiers to use. "Give 'em Watts, boys!" he supposedly instructed. Here, even worship was being weaponized![291]

Isn't this exactly what Rick Joyner was saying, even to the point of quoting Ecclesiastes 3, which speaks of a time for war? And isn't this exactly what the speakers at the Jericho March in DC on December 12, 2020, were saying, also pointing back to these early American clergymen who became known as the Black Robe Regiment?

Hartog notes that the situation was actually much more complex, writing that

> we should remember that there were several other cadres of black-robed ministers. Some eschewed politics altogether and sought to care for their flocks. Moravian missionaries, for instance, worked to shelter the Native Americans in their communities from depredations of both sides.
>
> Meanwhile, Loyalist clergy actively opposed the American Revolution. These articulate ministers—people like Jonathan Boucher, Charles Inglis, Samuel Seabury, and John Joachim Zubly—worked to convince Americans that the safest path for their liberties was in submission to the British crown. They insisted that Christian duty lay in following the monarch. Although marginalized and often muzzled, these ministers still preached their political Loyalism out of a sense of conviction. Theirs, too, was a Scripture-informed interpretation of the American Revolution.[292]

Still, even if a strong argument could be made that: (1) our forefathers did the right thing in God's sight to revolt against England, coining the slogan, "Rebellion against tyrants is obedience to God"; and (2) just because there were outspoken Christian clergy who helped fuel the flames and lead the way doesn't mean we are in this same situation today, let alone a situation similar to the Civil War where we butchered one another in the name of Jesus.

As I wrote in March 2021, "taking up arms is the last thing we should be thinking about since the biggest problem in our nation is the Church. Put another way, if even 10 to 20 percent of this nation's Christians started praying with holy desperation and gave themselves to repentance and evangelism and revival, God Himself would begin to intervene on our behalf. That's why I say that 'we have seen the enemy, and it is us.'"[293]

I explained further that, in the early 1980s, as a result of the publication of Francis Schaeffer's watershed book *A Christian Manifesto*, there was much discussion of the question: "At what point is it right for Christians to take up arms?" He wrote,

> There does come a time when force, even physical force, is appropriate. The Christian is not to take the law into his own hands and become a law unto himself. But when all avenues to flight and protest have closed, force in the defensive posture is appropriate. This was the situation of the American Revolution. The colonists used force in defending themselves. Great Britain, because of its policy toward the colonies, was seen as a foreign power invading America. The colonists defended their homeland. As such, the American Revolution was a conservative counter-revolution. The colonists saw the British as the revolutionaries trying to overthrow the legitimate colonial governments.[294]

He added, "A true Christian in Hitler's Germany and in the occupied countries should have defied the false and counterfeit state and hidden his Jewish neighbors from German SS troops. The government had abrogated its authority, and it had no right to make any demands. This brings us to a current issue that is crucial for the future of the church in the United States—the issue of abortion."

Yet Schaeffer was very careful in his language, offering strong cautions. As he explained, "we must make definite that we are in no way talking about any kind of a theocracy. Let me say that with great emphasis."[295]

He also noted that, "we must say that speaking of civil disobedience is frightening because there are so many kooky people around. People are always irresponsible in a fallen world. But we live in a special time of irresponsible people, and such people will in their unbalanced way tend to do the very opposite from considering the appropriate time and place. Anarchy is never appropriate."[296]

All the more should these points be emphasized today, when the age of internet has turned kookiness and lunacy into instant, national sensations. All the more should we be careful with the words we use and the calls we issue.

But that is not my biggest issue with the call to take up arms (or the call to prepare to take up arms). Rather, as stated by Douglas Wilson in a slightly different context, "I am against surrendering in any case, but I am really against surrendering before the battle is really joined."[297] And that, to me, is the crux of the problem. As the Church of America, we have barely joined the battle.

Really now, how many of us, aside from casting a pro-life vote, do anything on a regular basis to combat abortion? How many of us, while decrying the evils of pornography and sexual promiscuity, are ourselves bound by porn? How many of us, while denouncing the redefining of marriage, have winked at no-fault divorce in our own ranks? Shall I go on with the list? How many of us don't even vote?

And when it comes to earnestly contending for revival, which begins with repentance and intercession in the Church, how many of our congregations have at least one weekly prayer meeting—and I mean a well-attended, focused prayer meeting—devoted to intercession for national revival? How many of our congregations do this daily, let alone several times a day? Yet we're talking about taking up arms against the government? Seriously?

Go back and read about the history of awakenings and revivals in America and look at the profound impact they had.[298] What would happen if God moved again? What would happen if the Church simply started living like the Church?[299]

In the early to mid-1990s, as I was working with some strong pro-life Christians, the question about taking up arms came up in conversation. In response to this, while ministering in Finland in October 1995, I wrote in my journal words I believe apply today just as much as they did then:

The whole problem with the "Christian" call to take up arms is that if we were to be honest, we would have to admit that "we have seen the enemy, and it is us." America is aborting babies and exporting smut around the world because the "light that is within us is darkness." To be consistent, the call to violent activism would have to sound like this: "Kill the compromised clergy! Slaughter the sleeping saints! Shoot the sinning shepherds! Nuke the non-committed! Blow up the bankrupt believers! Wipe out the worldly watchmen!" Would you like to lead the attack? Who among us can throw the first stone—or shoot the first bullet?

I added, "Should the government forcefully attempt to disarm Americans, I'm sure Second Amendment advocates will have plenty to say. But that is not where we are today, and that is not where our emphasis needs to be. God has given us a solution. Let us avail ourselves of it and of Him."[300]

Despite all the opposition, the door is still wide open for us, the followers of Jesus, to make a dramatic impact on America—without the call to take up arms and without appeals to a militaristic Christian nationalism, which will only lead to death and destruction, leaving anything but the true Christian faith in its wake. There is a far better way. We cannot afford to miss it.

CHAPTER FOURTEEN

How We Failed the Test: Retracing Our Steps and Learning the Big Lessons

I n my October 2018 book, *Donald Trump Is Not My Savior: An Evangelical Leader Speaks His Mind About the Man He Supports as President*, I devoted a whole chapter to the subject of evangelicals and Donald Trump in which I wrote:

> I am personally thrilled that President Trump has a Faith Advisory Council. I am thrilled that he has a largely evangelical cabinet (some say the most evangelical ever, plus there is Vice President Mike Pence). I am thrilled that he seems steadfast in his pro-life, pro-liberty, pro-family, pro-Israel convictions. All this is wonderful, representing a push-back against a dangerous swing to the far left in recent years.
>
> Yet, when it comes to national transformation (in the best and highest sense of the word), we must not put our hope in President Trump. (Even less can we put our trust in the Republican Party as a whole, let alone in the political system.) We must remain more committed to the advancement of the gospel in America than to "making America great again." Put another way, we must be more concerned with the spiritual and moral transformation of our nation than with our world prominence and dominance.[301]

apter of the book, "Evangelicals and the
Do We Go From Here?" I noted that "these
have been a learning experience, and if we
chable moment, we'll be able build on our
nd learn from our mistakes. Here are seven
final points for consideration." Presented in bullet form here,
without further commentary, those seven points were:

1. We must rise above the political fray.
2. Regardless of party affiliation, we must remain independent.
3. We must stay involved.
4. God uses unlikely vessels, but character still matters.
5. We must stand for the issues near and dear to the Lord's heart.
6. Sometimes, we must function as the president's loyal opposition.
7. Our calling goes beyond patriotism.[302]

I closed the book with these words: "As the title of this book says, Donald Trump is not our Savior. But he is our president, and as such, one of the most powerful men in the world. Let's not scorn him; let's not glorify him; and by all means, let's not give up on him."[303]

Two years later, in July 2020, my book *Evangelicals at the Crossroads: Will We Pass the Trump Test?* was published, and by the "Trump test," I meant two things: First, could we vote for him and support him without losing our testimony in the process? Second, could we disagree about Trump while remaining united as followers of Jesus?

In my view, we failed miserably here, compromising our testimonies by our over-the-top support of Trump no matter what he said or did, and as followers of Jesus, dividing deeply over Trump rather than uniting around our Lord.

The last chapter of that book was titled, "T
Keys for Passing the Trump Test." There, I listed _
ten points (again, simply cited here without the commentary
provided in the book):

1. We must clearly and emphatically put the cross before the flag.
2. We must proclaim that Donald Trump is our president, not our Savior.
3. We must put greater emphasis on spiritual activity than on political activity.
4. We must not get caught up with election fever.
5. We must not justify carnality and unchristian behavior.
6. We must regain our prophetic voice.
7. We must be holistic Christians, truly pursuing justice and righteousness for all.
8. We must walk in love towards those who vilify us and oppose us.
9. We must unite around Jesus rather than divide over Trump.
10. We must lead the nation in repentance, knowing that repentance prepares the way of the Lord, opening a path for revival, visitation, and awakening.[304]

I ended this 2020 book with these words:

Let us, then, lead the nation in private and public repentance, in confession of sin and wrongdoing, of turning to righteousness, of turning to God. That is the great hope of America, not four more years of Donald Trump, or any political candidate, but a heaven-sent revival and awakening.

Until that time comes, we pray, we reach out, we serve, we speak, we love, and we get involved in the political process, but with our focus in the right place and our hopes firmly rooted in the Lord and the Lord alone. If we do this, we will pass the Trump test with flying colors. And who knows? Perhaps he too will be mightily touched by God and help lead the nation into deeper repentance and awakening. What is impossible with people is possible with God.[305]

How Did We Score?

Looking back from our vantage point today, it's easy to see where we got off track. Looking at my seven points for consideration (on page 248) and my ten keys for passing the Trump test (on page 249), let's see how well we did:

1. We did not rise above the political fray.
2. We made party affiliation the test for true devotion to God.
3. We did stay involved (this was positive).
4. We downplayed the destructive effects of Trump's serious character flaws.
5. We did emphasize a number of issues important to the Lord (such as the importance of every life, beginning in the womb) while forgetting other things of value to Him (such as loving one other deeply).
6. We often failed to speak truth to power, becoming deeply partisan.
7. We equated patriotism with Christian faith.
8. We conflated the cross with the flag.
9. We exalted Trump to the point of seeing him as the only man who could save America
10. Spiritual activity became so intertwined with political activity that, towards the end, the whole thrust of our prayers was focused on the elections.
11. We absolutely got caught up with election fever.

12. We did justify carnality and ungodly behavior, seeing it as a sign of strength, and at times, even emulating it ourselves.

13. We lost our prophetic voice through the false Trump prophecies and through being much more politically biased than prophetically based.

14. We often failed to pursue justice and righteousness for all, being moved more by right-wing talking points than by biblical justice and compassion.

15. We failed to walk in love towards those who vilified us or opposed us, often becoming just as ugly as them.

16. On a very large scale, we divided over Trump rather than united around Jesus.

17. We failed to lead the nation in repentance, resisting calls to recognize our idolatrous support of Trump, failing to see our descent into carnality, rebuking those who corrected the failed prophecies, not realizing the degree to which we wrapped the cross in the flag and conflated patriotism with spirituality, and not recognizing how divided and angry we had become.

By my count, then, we got 15 out of 17 points wrong, including quite a few of them very wrong, if not terribly wrong. Is it any surprise, then, that so many of us got so off track? Is it any surprise that so many of us were so easily deceived?

I received a Facebook message in September 2021 from a very solid Christian couple I have known for more than two decades. They asked, "Dr Brown can you send us a link on modern-day prophets and prophecy and how to know if someone is a prophet today. We're working with a young team of people in their thirties who are wrestling with this subject in light of the recent elections and what the prophets were saying."

I immediately sent them an important link and then began to ask some follow-up questions. The wife wrote back, explaining that she was heading down a Far Right–leaning path after following a well-known, female charismatic leader and a few others. "I listened to a message on the *Line of Fire* that set me straight! Thank God!!! You've always been a plumb line for us!"

I asked her to explain further in what ways she got off track, and she explained that she was thinking that Trump was the real President, and he was going to be put into office. She had been listening to not only the well-known, female charismatic leader and a highly respected, male charismatic leader, but a controversial prophet lady. "They kept saying he would be put into office."

She continued, "But you did a podcast on the *Line of Fire* and said, 'Listen to me! Trump isn't going to be President. It's over . . . . People who still believe so are delusional.' This brought me back to center. We're conservative in our voting and lifestyle and values, but I had swung way out there and was believing conspiracy theories and stuff."[306]

Thankfully, she did wake up to reality and came out of these dangerous delusions. But sadly, she was one of millions who fell into deception, and many of them, to this day, have not fully awakened, either failing to recognize how far they got off track or still believing in delusional lies.

For some, the error was joining patriotism together with strong Christian values and an abhorrence for the direction of the Left that led them into error. In other words, the things that opened the door for their political seduction were in and of themselves good and healthy. They simply took those good things to dangerous extremes until all perspective was lost.

For others, it was more of a charismatic spiritual deception, with Trump increasingly viewed as the chosen one, prophesied into office in 2016, a modern-day parallel to Cyrus in the Bible who was now declared president again by a host of prophets in 2020. Surely all these voices could not be wrong. And surely God would not scorn the prayers of millions of His people crying out for the good of America and praying against the anti-faith, anti-Bible sentiments of the Democrats and the Left.

For others still, conspiracy theories played a key role as the mainstream media was distrusted to the point that all kinds of other narratives were embraced. All anti-Trump news was deemed fake; all pro-Trump news was deemed true. And given our universal abhorrence of the subject of human trafficking and pedophilia, the idea that Trump was the key to exposing this alleged worldwide, Democrat-led abomination provided ample fuel for our fires. Soon all this would be revealed! And if this was not enough, the outrage over a supposedly stolen election pushed some Trump supporters over the deep end, to the point of rioting at the Capitol.

Added to all this was the rise of a particular form of Christian nationalism which believed that God had specially raised up America for an end-time purpose, with Donald Trump as the man uniquely positioned to help us fulfill our destiny. Thus, to be pro-God was to be pro-America, and to be pro-America was to be pro-Trump.

These, then, were some of the ingredients that merged together to create a perfect storm, and unless we recognize these trends clearly and renounce them decisively, we will only repeat the same errors in the years ahead. To be quite frank, if that happens, America may never recover. The situation really is that grave.

Two Messiahs

I was reminded of this on September 26, 2021, at a religious Jewish celebration taking place in Crown Heights,

Brooklyn, where thousands of ultra-Orthodox Jewish men danced in the streets on the last night of the Feast of Tabernacles (in Hebrew, Sukkot). As the crowds grew and the celebration intensified, some of the participants began to wave large yellow flags carrying the word "Messiah" (in Hebrew, "Moshiach") in honor of the leader of their movement, who was hailed by many of them as the Messiah even though he died in 1994.[307] A few others began to wave blue flags proclaiming, "Trump 2024."

When I pointed out these flags to my friend, Orthodox Rabbi Shmuley Boteach, who had invited me to join him in Brooklyn for the event, he said to me, "It's like two Messiahs." And he was right.

Of course, these religious Jewish men were focused on God, not Trump. In their minds, their deceased leader, whom they believe to be the Messiah, was in a different universe than Trump morally, intellectually, and spiritually. (Similarly, Christians do not confuse Trump with Jesus.) But as I wrote the day after the event, "At the same time, just as Christian prayer rallies shouting, 'Jesus! Jesus!' could in the next breath shout, 'Trump! Trump!', so also the appearance of these yellow and blue flags side by side was quite telling. And as far as I could see, there was not a syllable of protest about the presence of the Trump flags."[308]

And as far as I can tell today, in many of our conservative Christian circles, not only would Trump be welcomed back with enthusiasm, which is a subject that could be debated either way, but he would be hailed once again as God's appointed and anointed vessel, the only man who could save America from disaster, Donald Trump, our political messiah.

I fear we have not yet learned from our errors. In fact, to some extent, we have not even recognized our errors.

For those who say to me, "You just want to have it both ways. You voted for Trump and cheered him on when he was winning and then abandoned him when he was losing,"

I reply: please go back and re-read the opening pages of this chapter where I cite what I wrote in two books *as a Trump supporter*. The was first published in October 2018, two years after I voted for him in 2016. The second was published in July 2020, four months before I voted for him again in November 2020. In other words, *as an open supporter of President Trump*, I had serious concerns the whole time, sounding scores of warnings along the way, some of them in these very books.

Yet in the heat of the moment, it's all too easy to get caught up in the conflict, just like telling yourself to stay calm the next time your spouse or coworker or boss or friend gets into a heated argument with you, only to find yourself yelling and screaming the moment the conflict arises. It happened even to me. Having warned against getting caught up with election fever in July 2018, I had to fight that urge continually in the months leading up to the 2020 elections, often failing more than I succeeded. The drama was so engrossing, and the stakes were so high.

The Simple Ways That Many of Us Got Off Track

Let me share three words with you: *emphasis*, *priorities*, and *trajectory*. In many cases, this is how we got off track, placing too much *emphasis* on the elections and on the president, thereby getting our *priorities* out of line, as a result of which we ended up on a dangerous *trajectory*, starting a little off course and ending up way off course. A minor deviation led to a major deception.

It's as if we all became obsessed with politics to the point that we talked about Trump and the elections more than we talked about Jesus. (At least in our public postings and discussions we showed more passion about Trump and the elections then we did about Jesus and gospel issues, resulting in deep division and contention our churches, close circles of friends, and even within our own families.) Our political opinions began to sound more like religious convictions, and we judged others based on where they stood with Trump. Loyalty to him became the new dividing line and the test of true devotion to God.[309]

It's as if the whole Church had become a branch of the Family Research Council (or some other conservative political organization), with political issues dominating our hearts and minds, as if getting the right candidates in office and standing with President Trump had become our central calling. So rather than simply supporting these fine Christian organizations that were called by God to lobby in Congress and to educate us, we became their hands and feet and ears and mouth. Political issues, more than worship, more than evangelism, more than service, became our primary focus. And the more our country came under attack from within, the more patriotic we became, recognizing that our most fundamental freedoms were being threatened. What would the future hold for our kids and grandkids? In what kind of world would they raise their own children?

We felt certain that, if we didn't act now, America as we knew it would no longer exist, and there was only one way to stop our country's collapse. We needed four more years of Donald Trump together with a Republican Congress, and so we focused our prayers and efforts on the elections more than on revival or awakening or effective evangelism. (In some cases, we actually believed that Trump's reelection was the key to spiritual awakening.)

In our view, America was still the planet's best hope, the only superpower able to stand up to international tyrants. But our beloved homeland was suffering existential threats, which meant the fate of the entire world was at stake. How could we sit by on the sidelines and remain passive? How could we *not* focus on these critical political issues? Wasn't this the very reason we were in such a mess today, namely our lack of political involvement in the past and our failure to be true patriots?

Certainly, there is much truth in all of this, which explains why so many of us got so caught up in the outcome of the elections. The problem, once again, was one of emphasis, of putting too much stress on politics and patriotism and too little stress on the gospel and the kingdom of God, leading to wrong priorities and putting us on a dangerous trajectory. Added to this were all the prophetic words and visions and dreams and proclamations mixed with our distrust of the secular media and our increasing embrace of conspiracy theories, and before we knew it, we were grossly out of balance. Some of us even lost touch with reality, embracing the most bizarre and impossible theories, while others lost their moral compass. Carnality was justified (I mean our carnality). Preachers bashed Biden more loudly than they preached the cross. Insulting, crass memes were shared widely and enthusiastically (after all, the Democrats are baby killers). Meanness was considered more spiritual than meekness.

Speaking of preachers, in the eyes of many, the nastier you were the more anointed you were, and a sermon was not complete without some kind of pro-Trump, even pro-gun remark. "No one is going to shut me up. No one is going to take my guns. And no one is going to make me acknowledge crazy old Joe Biden as our president. In Jesus' name!" And the people shouted, "Amen!"

To be honest, as much as many of the critics of Trump evangelicals greatly overstated their cases, painting caricatured pictures and demonizing many fine people in the process—as I have often pointed out in these pages—the fact is they did not create their criticisms out of thin air. There is some truth to many of their concerns, and in some cases we *have* resembled the ugly caricatures that have been painted. It's hard not to wince when watching some online preaching posts that have gone viral. This is how we represent Jesus the Lord?

Unfortunately, there has been a real failure among Christian leaders to take responsibility for leading believers astray, and I'm not just talking about those who prophesied falsely, only to make ridiculous spiritual excuses or to claim that their words really did come to pass or to sweep things under the rug as if nothing happened at all. I'm talking about those leaders who worked their followers into a pro-Trump frenzy, even speaking of him as uniquely anointed to lead the nation like no other man and virtually cursing those who opposed him, only to return to normal ministry without acknowledging what they had done. This too is grievous.

There were also those who engaged in what I call bait and switch leadership. First, they were praying for Trump to win the elections. This, they told us, was essential for America's future. Then, when he apparently lost, they called us to pray for the fraud to be exposed, assuring us that the elections were stolen and that Trump would soon be reinstated, even focusing on key cities and telling us what would happen within specific time frames. The breakthrough is at hand, we were assured again and again. Then, when none of this happened, the prayers shifted to national awakening (where it should have been the whole time), without the slightest hint that their focus had been off and their assurances misguided.

One day we were praying for the elections and the next day we were praying for awakening, as if we had always been praying for awakening. This, too, is irresponsible. God's people need honest confessions from their leaders. The sheep deserve better from their shepherds. The Lord Himself certainly calls for it.

We live in very treacherous times, and it's all too easy for any of us to lose our bearings in the midst of all the turmoil. America certainly does hang in the balance, and the elections are quite important. But they are not as important as the gospel and Christian living, and for the sake of our nation— more importantly, for the sake of our souls—we must put our emphasis in the right place, reset our priorities, and straighten out our trajectory.

Perhaps the Worst of All

On October 1, 2021, a close friend of mine, Pastor David Harwood, sent an email to me and a few other colleagues that began:

> Here's a brief section of Scripture I believe the Holy Spirit made relevant to me.
>
> Then Jacob said to Simeon and Levi, "You have brought trouble on me by making me odious among the inhabitants of the land, among the Canaanites and the Perizzites; and my men being few in number, they will gather together against me and attack me and I will be destroyed, I and my household."
> But they said, "Should he treat our sister as a harlot?" (Genesis 34:30–31 NASB)

The word translated *odious* literally means a foul smell. I don't know why, but to me *odious* sounds a bit more dignified than *putrid*, or *smelly*. Jacob complained that the actions of his sons had made his reputation *stink*. After all, Jacob was the head of the household, and the entire family was now painted with the same brush.

Levi and Simeon refused to hear their father's rebuke. They justified themselves according to their understanding of honor.

I recently read this passage and thought it might be possible that, like Jacob with his sons, the Lord Jesus might have a reproof and a grievance against the church in our nation. Due to the fact that we are known for our angry demeanor and arrogant divisiveness amongst ourselves, due to our abusive and antagonistic political speech, due to the prevalence of our enthusiastically imbibing poorly researched conspiracy theories, due to how some of our well-known leaders have conducted themselves, due to publicly pronounced false prophecies (I could go on!), the most holy name of Jesus has fallen into great disrepute. We have made the Gospel, already offensive to the lost, less attractive. We "have given occasion to the enemies of the LORD to blaspheme (2 Samuel 12:14 NASB)."

As Simeon and Levi justified their actions, many of us justify our words, attitudes, and actions. But they were wrong and so are we.[310]

I believe Pastor Harwood was absolutely right. We have brought reproach on the name of the Lord. We have made Jesus look bad before a watching world. We have sullied our witness and hurt our reputation. We have become angry and ugly and carnal, behaving in the most unbecoming ways, and we have justified it as something holy, as if we were simply fulfilling our Christian duty. We were not. We became fleshly. We put too much trust in a man and leaned too heavily on the political system. We became as muddy as the DC swamp. And rather than elevate others, we were dragged down.

Jesus said that the world would know that we were His disciples by the love we had for each other. Tragically, we turned that saying upside down to the point that I wrote an article February 17, 2021, titled "And They Will Know We Are Christians by Our Hate."[311] May we never repeat this cycle again!

Ironically, in August 2020, some of the very Christian leaders who strongly criticized those of us who voted for Trump turned around and endorsed Joe Biden for president, looking to him to help "restore the soul of the nation" and to bring "moral leadership" and "moral clarity."[312] Looking back now, their endorsement rings more than hollow. In fact, it looks downright embarrassing. When will we learn?

During the 2016 Republican primaries, when I strongly opposed candidate Donald Trump, I wrote this in an open letter to Jerry Falwell after he enthusiastically endorsed Trump for president:

> [I]f we put the kingdom of God first (by which, of course, I do not mean trying to impose a theocracy but rather putting biblical values first), we can also rebuild the economy, address the immigration issue, and strengthen our national defense.
>
> But if we put nationalism first, the most pressing issues will be relegated to second place, and it will be a distant second place at that. And like Israel of old, we will look for a king to make us great rather than looking to the Lord.[313]

Yet look to a king we did, as if this one man could change the nation. Instead, for all the good he did, for which I am grateful and because of which I ultimately voted for him in 2016 and 2020, he did a lot of damage as well. And nowhere was that damage felt more acutely than within the Church itself, even though, to this moment, many still don't see it. In fact, the further away we get from 2020, the easier it is to forget just how frenzied we became, how fleshly, how divided, how nasty, how politicized, how worldly.

That's why in the second chapter I wrote of the Church's transcendent calling, as I wanted to remind us of that spiritual reality early in this book. It is absolutely imperative that we recover that sacred calling and, in doing so, reclaim our holy identity. As John wrote, "In this world we are like Jesus" (1 John 4:17 NIV), meaning that, while He sits enthroned in heaven, we are His representatives here on earth, as if to say, "If you want to know what Jesus is like, watch us." Even writing those words today stings.

Some will respond, "Well, Jesus overthrew the tables of the money changers and told His disciples to buy some swords. That's the Jesus I know. He also called the religious hypocrites snakes and vipers. I will follow His lead."

To that I say, first, nowhere in the New Testament are we told to follow His example of physically overturning the money tables of corrupt merchants in the Temple. Second, Jesus was not calling for a violent uprising.[314] It was this same Jesus, when talking about buying swords said, "Put your sword back in its place, for all who draw the sword will die by the sword" (Matthew 26:52 NIV). Third, whenever the New Testament tells us to follow the example of Jesus, it gives us directives like these:

> To this you were called, because Christ suffered for you, leaving you an example, that you should follow in his steps. "He committed no sin, and no deceit was found in his mouth." When they hurled their insults at him, he did not retaliate; when he suffered, he made no threats. Instead, he entrusted himself to him who judges justly. (1 Peter 2:21-23 NIV)

When it comes to our behavior and our attitude, this is how we are to live. As Paul wrote to the believers in Philippi, "Do everything without grumbling or arguing, so that you may become blameless and pure, 'children of God without fault in a warped and crooked generation.' Then you will shine among them like stars in the sky as you hold firmly to the word of life" (Philippians 2:14-16 NIV).

So let's all take a deep breath and ask the Lord (and ourselves) some honest questions: How did we fare with Donald Trump and the elections? How have we done from 2016 until today? Are we better known for our devotion to

Jesus or for our political affiliation? Have we set the cross infinitely higher than the flag? Do we look more like our Lord or like our political leaders? Are we living our lives here as sojourners and alien residents? Put another way, are we living our lives in the light of eternity, then bringing those eternal realities to bear in this world? Are we more passionate about the Bible than we are about party platforms?

On September 30, 2021, former Vice President Mike Pence said, "This is the greatest nation on earth, and I think it has fallen to us as conservatives and Republicans to defend and advance the freedom that's made this the greatest nation the world has ever known."[315] In many ways, he may be right. But we would be very wrong to think that America's freedoms will be advanced primarily through political means. Instead, while we should vote and stay involved politically, we must get our own houses in order; we must put first things first and make the main thing the main thing; and we must do what we are called to do, namely function as the salt of the earth and the light of the world. *And most of that will be done outside of politics.*

Make a List

I encourage you to ask yourself this question: If the Lord Himself tasked you and me with the assignment of bringing positive, lasting change to America, drawing up a strategic list of seven priorities for us as followers of Jesus, what would be on your list? As I answer this question for myself, thinking of the body of Christ in America, my list would look something like this, in order of priorities:

1) Personal and corporate repentance and turning to God for spiritual renewal.
2) Prayer and fasting.

3) Evangelism and church planting, with an emphasis on making solid disciples.
4) Getting our families healthy and strong, pouring into our spouses and kids.
5) Serving the hurting and the poor and the most vulnerable in our communities.
6) Positioning ourselves more deeply in the major sectors of society, from education to business and from media to entertainment, demonstrating how God's ways work best.
7) Staying politically involved by being informed, by voting, and by supporting those called to frontline political activity.

Your list might look a little different, and, depending on my own frame of mind, my own list might look slightly different at other times as well. But my hope is that by thinking of the Church on a national level, you would agree with me that political involvement should be toward the bottom of the list rather than toward the top, with the exception of those specially called to make that a priority.

God has given us wonderful, world-changing spiritual weapons and strategies, and to the extent that we implement those, we will see great and lasting victories. Nothing can stop the gospel! And to the extent that Jesus is our all in all and that knowing Him and making Him known remains the central focus of our lives, we will never be seduced again. We might even be surprised to see the amazing things our God will do. In fact, as we get recover our spiritual health and vitality, there is no telling what the Lord will do through us.

In the words of Charles Spurgeon, speaking with reference to the work of the British political leader William Wilberforce (1759–1833), who was responsible for abolishing the slave trade and then slavery itself in Great Britain and her colonies, "A healthy church kills error, and tears in pieces evil." Yes,

Spurgeon recalled, "Not so very long ago our nation tolerated slavery in our colonies. Philanthropists endeavored to destroy slavery; but when was it utterly abolished?" This was his answer:

It was when Wilberforce roused the church of God, and when the church of God addressed herself to the conflict, then she tore the evil thing to pieces. I have been amused with what Wilberforce said the day after they passed the Act of Emancipation. He merrily said to a friend when it was all done: "Is there not something else we can abolish?" That was said playfully, but it shows the spirit of the church of God. She lives in conflict and victory; her mission is to destroy everything that is bad in the land.[316]

As expressed by missionary pioneer Hudson Taylor (1832–1905), "We are a supernatural people; born again by a supernatural birth; we wage a supernatural fight and are taught by a supernatural teacher; led by a supernatural captain to assured victory." This is truth!

Let us, then, take our place here on earth as the Lord's priestly people, as ambassadors for the Lord Jesus, as citizens of heaven, as a Spirit-empowered community, as proclaimers of the living Word of the living God, as men and women driven and moved by sacrificial love. To the extent that this is who we are and this is how we live, we will bring about radical, dramatic, lasting change, for the glory and honor of our King. Are you with me?

Endnotes

[1] Peter Smith and Deepa Bharath, "Christian nationalism on the rise in some GOP campaigns," AP News, May 29, 2022, https://apnews.com/article/2022-midterm-elections-pennsylvania-religion-nationalism-8bf7a6115725f508a 37ef944333bc145.

[2] Elizabeth Dias and Ruth Graham, "The Growing Religious Fervor in the American Right," *The New York Times*, April 6, 2022, https://www.nytimes.com/2022/04/06/us/christian-right-wing-politics.html.

[3] John Fea, "Is there a difference between an evangelical worship service and a right-wing political rally?" Current, April 7, 2022, https://currentpub.com/2022/04/07/is-there-a-difference-between-an-evangelical-worship-service-and-a-right-wing-political-rally/.

[4] https://twitter.com/hemantmehta/status/1526048899810615301 (for the record, I have been attacked numerous times by this same "friendly atheist").

[5] Michael Brown, "When a Misguided Pastor Makes Threats About a Violent 'Christian' Insurrection," *The Stream*, May 19, 2022, https://stream.org/when-a-misguided-pastor-makes-threats-about-a-violent-christian-insurrection/.

[6] https://www.facebook.com/ASKDrBrown/posts/8236654256360104.

[7] For the broadcast with this pastor, see https://youtu.be/miX-vfYsKto.

[8] Brian Naylor, "Read Trump's Jan. 6 Speech, A Key Part Of Impeachment Trial," NPR, February 10, 2021, https://www.npr.org/2021/02/10/966396848/read-trumps-jan-6-speech-a-key-part-of-impeachment-trial.

[9] Tyler Olson, "Cops blame Trump, Republicans for allegedly inspiring and then downplaying Jan. 6 Capitol attack" Fox News, July 27, 2021, https://www.foxnews.com/politics/jan-6-commission-hearing-cops-trump-republicans-capitol-attack.

[10] Sarah Posner, "How the Christian Right Helped Foment Insurrection," *Rolling Stone*, January 31, 2021, https://www.rollingstone.com/culture/culture-features/capitol-christian-right-trump-1121236/.

[11] Emma Green, "A Christian Insurrection," *The Atlantic*, January 8, 2021, https://www.theatlantic.com/politics/archive/2021/01/evangelicals-catholics-jericho-march-capitol/617591/.

[12] Matthew Avery Sutton, "The Capitol Riot Revealed the Darkest Nightmares of White Evangelical America," *The New Republic*, January 14, 2021, https://newrepublic.com/article/160922/capitol-riot-revealed-darkest-nightmares-white-evangelical-america.

[13] Elizabeth Dias and Ruth Graham, "How White Evangelical Christians Fused With Trump Extremism," *The New York Times*, January 11, 2021, https://www.nytimes.com/2021/01/11/us/how-white-evangelical-christians-fused-with-trump-extremism.html.

[14] David French, "Only the Church Can Truly Defeat a Christian Insurrection," *The Dispatch*, January 10, 2021, https://frenchpress.thedispatch.com/p/only-the-church-can-truly-defeat; the December 13, 2020 article he referenced was David French, "The Dangerous Idolatry of Christian Trumpism," *The Dispatch*, December 13, 2020, https://frenchpress.thedispatch.com/p/the-dangerous-idolatry-of-christian. See also Bob Smietana, "Jericho March Returns to DC to Pray for a Trump Miracle," *Christianity Today*, January 5, 2021, https://www.christianitytoday.com/news/2021/january/jericho-march-dc-election-overturn-trump-biden-congress.html.

[15] Rachel Martin, "'How Did We Get Here?' A Call For An Evangelical Reckoning On Trump," NPR, January 13, 2021, https://www.npr.org/sections/insurrection-at-the-capitol/2021/01/13/955801878/how-did-we-get-here-a-call-for-an-evangelical-reckoning-on-trump.

[16] For a historical critique, see Anthea Butler, *White Evangelical Racism: The Politics of Morality in America* (Chapel Hill, NC: The University of North Carolina Press, 2021).

[17] Rob Dreher, "What I Saw At The Jericho March," *The American Conservative*, December 12, 2020, https://www.theamericanconservative.com/dreher/what-i-saw-at-the-jericho-march/.

[18] Joshua Feuerstein at the "Stop the Steal" rally, January 5, 2021, https://vimeo.com/505819544?embedded=true&source=vimeo_logo&owner=5657100.

[19] Michael Brown, "No! It Was Not Jesus-Loving Evangelicals Who Vandalized the Capitol," *The Stream*, January 14, 2021, https://stream.org/no-it-was-not-jesus-loving-evangelicals-who-vandalized-the-capitol/.

[20] Jack Jenkins, "More than 1,400 evangelicals, other faith leaders condemn religion at insurrection as 'heretical'," *The Washington Post*, February 26, 2021, https://www.washingtonpost.com/religion/evangelicals-condemn-attack-on-capitol-jan-6/2021/02/26/c0d8a26e-779b-11eb-948d-19472e683521_story.html

[21] For a typical statement from a colleague of mine, see here: Jeremy Finley, "Governor Lee's pastor apologizes for his account of DC riots," News 4 Nashville, January 7, 2021, https://www.wsmv.com/news/governor-lees-pastor-apologizes-for-his-account-of-dc-riots/article_24a3a080-5156-11eb-9f75-371cdbbda8bd.html.

[22] Michael Brown, Twitter Post, January 12, 2021, https://twitter.com/DrMichaelLBrown/status/1349199343367159814.

[23] Craig Timberg, Drew Harwell, and Marissa J. Lang, "Capitol siege was planned online. Trump supporters now planning the next one," *The Washington Post*, January 9, 2021, https://www.washingtonpost.com/technology/2021/01/09/trump-twitter-protests/

[24] Tucker Carlson, "Tucker Carlson: Media will never admit there was no insurrection," Fox News, September 24, 2021, https://www.foxnews.com/opinion/tucker-carlson-media-insurrection.

[25] MindShift Podcast, Twitter Post, January 8, 2021, https://twitter.com/MindShift2018/status/1347580234216988675.

[26] Michelle Boorstein, "A horn-wearing 'shaman.' A cowboy evangelist. For some, the Capitol attack was a kind of Christian revolt," *The Washington Post*, July 6, 2021 https://www.washingtonpost.com/religion/2021/07/06/capitol-insurrection-trump-christian-nationalism-shaman/.

[27] Steve Rabey, "Additional Church Leaders Arrested in Relation to January 6 Attack on U.S. Capitol," Ministry Watch, July 9, 2021, https://ministrywatch.com/additional-church-leaders-arrested-in-relation-to-january-6-attack-on-u-s-capitol/.

[28] Michael T. Flynn, "On the Occasion of the Jericho March," UncoverDC, December 10, 2020, https://uncoverdc.com/2020/12/10/on-the-occasion-of-the-jericho-march/.

[29] Francis Schaeffer, *Christian Manifesto* (Wheaton, Ill., Crossway Books, 1981), 121. He had issued this warning in a number of his other writings as well.

[30] Reed Richardson, "Trump Campaign Lawyer Joe diGenova Says Fmr DHS Official Chris Krebs Should Be 'Taken Out at Dawn and Shot'," Mediaite, November 30th, 2020, https://www.mediaite.com/election-2020/trump-campaign-lawyer-joe-digenova-says-fmr-dhs-official-chris-krebs-should-be-taken-out-at-dawn-and-shot/.

[31] "Joint Statement From Elections Infrastructure Government Coordinating Council & The Election Infrastructure Sector Coordinating Executive Committees," Cybersecurity & Infrastructure Security Agency, November 12, 2020, https://www.cisa.gov/news/2020/11/12/joint-statement-elections-infrastructure-government-coordinating-council-election.

[32] Alana Wise, "Trump Fires Election Security Director Who Corrected Voter Fraud Disinformation," NPR, November 17, 2020, https://www.npr.org/2020/11/17/936003057/cisa-director-chris-krebs-fired-after-trying-to-correct-voter-fraud-disinformati.

[33] AskDrBrown, Facebook Post, November 30, 2020, https://www.facebook.com/AskDrBrown/posts/5431749626850595.

[34] Dr. Michael L. Brown, Twitter Post, November 30, 2020, https://twitter.com/DrMichaelLBrown/status/1333618588427689985.

[35] AskDrBrown, Facebook Video, November 30, 2020, https://www.facebook.com/AskDrBrown/videos/382311162979932. For the related article, see Michael Brown, "Have We Completely Lost Our Minds and Our Souls?" *The Stream*, December 1, 2020, https://stream.org/have-we-completely-lost-our-minds-and-our-souls/.

[36] Gerald R. Sittser, *Resilient Faith: How the Early Christian "Third Way" Changed the World* (Grand Rapids, MI: Brazos Press, 2019), 4.

[37] Alexandr Solzhenitsyn, "A World Split Apart," June 8, 1978, Harvard University, Cambridge, MA. Available online at "Alexandr Solzhenitsyn: A World Split Apart, American Rhetoric, https://www.americanrhetoric.com/speeches/alexandersolzhenitsynharvard.htm.

[38] Kristin Kobes Du Mez, *Jesus and John Wayne: How White Evangelicals Corrupted a Faith and Fractured a Nation* (New York, NY: Liveright Publishing Corporation, 2020), 3.

[39] Du Mez, *Jesus and John Wayne*, 3.

[40] Du Mez, *Jesus and John Wayne*, 6-7.

[41] Angela Denker, *Red State Christians: Understanding the Voters Who Elected Donald Trump* (Minneapolis, MN: Fortress Press, 2019), 8-9. Note that Denker seeks to be fair in her assessment, writing, "In addition to the many wise, kind, and genuine Red State Christians I met across America, others were committed to division, destruction, and perversion of the story of Jesus to support their own wealth and power. Most of these people were pastors, and most of the divisive and damaging rhetoric I heard from Christians across America came either from manipulative pastors or from partisan media" (4).

[42] Mike Huckabee, *God, Guns, Grits, and Gravy* (New York, NY: St. Martin's Press, 2014); idem and Steve Feazel, *The Three Cs That Made America Great: Christianity, Capitalism, and the Constitution* (Tustin, CA: Trilogy Christian Publishing, 2020).

[43] For more on this, see Michael L. Brown, *The Silencing of the Lambs: The Ominous Rise of Cancel Culture and How We Can Overcome It* (Lake Mary, FL: Frontline, 2022).

[44] Lindsay Kornick, "CNN's Brian Stelter compares Donald Trump supporters to Jonestown cult members," Fox News, August 1, 2021, https://www.foxnews.com/media/cnn-brian-stelter-compares-trump-supporters-jonestown-cult.

[45] Joshua Klein, "Outrage over George W. Bush 9/11 Speech Attacking American 'Extremists'—'Americans Are the New Terrorists'," Breitbart, September 12, 2021, https://www.breitbart.com/politics/2021/09/12/outrage-george-w-bush-9-11-speech-attacking-american-extremists-americans-new-terrorists/.

[46] Joe Kent, Twitter Post, September 11, 2021, https://twitter.com/joekent16jan19/status/1436752311305465861?ref_src=twsrc%5Etf-w%7Ctwcamp%5Etweetembed%7Ctwterm%5E1436752311305465861%7Ctwgr%5E%7Ctwcon%5Es1_&ref_url=https%3A%2F%2Fwww.breitbart.com%2Fpolitics%2F2021%2F09%2F12%2Foutrage-george-w-bush-9-11-spe ech-attacking-american-extremists-americans-new-terrorists%2F.

[47] Jack Posobiec, Twitter Post, September 11, 2021, https://twitter.com/JackPosobiec/status/1436718256245678084?ref_src=twsrc%5Etf-w%7Ctwcamp%5Etweetembed%7Ctwterm%5E1436718256245678084%7Ctwgr%5E%7Ctwcon%5Es1_&ref_url=https%3A%2F%2Fwww.breitbart.com%2Fpolitics%2F2021%2F09%2F12%2Foutrage-george-w-bush-9-11-speech-attacking-american-extremists-americans-new-terrorists%2F.

[48] Gianno Caldwell, "Why the supposedly racist Trump grew his numbers with black and Latino voters," *New York Post*, November 7, 2020, https://nypost.com/2020/11/07/why-trump-grew-his-numbers-with-black-and-latino-voters/.

[49] Michael L. Brown, "The Case Against Trump and Why He Still Gets My Vote," AskDrBrown Ministries, November 2, 2020, https://askdrbrown.org/library/case-against-trump-and-why-he-still-gets-my-vote.

[50] Michael Brown, "Once Again, Why So Many Evangelical Christians Strongly Support Trump," *The Stream*, October 5, 2020, https://stream.org/once-again-why-so-many-evangelical-christians-strongly-support-trump/.

[51] "Resolution On Moral Character Of Public Officials," Salt Lake City, Utah, 1998. Southern Baptist Convention, https://www.sbc.net/resource-library/resolutions/resolution-on-moral-character-of-public-officials/. See further *Evangelicals at the Crossroads*.

[52] Foreword to Rodney Wallace Kennedy, *The Immaculate Mistake: How Evangelicals Gave Birth to Donald Trump* (Eugene, OR: Cascade Books, 2021), ix.

[53] Cited by John Fea, "What James Dobson Said in 1998 About Moral Character and the Presidency," *Current*, June 25, 2016, https://currentpub.com/2016/06/25/james-dobson-on-the-character-of-the-president-of-the-united-states/.

[54] David French, "How Do Christian Patriots Love Their Country Well?" *The Dispatch*, July 4, 2021, https://frenchpress.thedispatch.com/p/how-do-christian-patriots-love-their.

[55] Obery M. Hendricks, *Christians Against Christianity: How Right-Wing Evangelicals Are Destroying Our Nation and Our Faith* (Boston, MA: Beacon Press, 2021), xi-xii.

[56] Hendricks, *Christians Against Christianity*, 117.

[57] Karl Zinsmeister, "Less God, Less Giving? Religion and generosity feed each other in fascinating ways," *Philanthropy Roundtable*, Winter 2019, https://www.philanthropyroundtable.org/philanthropy-magazine/less-god-less-giving.

[58] See, e.g., Sarah Eekhoff Zylstra, "How Foster Care Became a Christian Priority—Just in Time," The Gospel Coalition, September 24, 2018, https://www.thegospelcoalition.org/article/how-foster-care-became-christian-priority-just-time/ and Bob Smietana, "How Protestant Churches Are Involved with Adoption and Foster Care," *Christianity Today*, January 24, 2018, https://www.christianitytoday.com/news/2018/january/how-protestant-churches-involved-adoption-foster-care.html; Evangelicals have become so active in adopting children that they are now being criticized for it! See Kathryn Joyce, "Orphan Fever: The Evangelical Movement's Adoption Obsession," May/June 2013, Mother Jones, https://www.motherjones.com/politics/2013/04/christian-evangelical-adoption-liberia/.

[59] Hendricks, *Christians Against Christianity*, 103.

[60] See "Who Gives Most to Charity?" *Philanthropy Roundtable*, https://www.philanthropyroundtable.org/almanac/statistics/who-gives; Karl Zinsmeister, "Less God, Less Giving? Religion and generosity feed each other in fascinating ways," *Philanthropy Roundtable*, Winter 2019, https://www.philanthropyroundtable.org/philanthropy-magazine/less-god-less-giving.

[61] Hendricks, *Christians Against Christianity*, 25-26.

[62] In the aftermath of surprising victory of the Republican gubernatorial candidate Glenn Youngkin in Virginia in November 2021, the reactions from many pundits on the left were the same: this is another manifestation of white nationalism and racism. See, for example, The Editorial Board, "The Big 'Racist' Fail in Virginia," *The Wall Street Journal*, November 3, 2021, https://www.wsj.com/articles/virginia-governor-election-glenn-youngkin-race-11635979212. See also this tweet from sports journalist Jemele Hill, with 1.4 million followers on Twitter: "It's not the messaging, folks. This country simply loves white supremacy"; https://twitter.com/jemelehill/status/1455766504650067971.

[63] Hendricks, *Christians Against Christianity*, 76.

[64] Hendricks, *Christians Against Christianity*, 77, his emphasis.

[65] Craig Borlase, *God's Hostage: A True Story of Persecution, Imprisonment, and Perseverance* (Grand Rapids, MI: Baker, 2019), 172.

[66] Borlase, *God's Hostage*, 196.

[67] Borlase, *God's Hostage*, 211.

[68] Borlase, *God's Hostage*, 231.

[69] Borlase, *God's Hostage,* 110.

[70] These are not exact quotes but accurately represent the substance of the interaction.

[71] In my anti-Trump days, during the 2016 primaries, I actually warned my fellow evangelicals not to look to Trump as our protector and defender. See Michael Brown, "Donald Trump is Not Your Protector: A Warning to Conservative Christians," *The Stream*, April 22, 2016, https://stream.org/donald-trump-not-protector-warning-conservative-christians/. I was one of those who was pleasantly surprised when he kept his promises.

[72] Steven Mosher, "Repeal the Christian Gag Rule: Johnson Amendment Allows Continued IRS Targeting," Breitbart, August 18, 2016, https://www.breitbart.com/politics/2016/08/18/donald-trump-addresses-values-voters-irs-christians/.

[73] Charles Spiering, "Trump Celebrates America's Faith-Based Foundation, Vows to Defend Religious Values," Breitbart, February 2, 2017, https://www.breitbart.com/politics/2017/02/02/trump-celebrates-americas-faith-based-foundation-vows-defend-religious-values/.

[74] David S. Miller and Yomarie S. Habenicht, "President Trump Signs "Johnson Amendment" Executive Order Limiting Treasury's Actions Against Religious Organizations Engaged in Political Campaign Activities," *The National Law Review*, May 10, 2017, https://www.natlawreview.com/article/president-trump-signs-johnson-amendment-executive-order-limiting-treasury-s-actions; emphasis in the original.

[75] Penny Starr, "Exclusive—Tony Perkins: Trump's Commitment to Religious Liberty is Most Important Promise He's Kept," Breitbart, October 14, 2017, https://www.breitbart.com/politics/2017/10/14/exclusive-tony-perkins-trumps-commitment-to-religious-liberty-is-most-important-promise-hes-kept/.

[76] Adiel Kaplan, David Mora, Maya Miller and Andrew R. Calderon, "Trump admin files more briefs in religious liberty cases than Obama, Bush," NBC News,

February 24, 2019, https://www.nbcnews.com/politics/justice-department/trump-admin-files-more-briefs-religious-liberty-cases-obama-bush-n974531.

[77] Marc A. Thiessen, "Trump might be the most pro-religion president ever," *Des Moines Register*, March 29, 2018, https://www.desmoinesregister.com/story/opinion/columnists/2018/03/29/trump-pro-religion-president-christian-conservatives/470261002/.

[78] Thiessen, "Trump might be the most pro-religion president ever."

[79] Thiessen, "Trump might be the most pro-religion president ever."

[80] Jeffery C. Mays, "New York City Is Ending a Ban on Gay Conversion Therapy. Here's Why," *The New York Times*, September 12, 2019, https://www.nytimes.com/2019/09/12/nyregion/conversion-therapy-ban-nyc.html.

[81] Mays, "New York City Is Ending a Ban on Gay Conversion Therapy."

[82] "Trump says he moved US embassy to Jerusalem 'for the evangelicals'," *The Times of Israel*, August 18, 2020, https://www.timesofisrael.com/trump-says-he-moved-us-embassy-to-jerusalem-for-the-evangelicals/.

[83] David Rubin, *Confronting Radicals: What America Can Learn From Israel* (Shiloh, Israel: Shiloh Israel Press, 2021), 32–34.

[84] "Trump to Kim: My nuclear button is 'bigger and more powerful'," BBC News, January 3, 2018, https://www.bbc.com/news/world-asia-42549687.

[85] Rich Kiper, "Rich Kiper: We're coming for your guns," *Leavenworth Times*, July 16, 2020, https://ourgunfreedoms.com/rich-kiper-were-coming-for-your-guns/.

[86] Private communication, printed with permission.

[87] At Trump's major rally in Iowa in October 2021, one which further fueled speculation that he would run in 2024, while frequently praising his Republican Party and criticizing the Democrats, he also called on Republicans in Congress to stand strong, noting, "they just don't seem to have the spine, some of them." See "Donald Trump Des Moines, Iowa, Rally Speech Transcript, October 9," Rev.com, October 9, 2021, https://www.rev.com/blog/transcripts/donald-trump-des-moines-iowa-rally-speech-transcript-october-9.

[88] Jennifer Slattery, "10 Common Idols in Our Lives and How to Resist Them," Bible Study Tools, December 4, 2019, https://www.biblestudytools.com/bible-study/topical-studies/idols-that-sneak-into-our-lives-and-how-to-resist-them.html.

[89] Shneur Zalman of Liadi as quoted in Paul Steinberg, *Spiritual Growth: A Contemporary Jewish Approach*, (Santa Fe: Terra Nova Books, 2018), 32–33.

[90] Michael Brown, "Christian Friends, Remember: There is Only One Messiah," *The Stream*, November 29, 2020, https://stream.org/christian-friends-remember-there-is-only-one-messiah/.

[91] See, e.g., Michael Brown, "This is What Idolatry Looks Like," *The Stream*, March 1, 2021, https://stream.org/this-is-what-idolatry-looks-like/.

[92] Bliss Zechman, "Pastor criticizes now-removed Fort Oglethorpe billboard comparing Trump to Jesus," ABC 13 News, September 23, 2021, https://wset.com/news/nation-world/pastor-criticizes-now-removed-fort-oglethorpe-billboard-comparing-trump-to-jesus-09-23-2021; see also

Bill Bond, Twitter Post, September 10, 2021, https://twitter.com/wcbj/status/1436473573833650181.

[93] Michael Brown, "Christian Friends, Remember: There is Only One Messiah," *The Stream*, November 29, 2021, https://stream.org/christian-friends-remember-there-is-only-one-messiah/.

[94] Stanley Hauerwas, "Christians Don't Be Fooled: Trump Has Deep Religious Convictions," *Washington Post*, January 27, 2017, https://www.washing-tonpost.com/news/acts-of-faith/wp/2017/01/27/christians-dont-be-fooled-trump-has-deep-religious-convictions/.

[95] Alex Pfeiffer, "Ann Coulter Is Worried The 'Trump-Haters Were Right'," *Daily Caller*, May 14, 2017, http://dailycaller.com/2017/05/14/ann-coulter-is-worried-the-trump-haters-were-right/.

[96] Lindsey Ellefson, "Ann Coulter Doubles Down on Trump Criticism: 'Jackass President Being a Big Baby'," *The Wrap*, Mary 26, 2020, https://www.thewrap.com/ann-coulter-doubles-down-on-trump-criticism-jackass-president-being-a-big-baby/.

[97] Rosemary Rossi, "Ann Coulter Turns on 'Disloyal Actual Retard' Trump in Twitter Rant," *The Wrap*, May 24, 2020, https://www.thewrap.com/ann-coulter-turns-on-disloyal-actual-retard-trump-in-twitter-rant/.

[98] AskDrBrown, Facebook Post, February 28, 2021, https://www.facebook.com/ASKDrBrown/posts/5843546125670941 and Dr. Michael L. Brown, Twitter Post, February 28, 2021, https://twitter.com/DrMichaelLBrown/status/1366156173448200192.

[99] Check out this call to my radio show for a good example. ASKDrBrown, "Should We Pray Imprecatory Psalms On Our Political Opponents?" YouTube, March 3, 2021, https://youtu.be/nM2Q00D73oI.

[100] Johnny + Elizabeth Enlow, Facebook post, April 30, 2021, https://www.face-book.com/Restore7/posts/3163745300558955.

[101] More broadly, see Mollie Hemingway, *Rigged: How the Media, Big Tech, and the Democrats Seized Our Elections* (Washington, DC: Regnery Press, 2021).

[102] Michael Brown, "With Full Appreciation for the Good Trump Did, He is Not Being Reinstated on August 13," *The Stream*, August 10, 2021, https://stream.org/with-full-appreciation-for-the-good-trump-did-he-is-not-being-reinstated-on-august-13/; idem, "Newsflash: Trump Will Not Be Reinstated to the Presidency This Year," *The Stream*, June 30, 2021, https://stream.org/newsflash-trump-will-not-be-reinstated-to-the-presidency-this-year/.

[103] I took screenshots of some of these predictions, including the announcement that Trump was about to be reinstated in September.

[104] See https://propheticstandards.com/; along with Dr. Joe Mattera, I helped organize the leaders who put this statement together.

[105] Johnny + Elizabeth Enlow, Facebook post, April 30, 2021, https://www.face-book.com/Restore7/posts/3163745300558955.

[106] Johnny + Elizabeth Enlow, Facebook post, April 30, 2021.

[107]See 1 Corinthians 14:29; 1 Thessalonians 5:19–22; more broadly, see Matthew 7:15–20.

[108]Lake Mary, FL: Charisma House, 2018.

[109]See, e.g., Michael L. Brown, *Whatever Happened to the Power of God: Is the Charismatic Church Slain in the Spirit of Down for the Count* (Shippensburg, PA: Destiny Image, 1991); idem, *Authentic Fire: A Response to John MacArthur's Strange Fire* (Lake Mary, FL: Creation House, 2015).

[110]Michael Brown, "This is a Great Time to Test Contemporary Prophetic Words," *The Stream*, March 30, 2021, https://stream.org/this-is-a-great-time-to-test-contemporary-prophetic-words/.

[111]Michael Brown, "To My Prophetic Friends: You Were Either Right or You Were Wrong," *The Stream*, December 15, 2020, https://stream.org/to-my-prophetic-friends-you-were-either-right-or-you-were-wrong/.

[112]Michael Brown, "A Strong Appeal to Those Who Prophesied Trump's Reelection," *The Stream*, January 21, 2021, https://stream.org/a-strong-appeal-to-those-who-prophesied-trumps-reelection/.

[113]These comments were all screenshotted from the AskDrBrown Facebook or YouTube pages.

[114]For the large picture, see Julia Duin, "The Christian Prophets Who Say Trump Is Coming Again," *Politico*, February 18, 2021, https://www.politico.com/news/magazine/2021/02/18/how-christian-prophets-give-credence-to-trumps-election-fantasies-469598. Among those who issued threats to those who would speak against the prophets were Kat Kerr and Hank Kunneman. For a response to this, see my video "Don't Let Anyone Threaten You with Prophetic Manipulation," YouTube, January 5, 2021, https://youtu.be/wn7OJ4u2MUE.

[115]Johnny + Elizabeth Enlow, Facebook Post, July 5, 2021, https://www.facebook.com/Restore7/posts/3212593472340804.

[116]See Daniel Villarreal, "Pastor Robin Bullock Says It's a Sin to Recognize Joe Biden as President," *Newsweek*, May 3, 2021, https://www.newsweek.com/pastor-robin-bullock-says-its-sin-recognize-joe-biden-president-1588361; Jenni Fink, "Evangelical 'Prophet' Jeff Jansen Still Sees Trump Returning to Office After April Prediction Fails," *Newsweek*, June 8, 2021, https://www.newsweek.com/evangelical-prophet-jeff-jansen-still-sees-trump-returning-office-after-april-prediction-fails-1598745; The Editorial Board, "Calling out so-called 'prophets' who miscalled Trump's election victory," *Saint Louis Dispatch*, July 24, 2021, https://www.stltoday.com/opinion/editorial/editorial-calling-out-so-called-prophets-who-miscalled-trumps-election-victory/article_3bff4dab-2db9-5b84-b10b-0259f41fb6c4.html; Benjamin Fearnow, "Pastor Greg Locke Says Biden Is 'Demon-Possessed,' Insists Trump Is 'Legitimate President'," *Newsweek*, June 27, 2021, https://www.newsweek.com/pastor-greg-locke-says-biden-demon-possessed-insists-trump-legitimate-president-1604528.

[117]Ruth Graham, "Christian Prophets Are on the Rise. What Happens When They're Wrong?" *The New York Times*, February 11, 2021, https://www.nytimes.com/2021/02/11/us/christian-prophets-predictions.html.

[118]This was the relevant chapter title in his book *The Purpose, Power, and Process of Prophetic Ministry* (Chambersburg, PA: eGenCo, 2021).

[119]Johnny + Elizabeth Enlow, Facebook post, April 30, 2021, https://www.facebook.com/Restore7/posts/3163745300558955.

[120]For the record, contrary to what Enlow wrote, no one who was part of the leadership group mentioned by Enlow ever saw Trump in such exalted terms, even though most all of us voted for him. So, Enlow is quite wrong here as well.

[121]Steve Rabey, "Prophets' Political Words Bring Division, Derision," Ministry Watch, July 27, 2021, https://ministrywatch.com/prophets-political-words-bring-division-derision/. For the record, James Beverley is a good friend of mine, known for his sober-minded and meticulous scholarly research.

[122]For a broader compilation, see Kyle Mantyla, "The Trump Prophecies: A Look Back at Some of the Self-Proclaimed 'Prophets' Who Guaranteed Trump's Second Term," Right Wing Watch, January 20, 2021, https://www.rightwingwatch.org/post/the-trump-prophecies-a-look-back-at-some-of-the-self-proclaimed-prophets-who-guaranteed-trumps-second-term/.

[123]Kyle Mantyla "Hank Kunneman Says Christians Must Continue to Trust the 'Prophets' Who Guaranteed Trump's Reelection," Right Wing Watch, April 2, 2021, https://www.rightwingwatch.org/post/hank-kunneman-says-christians-must-continue-to-trust-the-prophets-who-guaranteed-trumps-reelection/.

[124]I have had the honor of being mentioned more than 100 times on their website, according to their official list, normally related to my stand on LGBTQ issues. For specifics, see "Michael Brown," Right Wing Watch, https://www.rightwingwatch.org/people/michael-brown/.

[125]See Deuteronomy 13:1–5; 18:14–22; Jeremiah 23:9-40; Ezekiel 13:1–23; Matthew 7:15–20.

[126]Steve Rabey, "Prophets' Political Words Bring Division, Derision," Ministry Watch, July 27, 2021, https://ministrywatch.com/prophets-political-words-bring-division-derision/.

[127]For a full list of all the prophecies, see Beverley, *God's Man in the White House.*

[128]Brown, *Playing with Holy Fire*, 117-137.

[129]See Mark Taylor, *The Trump Prophecies: The Astonishing True Story of the Man Who Saw Tomorrow . . . and What He Says Is Coming Next: UPDATED AND EXPANDED* (Crane, MO: Defender, 2019).

[130]I'm speaking here of Bill Hamon, founder of Christian International Ministries, and Cindy Jacobs, co-founder of Generals International, respectively.

[131]See Ron Cantor, "What (I felt) God told me about the Election in September," Messiah's Mandate, November 8, 2020, https://messiahsmandate.org/what-i-felt-god-told-me-about-the-election-in-september/; Michael Brown, "Michael Brown on The Trump Reelection Prophecy That You Never Heard About," *The Stream*, May 2021, https://stream.org/the-trump-reelection-prophecy-that-you-never-heard-about/.

[132] https://www.facebook.com/AskDrBrown/posts/this-was-the-prophetic-word-from-jeremiah-johnson-last-july-regarding-donald-tru/165195425 8163503/

[133] https://livingfaithforum.com/discussing-politics/9374-urgent-message-jeremiah-johnson.html.

[134] James A. Beverley, with Larry N. Willard, *God's Man in the White House: Donald Trump in Modern Christian Prophecy* (Paris, Ontario, Canada; Castle Quay Books, 2020). As for evangelical commentators who supported Trump, Dr. Beverley told me that I was the only he read who also issued warnings and raised concerns about Trump. How could this be?

[135] Jeremiah Johnson, "Jeremiah Johnson: My Public Apology and Process," Charisma News, January 7, 2021, https://www.charismanews.com/opinion/83947-jeremiah-johnson-my-public-apology-and-process.

[136] *Conservative Judaism*, Vol. 33, No. 3, 1980, 25-37.

[137] Michael Brown, *Donald Trump Is Not My Savior: An Evangelical Leader Speaks His Mind About the Man He Supports As President* (Shippensburg, PA: Destiny Image, 2018), 326-327.

[138] See further Mattera, *Purpose, Power, and Process of Prophecy.*

[139] I do not have the original source for this quote; it is found with source not cited in Arthur Wallis, *In the Day of Thy Power* (repr.; Fort Washington, PA: CLC Publications, 2010); see 279, n. 7.

[140] Michael Sebastian and Gabrielle Bruney, "Years After Being Debunked, Interest in Pizzagate Is Rising—Again," *Esquire*, July 24, 2020, https://www.esquire.com/news-politics/news/a51268/what-is-pizzagate/.

[141] James A. Beverley, *The QAnon Deception: Everything You Need to Know about the World's Most Dangerous Conspiracy Theory* (Concord, NC: EqualTime Books, 2020), 30.

[142] James A. Beverley, with Annette Johnson and Rick Anderson, *The QAnon Resource Guide: 2400 Linked News Reports, Articles & Opinion Pieces* (n.p.: James Beverley Resources, 2021).

[143] Mike Wendling, "QAnon: What is it and where did it come from?" BBC News, January 6, 2021, https://www.bbc.com/news/53498434.

[144] Brett Forrest, "What Is QAnon? What We Know About the Conspiracy-Theory Group," *The Wall Street Journal*, February 4, 2021, https://www.wsj.com/articles/what-is-qanon-what-we-know-about-the-conspiracy-theory-11597694801.

[145] Wendling, "QAnon: What is it and where did it come from?"

[146] Justin Vallejo and Phil Thomas, "Why some QAnon believers think JFK Jr is still alive — and about to become vice president," *The Independent*, July 22, 2021, https://www.independent.co.uk/news/world/americas/us-politics/john-f-kennedy-jr-qanon-b1884724.html. On November 2, 2021, Meryl Kornfeld reported that, "At the site overlooking where President John F. Kennedy was assassinated nearly six decades ago, scores of QAnon believers outfitted with "Trump-Kennedy 2024" shirts, flags and other merchandise gathered. They forecast the president's son John F. Kennedy Jr., who has been dead for over 20

years, would appear at that spot, emerging from anonymity to become Donald Trump's vice president when the former president is reinstated. The prophecy foretold online, of course, did not come true." See, "Why hundreds of QAnon supporters showed up in Dallas, expecting JFK Jr.'s return," *The Washington Post*, https://www.washingtonpost.com/nation/2021/11/02/qanon-jfk-jr-dallas/.

[147] Beverley, *QAnon Deception*, 41.

[148] The interview is here: ASKDrBrown, "The Shocking Truth About QAnon," YouTube Video, December 28, 2020, https://youtu.be/b9t_-6M_HfA.

[149] See https://freedomneedstruth.medium.com/freedom-needs-truth-5224c63 2557b.

[150] Beverley, *QAnon Deception*, 39.

[151] Beverley, *QAnon Deception*, 31.

[152] Joseph Menn Elizabeth Culliford, Katie Paul and Carrie Monahan, "'We've been had': Biden inauguration has QAnon followers confused," *National Post*, January 20, 2021, https://nationalpost.com/news/no-plan-no-q-nothing-qanon-followers-reel-as-biden-inaugurated.

[153] Jack Brewster, " 'We All Got Played': QAnon Followers Implode After Big Moment Never Comes," *Forbes*, January 20, 2021, https://www.forbes.com/sites/jackbrewster/2021/01/20/we-all-got-played-qanon-followers-implode-after-big-moment-never-comes/?sh=2745e8d73a06.

[154] Brewster, " 'We All Got Played' ".

[155] For Catholics, see Kathryn Joyce, "Deep State, Deep Church: How Qanon And Trumpism Have Infected The Catholic Church," *Vanity Fair*, October 30, 2020, https://www.vanityfair.com/news/2020/10/how-qanon-and-trumpism-have-infected-the-catholic-church.

[156] John General and Richa Naik, "QAnon is spreading amongst evangelicals. These pastors are trying to stop it," CNN, May 23, 2021, https://www.cnn.com/2021/05/23/business/qanon-evangelical-pastors/index.html.

[157] Dalia Mortada, Rachel Martin, and Bo Hamby, "Disinformation Fuels A White Evangelical Movement. It Led 1 Virginia Pastor To Quit," NPR, February 21, 2021, https://www.npr.org/2021/02/21/969539514/disinformation-fuels-a-white-evangelical-movement-it-led-1-virginia-pastor-to-qu.

[158] Kaleigh Rogers, "Why QAnon Has Attracted So Many White Evangelicals," FiveThirtyEight, March 4, 2021, https://fivethirtyeight.com/features/why-qanon-has-attracted-so-many-white-evangelicals/.

[159] Mark Lewis, "Why So Many Evangelicals Are Susceptible to QAnon Craziness," *The Daily Beast*, April 27, 2021, https://www.thedailybeast.com/why-so-many-evangelicals-are-susceptible-to-qanon-craziness.

[160] Aila Slisco, "One-Quarter of White Evangelicals Believe QAnon 'Storm' Is Coming to 'Restore Rightful Leaders'," *Newsweek*, May 28, 2021, https://www.newsweek.com/one-quarter-white-evangelicals-believe-qanon-storm-coming-restore-rightful-leaders-1596086.

[161] Jason Springs, "QAnon, Conspiracy, and White Evangelical Apocalypse," *Contending Modernities*, June 16, 2021, https://contendingmodernities.nd.edu/ theorizing-modernities/qanon-evangelical-apocalypse/.

[162] See, for example, Jason Jones and John Zmirak, "What We Can Learn About Christian Citizenship From David French and the Rest of the Sorority Beta Dogma Stigma," *The Stream*, October 11, 2021, https://stream.org/ what-we-can-learn-about-christian-citizenship-from-david-french-and-the-rest-of-the-sorority-beta-dogma-stigma/; https://spectator.org/david-french-the-principled-conservative/; Sohrab Ahmari, "Against David French-ism," *First Things*, May 29, 2019, https://www.firstthings.com/web-exclusives/2019/05/ against-david-french-ism; for a summary of some of the attacks on French along with a response, see Tyler O'Neil, "Bizarre: Mainstream Conservative Leaders Are Gunning for David French," PJ Media, June 5, 2019, https:// pjmedia.com/news-and-politics/tyler-o-neil/2019/06/05/the-bizarre-conservative-twitter-mob-gunning-for-david-french-n66282. For a response from French, see David French, "What Sohrab Ahmari Gets Wrong," *National Review*, May 30, 2019, https://www.nationalreview.com/2019/05/ david-french-response-sohrab-ahmari/.

[163] David French, "The Dangerous Idolatry of Christian Trumpism," *The Dispatch*, December 13, 2020, https://frenchpress.thedispatch.com/p/the-dangerous-idolatry-of-christian.

[164] Morgan Chalfant, "Trump: 'The only way we're going to lose this election is if the election is rigged'," *The Hill*, August 17, 2020, https://thehill.com/home-news/administration/512424-trump-the-only-way-we-are-going-to-lose-this-election-is-if-the.

[165] Nick Coltrain, Ian Richardson, Stephen Gruber-Miller, Andrea May Sahouri, "Donald Trump tells thousands at a rally in Iowa, 'We're going to take America back'" Des Moines Register, October 9, 2021, https://www.desmoinesregister.com/story/news/politics/2021/10/09/donald-trump-rally-iowa-state-fair-grounds-schedule-2020-election/6035496001/; Mollie Ziegler Hemingway, Rigged: How the Media, Big Tech, and the Democrats Seized Our Elections (Washington, DC: Regnery, 2022).

[166] Paul Bois, "Trump: 'Republicans Will Not Be Voting' in Future Elections Unless 2020 Fraud Resolved," *Breitbart*, October 13, 2021, https://www.breitbart.com/politics/2021/10/13/trump-republicans-will-not-be-voting-in-future-elections-unless-2020-fraud-resolved/. Trump continued to push this narrative into 2022, hosting the 2,000 Mules documentary in Mara Lago.

[167] See Ewan Palmer. "Donald Trump Holds Screening Of '2,000 Mules' Documentary At Mar-a-Lago," May 5, 2022, *Newsweek*, https://www. newsweek.com/donald-trump-2000-mules-film-election-fraud-dsouza-rittenhouse-1703680.

[168] Christopher Hutton, "Actor Jim Caviezel appears at QAnon-adjacent conference and channels Braveheart in speech," *Washington Examiner*, October 25,

2021, https://www.washingtonexaminer.com/news/jim-caviezel-channels-braveheart-qanon-conference.

[169] We have all these emails and comments on file.

[170] David Watson, "A Jesus I Do Not Know: Christians and the Capitol Riot," *Firebrand*, January 11, 2021, https://firebrandmag.com/articles/a-jesus-i-do-not-know-christians-and-the-capitol-riot?fbclid=IwAR3ubNTYsgkKvkU9Jyx-57g5rwZ5WAg59SVXubi9az4yDkxhVvSRorIUxf7o.

[171] Francis A. Schaeffer, *The Great Evangelical Disaster* (Wheaton, IL: Crossway Books, 1984), 118. He added, "But we must equally stand against those who would accommodate to the world spirit of this age under the guise of scholarship, and in the process not only distort the facts of history but Christian truth as well."

[172] Schaeffer, *The Great Evangelical Disaster*, 116.

[173] For a convenient but academically based statement, see Donald M. Scott, Scott, Donald M. "The Religious Origins of Manifest Destiny," Divining America, TeacherServe. National Humanities Center, http://nationalhumanitiescenter.org/tserve/nineteen/nkeyinfo/mandestiny.htm.

[174] "Mayflower and Mayflower Compact," Plimoth Patuxet Museums, https://plimoth.org/for-students/homework-help/mayflower-and-mayflower-compact.

[175] See https://www.mtsu.edu/first-amendment/article/1032/old-deluder-satan-act-of-1647.

[176] See "Massachusetts," Harvard GSAS Christian Community, http://www.hcs.harvard.edu/~gsascf/shield-and-veritas-history/. Under Rev. John Leverett, president of Harvard from 1708-1724, standards temporarily declined and there were complaints of "profane swearing," "riotous Actions," and "bringing Cards into the College." Can you imagine such actions creating a stir on our campuses today, especially "bringing Cards into the College"?.

[177] Stephen McDowell, *The Bible: America's Source of Law and Liberty*, (Charlottesville, VA: Providence Foundation, 2016), Kindle locations 638–40.

[178] For the politically related sermons of New England clergy prior to the Revolutionary War, see Alice M. Baldwinn, edited and introduced by Joel McDurmon, *The New England Pulpit and the American Revolution: When American Pastors Preached Politics, Resisted Tyranny, and Founded a Nation on the Bible* (second edition; Dallas, GA: Devoted Books, 2019); McDurmon's substantial introduction is also important for historical context.

[179] Benjamin F. Morris, *Christian Life and Character of the Civil Institutions of the United States* (repr., Powder Springs, GA: American Vision, 2007), 23.

[180] Morris, *Christian Life and Character*, 27-28.

[181] Morris, *Christian Life and Character*, 28.

[182] Denker, *Red State Christians*, 11.

[183] Denker, *Red State Christians*, 10.

[184] Denker, *Red State Christians*, 11.

[185] Michael Brown, "The Demonization of the Democrat Party," AskDrBrown, September 2, 2019, https://askdrbrown.org/library/demonization-democrat-party.

[186] Michael Brown, "Is the Republican Party the Party of God?" *Townhall*, September 17, 2012, https://townhall.com/columnists/michaelbrown/2012/09/17/is-the-republican-party-the-party-of-god-n1187870.

[187] Dutch Sheets, "Manifest Destiny," http://www.christsbondservants.org/Key_Issues/wys-Key%20Manifest%20Judgment%20sheets.pdf.

[188] Francis Schaeffer, *Christian Manifesto* (Wheaton, Ill., Crossway Books, 1981), 121.

[189] Marguerite Michaels, "Billy Graham: America Is Not God's Only Kingdom," *Parade*, February 1, 1981, 6.

[190] Peter Lillback, "Dr. Martin Luther King, Jr.: Are You a Thermometer or a Thermostat?" Providence Forum, January 15, 2018, https://providenceforum.org/blog/dr-martin-luther-king-jr-thermometer-thermostat/.

[191] See Kathryn Jean Lopez, "The Church Must Be the Conscience of the State," *National Review*, January 25, 2021, https://www.nationalreview.com/2021/01/the-church-must-be-the-conscience-of-the-state/.

[192] Written May 16, 2021, during a personal prayer retreat.

[193] M. R. Reese, "The Madness of Caligula: Rome's Cruelest Emperor?" Ancient Origins, March 29, 2019.

[194] Rachel Seigel, "Disturbed Facts About Caligula, The Mad Emperor," Factinate, https://www.factinate.com/people/42-disturbed-facts-caligula/.

[195] William Stearns, *Readings in Ancient History* (Norwood, Mass., Norwood Press, 1913), 286-87.

[196] See the many books by Paul Hattaway documenting this growth, as well as documenting the many Chinese Christian martyrs.

[197] For a short summary, see https://operationworld.org/locations/iran/.

[198] Laura Geggel, "Same-Sex Marriage in History: What the Supreme Court Missed," *Live Science*, May 5, 2015, https://www.livescience.com/50725-same-sex-marriage-history.html#:~:text=Emperor%20Nero%20(ruled%20A.D.%2054,69).

[199] Gene Edward Veith, "The Good, the Bad, and the Ugly." Ligonier Ministries, August 1, 2004, https://www.ligonier.org/learn/articles/good-bad-and-ugly/.

[200] "The Mystery of Iniquity," Wesley Center Online, 1999, http://wesley.nnu.edu/john-wesley/the-sermons-of-john-wesley-1872-edition/sermon-61-the-mystery-of-iniquity/.

[201] Veith, "The Good, the Bad, and the Ugly."

[202] Veith, "The Good, the Bad, and the Ugly."

[203] Kevin Kinghorn, "John Wesley's Focus on Money," Seedbed, July 30, 2015, https://www.seedbed.com/john-wesleys-focus-money/.

[204] Michael Brown, "Christian Friends, Remember: There is Only One Messiah," *The Stream*, November 29, 2020, https://stream.org/christian-friends-remember-there-is-only-one-messiah/; Michael Brown, "Christ, Not Trump, is the

Solid Rock on Which We Stand," *The Stream*, June 29, 2020, https://stream. org/christ-not-trump-is-the-solid-rock-on-which-we-stand/.

[205] Sittser, *Resilient Faith*, 51.

[206] Sittser, *Resilient Faith*, 52.

[207] Sittser, *Resilient Faith*, 52.

[208] To quote Sittser again (*Resilient Faith*, 52), "God's people are not always on the 'winning' side. Perhaps they never are, or at least never should be."

[209] Alexander Roberts, James Donaldson, and A. Cleveland Coxe, eds., "The Epistle of Mathetes to Diognetus," in *The Apostolic Fathers with Justin Martyr and Irenaeus, vol. 1, The Ante-Nicene Fathers* (Buffalo, NY: Christian Literature Company, 1885), 26–27.

[210] Aleksandra Sandstrom, "Biden is only the second Catholic president, but nearly all have been Christians," Pew Research Center, January 20, 2021, https:// www.pewresearch.org/fact-tank/2021/01/20/biden-only-second-catholic-president-but-nearly-all-have-been-christians-2/.

[211] "Global Christianity—A Report on the Size and Distribution of the World's Christian Population," Pew Research Center, December 19, 2011, https:// www.pewforum.org/2011/12/19/global-christianity-exec/.

[212] I first encountered this quote in the 1980s, but to this day, I cannot trace its original source.

[213] Myles Munroe, *Reclaiming God's Original Purpose for Your Life: God's Big Idea* (Shippensburg, PA: Destiny Image Publishers, 2012).

[214] Cited in John W. Whitehead, "The Rise of Dominionism and the Christian Right," *Liberty Magazine*, July/August 2006, http://www.libertymagazine.org/ article/the-rise-of-dominionism-and-the-christian-right.

[215] Pat Robertson cited in John W. Whitehead, "The Rise of Dominionism.

[216] D. James Kennedy at Reclaiming America for Christ conference, February 2005.

[217] See, e.g., John Fea, "Ted Cruz's campaign is fueled by a dominionist vision for America," *The Washington Post*, February 4, 2016, https://www. washingtonpost.com/national/religion/ted-cruzs-campaign-is-fueled-by-a-do-minionist-vision-for-america-commentary/2016/02/04/86373158-cb6a-11e5-b9ab-26591104bb19_story.html.

[218] Wayne Besen, "We are now all members of Billy Graham's church... whether we like it or not," LGBTQ Nation, May 3, 2012, https://www. lgbtqnation.com/2012/05/we-are-now-all-members-of-billy-grahams-church-whether-we-like-it-or-not/.

[219] John McCandlish Phillips, "When Columnists Cry 'Jihad'," *The Washington Post*, May 4, 2005, https://www.washingtonpost.com/wp-dyn/content/ article/2005/05/03/AR2005050301277.html

[220] For further discussion of Matthew 28:19, see Donald A. Hagner, *Matthew 14–28, Word Biblical Commentary* (Dallas: Word, 1995), 886–888.

[221] Jonathan Edwards, "Works of Jonathan Edwards, Volume One," Christian Classics Ethereal Library, https://www.ccel.org/ccel/edwards/works1.ix.iii.ii.html.

[222] Steven R. Pointer, "American Postmillennialism: Seeing the Glory," Christian History Institute, https://christianhistoryinstitute.org/magazine/article/american-postmillennialism-seeing-the-glory.; see further James D. Bratt, "The Reorientation of American Protestantism, 1835–1845," *Church History*, Vol. 67, No. 1 (March 1998), 52–82.

[223] Cited in Robert T. Handy, *A Christian America: Protestant Hopes and Realities* (New York, NY: Oxford University Press, 1971).

[224] Steven R. Pointer, "American Postmillennialism".

[225] Tim Stafford, "The abolitionists," Christian History Institute, https://christianhistoryinstitute.org/magazine/article/abolitionists.

[226] "Bill Johnson Quotes," AZ Quotes, https://www.azquotes.com/quote/1318569?ref=dominion.

[227] Michelle Goldberg, "Dominionism: Michele Bachmann and Rick Perry's Dangerous Religious Bond," The Daily Beast, July 13, 2017, https://www.thedailybeast.com/dominionism-michele-bachmann-and-rick-perrys-dangerous-religious-bond.

[228] Bill Johnson and Wallnau, Lance, *Invading Babylon: The 7 Mountain Mandate* (Shippensburg, PA: Destiny Image Publishing, 2013), 21–22.

[229] Brad Christerson, "How a Christian movement is growing rapidly in the midst of religious decline," Religion News Service, March 18, 2017, https://religionnews.com/2017/03/18/how-a-christian-movement-is-growing-rapidly-in-the-midst-of-religious-decline/.

[230] From his book, *The Changing of the Guard (The Vital Role Christians Must Play in America's Unfolding Political and Cultural Drama)* (Nashville, TN: Broadman & Holman, 1995), cited by Michelle Goldberg, "What Is Christian Nationalism?" May 14, 2006 (updated May 25, 2011), https://www.huffpost.com/entry/what-is-christian-nationa_b_20989.

[231] Author, strategist, and futurist Lance Wallnau, however, would emphasize that a well-placed, strategically thinking minority can influence an entire nation and so, it is not simply a matter of numbers.

[232] For a convenient presentation of the main lexical evidence, see my Line of Fire broadcast from December 7, 2020, "Is the Church God's Governing Authority on the Earth?" YouTube, https://youtu.be/3a-qfq-Z18Y; For a serious study of the subject, focusing on our spiritual authority, and with some concepts with which I would differ, see Dean Briggs, *Ekklesia Rising: The Authority of Christ in Communities of Prayer* (Kansas City, MO: Champion Press, 2014).

[233] Frederick Clarkson, "Dominionism Rising A Theocratic Movement Hiding in Plain Sight," Political Research Associates, August 18, 2016, https://www.politicalresearch.org/2016/08/18/dominionism-rising-a-theocratic-movement-hiding-in-plain-sight.

234"The Laws of Virginia (1610–1611)," Le Projet Albion/Puritan Studies on the Web/Primary Sources, http://puritanism.online.fr/puritanism/sources/valaws1611.html.

235Andrew T. Walker, "American Culture Is Broken. Is Theonomy the Answer?" The Gospel Coalition, March 31, 2021, https://www.thegospelcoalition.org/article/theonomy/.

236Walker, "American Culture Is Broken."

237Walker, "American Culture Is Broken."

238Quoted Walker, "American Culture Is Broken."

239"The Seven Mountains of Societal Influence," Generals International, https://www.generals.org/the-seven-mountains.

240"What is the seven mountain mandate, and is it biblical?" Got Questions, https://www.gotquestions.org/seven-mountain-mandate.html.

241For other negative assessments, see Jack Matirko, "Dominionism is America Part 5: The Seven Mountains Mandate," February 20, 2019, https://www.patheos.com/blogs/infernal/2019/02/dominionism-in-america-part-5-the-seven-mountains-mandate/, accessed on MMMM, DD, YYYY, and Marsha West, "7 Mountain Politics and Theology," Berean Research, https://bereanresearch.org/7-mountain-politics-theology/. For another positive assessment, see https://www.the7mountains.com/history-of-the-7-mountains. See further Johnson and Wallnau, *Invading Babylon*.

242U.S. Cont. amend. I, § 1.

243Martin Luther King, Jr., "How Should A Christian View Communism?" Sermon from 1963.

244Cited in Michael Brown, "Is the '7 Mountains Mandate' Biblical or Heretical?" AskDrBrown, March 5, 2020, https://askdrbrown.org/library/%E2%80%987-mountains-mandate%E2%80%99-biblical-or-heretical.

245R.J. Rushdoony, *The Philosophy of the Christian Curriculum.*

246Cited in Whitehead, "The Rise of Dominionism and the Christian Right."

247As quoted in R. J. Rushdoony, "Institutes of Biblical Law: Introduction to the Law," Christ Rules, November 4, 2009, https://www.christrules.com/biblical-law/.

248R. J. Rushdoony, *A Word in Season: Daily Messages on the Faith for All of Life, vol. 2* (Vallecito, CA: Chalcedon/Ross House Books, 2012), 103.

249John W. Whitehead, "The Rise of Dominionism and the Christian Right," *Liberty Magazine*, July/August 2006, http://www.libertymagazine.org/article/the-rise-of-dominionism-and-the-christian-right; all emphasis in the original. With reference to Whitehead's book *The Second American Revolution*, Schaeffer said: "If there is still an entity known as 'the Christian church' by the end of this century, operating with any semblance of liberty within our society here in the United States, it will probably have John Whitehead and his book to thank." According to Wikipedia, Whitehead was described by jazz historian and civil libertarian Nat Hentoff as "this nation's Paul Revere of protecting civil liberties." "Rutherford Institute," Wikipedia, last edited date June 12, 2021, https://en.wikipedia.org/wiki/Rutherford_Institute.

[250]Beth Moore, Twitter Post, December 13, 2020, https://twitter.com/BethMooreLPM/status/1338134290647953410. As of September 20, 2021, the tweet had received 146.5K likes and was retweeted 22.3K times.

[251]Elizabeth Dias and Ruth Graham, "How White Evangelical Christians Fused With Trump Extremism," *The New York Times*, January 11, 2021, https://www.nytimes.com/2021/01/11/us/how-white-evangelical-christians-fused-with-trump-extremism.html.

[252]The leader was from the Oath Keeper's group. Right Wing Watch, Twitter Post, December 12, 2020, https://twitter.com/RightWingWatch/status/1337835464334708738.

[253]Right Wing Watch, Twitter Post, December 12, 2020, https://twitter.com/RightWingWatch/status/1337819203852709888.

[254]Andrew L. Whitehead, Joseph O. Baker, and Samuel L. Perry, "Despite porn stars and Playboy models, white evangelicals aren't rejecting Trump. This is why," *The Washington Post*, March 26, 2018, https://www.washingtonpost.com/news/monkey-cage/wp/2018/03/26/despite-porn-stars-and-playboy-models-white-evangelicals-arent-rejecting-trump-this-is-why/

[255]Andrew L. Whitehead and Samuel L. Perry, *Taking America Back for God* (Oxford: Oxford University Press, 2020), loc. 444–545, Kindle.

[256]Whitehead and Perry, *Taking America Back for God*, loc. 404–411.

[257]John Zmirak, "Turning 'Christian Nationalism' Into a Slur," *The Stream*, December 22, 2020, https://stream.org/turning-christian-nationalism-into-an-slur/.

[258]John Zmirak, "Why I'm a Christian Nationalist and You Should Be Too," *The Stream*, December 26, 2020, https://stream.org/why-im-a-christian-nationalist-and-you-should-be-too/.

[259]Zmirak, "Why I'm a Christian Nationalist."

[260]Joseph Mattera, "Contrasting the Kingdom of God and Christian Nationalism Part 1," Josephmattera.org, January 5, 2021, https://josephmattera.org/contracting-kingdom-christian-nationalism/.

[261]https://stream.org/was-beth-moore-right-to-sound-the-alarm-about-christian-nationalism/, citing https://christianchronicle.org/what-is-christian-nationalism/ at the end of the quote.

[262]Joseph Mattera, "Contrasting the Kingdom of God and Christian Nationalism Part 1," Josephmattera.org, January 5, 2021, https://josephmattera.org/contracting-kingdom-christian-nationalism/.

[263]Mattera, "Contrasting the Kingdom of God and Christian Nationalism."

[264]Mattera, "Contrasting the Kingdom of God and Christian Nationalism."

[265]Dr. Michael L. Brown, Twitter Post, December 13, 2020, https://twitter.com/DrMichaelLBrown/status/1338235283502985218.

[266] Michael Brown, "Was Beth Moore Right to Sound the Alarm About Christian Nationalism?" *The Stream*, December 14, 2020, https://stream.org/was-beth-moore-right-to-sound-the-alarm-about-christian-nationalism/.

[267] For example, see Michael Brown, "White Evangelical Support for Trump Was Not About Whiteness," *The Stream*, December 9, 2020, https://stream.org/white-evangelical-support-for-trump-was-not-about-whiteness/.

[268] Michael Brown, "Why I reject the 'Christian nationalist' label," *The Christian Post*, December 30, 2020, https://www.christianpost.com/voices/why-i-reject-the-christian-nationalist-label.html.

[269] See George Thomas, "India's Christians Under Fire, Campaign to Make Country More Hindu Intensifies," CBN News, August 31, 2020, https://www1.cbn.com/cbnnews/world/2020/august/indias-christians-under-fire-campaign-to-make-country-more-hindu-intensifies.

[270] Ethan Goodnight, "William Apess, Pequot Pastor: A Native American Revisioning of Christian Nationalism in the Early Republic," *Religion*, ed. by Mark T. Edwards, *Christian Nationalism in the United States* (Basel, Switzerland: MDPI, 2016–2017), 16.

[271] Sam Haselby, "What politicians mean when they say the United States was founded as a Christian nation," *The Washington Post*, July 4, 2017, https://www.washingtonpost.com/news/posteverything/wp/2017/07/04/what-politicians-mean-when-they-say-america-was-founded-as-a-christian-nation/. More fully, see Sam Haselby, *The Origins of American Religious Nationalism* (New York, NY: Oxford University Press, 2015).

[272] Haselby, "What politicians mean."

[273] Quoted in John Sides, "Why most American Jews vote for Democrats, explained," *The Washington Post*, March 24, 2015, https://www.washingtonpost.com/news/monkey-cage/wp/2015/03/24/why-most-american-jews-vote-for-democrats-explained/.

[274] Kristin Kobes Du Mez, *Jesus and John Wayne: How White Evangelicals Corrupted a Faith and Fractured a Nation* (New York: Liveright, 2020), 303.

[275] Kristin Kobes Du Mez, *Jesus and John Wayne*, 301.

[276] For books emphasizing positive aspects of Christian masculinity, but in a certain sense, applicable for all believers, see, e.g., Erwin Raphael McManus, *The Barbarian Way: Unleash the Untamed Faith Within* (Nashville, TN: Thomas Nelson, 2005). For the argument that "the Western church has become effeminate and weak," see Zachary Garris, *Masculine Christianity* (Ann Arbor, MI: Reformation Zion Publishing, 2020).

[277] Denker, *Red State Christians*, 15.

[278] Denker, *Red State Christians*, 16.

[279] Denker, *Red State Christians*, 16–17.

[280] Mary Lynn Smith, "Minnesota pastor says on video to be ready to 'arm up' as a citizen militia force," *Star Tribune*, January 18, 2021, https://www.startribune.com/minnesota-pastor-says-on-video-to-be-ready-to-arm-up-as-a-citizen-militia-force/600010291/.

[281] Jason Lemon, "Evangelical Pastor Urges Christians to 'Mobilize' to Fight Civil War Against Left-Wing Activists," *Newsweek*, January 14, 2020, https://www.newsweek.com/evangelical-pastor-urges-christians-mobilize-fight-civil-war-against-left-wing-activists-1531827, quoting Luke 22; *Real Kosher Jesus* critique.

[282] Benjamin Fearnow, "Pastor Rick Joyner Urges American Christians to Prepare for Civil War," *Newsweek*, March 16, 2021, https://www.newsweek.com/pastor-rick-joyner-urges-american-christians-prepare-civil-war-1576570.

[283] Stephen Strang, "Stephen Strang: Is America Headed for Civil War?" *Charisma Magazine*, July 2021, https://www.charismamag.com/life/culture/49746-stephen-strang-is-america-headed-for-civil-war.

[284] Strang, "Is America Headed for Civil War?"

[285] BU Today Staff, "BU Historian Answers: Are We Headed for Another Civil War?" BU Today, Marcy 27, 2019, https://www.bu.edu/articles/2019/are-we-headed-for-another-civil-war/.

[286] For talk about secession from the union, see Daniel Villarreal, "Majority of Trump Voters Want to Split the Nation Into 'Red' and 'Blue' Halves," *Newsweek*, September 30, 2021, https://www.newsweek.com/majority-trump-voters-want-split-nation-red-blue-halves-1634523.

[287] Cameron Hilditch, "Christianity as Ideology: The Cautionary Tale of the Jericho March," *National Review*, December 18, 2020, https://www.nationalreview.com/2020/12/christianity-as-ideology-the-cautionary-tale-of-the-jericho-march/.

[288] Julia Duin, "Jericho march in DC: Coming-out party for a movement journalists haven't really covered," Get Religion, December 15, 2020, https://www.getreligion.org/getreligion/2020/12/14/jericho-march-in-dc-coming-out-party-for-movement-journalists-havent-really-covered.

[289] Rob Dreher, "What I Saw At The Jericho March," The American Conservative, December 12, 2020, https://www.theamericanconservative.com/dreher/what-i-saw-at-the-jericho-march/.

[290] John L. Allen, *The Global War on Christians* (New York: The Crown Publishing Group2016), 7.

[291] Jonathan Den Hartog, "What the Black Robe Regiment Misses About Revolutionary Pastors," *Christianity Today*, January 20, 2021, https://www.christianitytoday.com/ct/2021/january-web-only/black-robe-regiment-revolutionary-war-pastor-election-trump.html.

[292] Hartog, "What the Black Robe Regiment Misses."

[293] Michael Brown, "The Whole Problem With a Christian Call to Take Up Arms Against the Government," *The Stream*, March 23, 2021, https://stream.org/the-whole-problem-with-a-christian-call-to-take-up-arms-against-the-government/.

[294] Francis Schaeffer, *Christian Manifesto* (Wheaton, Ill., Crossway Books, 1981), 117.

[295] Schaeffer, *Christian Manifesto*, 120.

296 Schaeffer, *Christian Manifesto*, 126.

297 Douglas Wilson, "In Which First Things Does Some Fourth Things," Blog and Mablog, November 14, 2014, https://dougwils.com/books-and-culture/s7-engaging-the-culture/in-which-first-things-does-some-fourth-things.html.

298 See, for example, Keith J. Hardman, *Seasons of Refreshing: Evangelism and Revivals in America* (Eugene, OR: Wipf & Stock, 2006).

299 See Michael L. Brown, *Revival Or We Die: A Great Awakening Is Our Only Hope* (Shippensburg, PA: Destiny Image, 2021).

300 Michael Brown, "The Whole Problem With a Christian Call to Take Up Arms Against the Government," *The Stream*, March 23, 2021, https://stream.org/the-whole-problem-with-a-christian-call-to-take-up-arms-against-the-government/.

301 Brown, *Donald Trump Is Not My Savior*, 21–22.

302 Brown, *Donald Trump Is Not My Savior*, 323–328.

303 Brown, *Donald Trump Is Not My Savior*, 328.

304 Brown, *Evangelicals at the Crossroads*, 207–226.

305 Brown, *Evangelicals at the Crossroads*, 230.

306 She was referring to my *Line of Fire* broadcast on January 6, 2020, live during the storming of the Capitol.

307 See Michael L. Brown, *Resurrection: Investigating a Rabbi from Brooklyn, a Preacher from Galilee, and an Event that Changed the World* (Lake Mary, FL: Charisma House, 2020).

308 Michael Brown, "Ultra-Orthodox Jews Proclaim 'Trump 2024' in the Midst of a Religious Celebration," *The Stream*, September 28, 2021, https://stream.org/ultra-orthodox-jews-proclaim-trump-2024-in-the-midst-of-a-religious-celebration/; for comparisons between ultra-Orthodox and evangelical voting patterns, see Michael Brown, "Will American Jews Abandon the Democratic Party?" *The Stream*, September 23, 2021, https://stream.org/will-american-jews-abandon-the-democratic-party/.

309 See Brown, *Evangelicals at the Crossroads*, Chapter Two, "Since When Was Loyalty to Trump the Dividing Line for Christians?" 12–18.

310 Pastor David Harwood, email to the author, October 1, 2021, used with permission.

311 Michael Brown, "And They Will Know We are Christians by Our Hate," *The Stream*, February 17, 2021, https://stream.org/and-they-will-know-we-are-christians-by-our-hate/.

312 See Michael Brown, "When 350 Faith Leaders Endorsed Candidate Joe Biden to 'Restore the Soul' of the Nation," *The Stream*, October 3, 2021, https://stream.org/when-350-faith-leaders-endorsed-candidate-joe-biden-to-restore-the-soul-of-the-nation/.

313 Michael Brown, "An Open Letter to Jerry Falwell Jr. on His Trump Endorsement," *The Christian Post*, January 27, 2016, https://www.christianpost.com/news/open-letter-jerry-falwell-jr-trump-endorsement-liberty.html.

[314]See Michael L. Brown, *The Real Kosher Jesus: Revealing the Mysteries of the Hidden Messiah* (Lake Mary, FL: Frontline, 2012).

[315]Joseph A. Wulfsohn, "Pence says he's spoken with Trump 'probably a dozen times' since leaving office," Fox News, September 30, 2021, https://www.foxnews.com/media/mike-pence-donald-trump-ruthless-podcast.

[316]From his message *The Best Warcry,* March 4th, 1883, "Charles Haddon Spurgeon—Prince of Preachers," West Park Baptist Church, October 29, 2018, https://westpark-baptist.com/charles-haddon-spurgeon-prince-of-preachers/.

CPSIA information can be obtained
at www.ICGtesting.com
Printed in the USA
BVHW041754310822
645866BV00021B/144

9 781954 618497